MW00588451

WITNESS LEE

GOSPEL
OUTLINES

Living Stream Ministry
Anaheim, California • www.lsm.org

First Edition, December 1980.

ISBN 978-0-87083-039-6

Published by

Living Stream Ministry
2431 W. La Palma Ave., Anaheim, CA 92801 U.S.A.
P. O. Box 2121, Anaheim, CA 92814 U.S.A.

Printed in the United States of America

08   09   10   11   12   13   /   12   11   10   9   8   7

CONTENTS

FOREWORD

Gospel Outlines is a record of the messages given in a special training on service with the church in Taipei during October 1954. How we thank the Lord that in these days, as He is recovering the preaching of the gospel among us, He has seen fit to release this treasury of gospel material to His Body! These outlines abound with the riches of Christ, embodied in the gospel truths. Thus, our gracious Lord has freshly fortified us to "preach the unsearchable riches of Christ as the gospel."

This book is more than just a compilation of riches; it is also a practical training in gospel preaching. The outline style mingles the points of the gospel messages with valuable instruction on how to preach the gospel. The reader is helped, therefore, not only in what to preach, but also in how to do it most effectively. We can testify that as we have put this material to use we have been greatly helped in our preaching, and have experienced the Lord's rich blessing upon our meetings!

Part I of this volume consists of sixty gospel messages taken from the Old Testament. *Part II* comprises one hundred fifty messages covering New Testament subjects. In addition, *Part III* consists of an eight part series of special topics for gospel preaching. An index has been included in which the messages are classified according to category. This allows the reader to cross-reference other messages in the same category.

Although much has been prepared for us in these outlines, still, on our part, much is required. The riches provided here by our brother must be applied with much prayer and in the spirit of gospel preaching. Many of the outlines are rich and lengthy, demanding less additional development. Others, particularly toward the end of this volume, are presented in a simpler outline form, and require more "cooking." However, only a fresh burden from the living Lord and the anointing of the Spirit can assure that these outlines will fulfill the purpose for which they were intended. May the Lord provide all the gospel preachers the grace to labor together with Him to make His gospel so rich, so convincing, and so prevailing.

Finally, it should be noted that these outlines have not been reviewed in translation or composition by the speaker and any inaccuracies are the sole responsibility of the editors. We gratefully acknowledge the joint effort of many in the production of this work. May the Lord use this book to gain His own glory in the church through the gospel.

Fullerton, California   *The Editors*
December 1980

Part I
Old Testament
Subjects

Subject One

THE ORIGIN OF THE UNIVERSE—GOD

Scripture: Gen. 1

Such a subject is best suited for speaking to high school and college students. The first seven subjects form a group, which may be called, "The Story of the Universe."

I. Men's presumptions

Begin with what the world's famous men of all cultures and all ages have had to say about the universe. Include philosophers, sages, and scholars, past and present; Chinese, Egyptian, Babylonian, and Greek. Include also the presumptions of the common people. For this you need to refer to history and literature.

II. The revelation of the Bible

Every time in preaching the gospel begin with what people in the past have had to say, and then point out what the Bible reveals. This is a principle in gospel preaching. Based on the Bible, refute men's false presumptions.

A. First find some good verses in the Old Testament about the heavens, the earth, and all things that were created by God.

B. Then find what Jesus had to say about creation.

C. Lastly look at what the Apostles had to say.

III. The evidence of all things in the universe

A. The material evidence: the vastness of the universe, the wonder of the way the earth revolves on its axis, the wonder of the air, of the water, and of the stars all prove that the universe was created by God.

B. The circumstantial evidence: great events have occurred in the universe which prove God's existence and His ruling. Examples of such events are: (1) the long day recorded in the book of Joshua, when the sun stood still for twenty-four hours (Josh. 10:12-14), and (2) at the time of Hezekiah, when the sun went backward ten degrees on the sundial (2 Kings 20:8-11).

IV. **The evidence of laws and principles**

Mention some physical laws and principles of the universe and then point out that not one law or principle can exist by accident. A law is a law, and there must be One in the universe who establishes the law; a principle is a regulation, and there must be One in the universe who regulates.

Points III and IV testify to the revelation of the Bible which declares that God is the origin of the universe.

Subject Two

THE MEANING OF THE UNIVERSE—GOD

Scripture: Gen. 1

I. **The universe is a mystery**

For centuries people have regarded the universe as a mystery. You need to search out their presumptions, with which they attempt to explain this mystery.

This is a point that can touch people, so the more good material you have the better.

II. **Can the universe be meaningless?**

Point out numerous principles of physics and other matters to prove that the universe is not meaningless. If a man's house is decorated, orderly, and meaningful; how much more meaningful is the universe created by God, which is so bright, so comely, and arranged in such an orderly fashion! For instance, the earth revolves on its axis every twenty-four hours; the sun and the moon rise according to certain set times; and there are so many beautiful days and scenic places. Can all of these things be meaningless?

III. **The universe is the proof of God's existence**

The greatest meaning of the universe is to prove the existence of God.

A. The scriptural basis: Psa. 19:1-2; Rom. 1:20; Acts 14:15-17; 17:23-31.

These four passages show us that the meaning of the universe is to prove the existence of God.

B. The material for this subject can be used together with that of the previous subject, "The Origin of the Universe," along with examples of all kinds of phenomena to prove God's existence.

IV. The universe is the manifestation of God's glory

Psalm 19 says that God's glory is the manifestation of God in six aspects:

A. The greatness of the universe: so great is the universe that even today no one could tell how great it is. A man viewing the ocean from a big ship is just like a little fish in the ocean. The greatness of the universe manifests the greatness of God.

B. The wonder of the universe: the arrangement and movement of the stars and also the distinction of the four seasons manifest how wonderful God is.

C. The brightness of the universe: the brightness of the sun, the moon, and the stars declare that God is a God of light.

D. The beauty of the universe: mornings and evenings, flowers, grass and trees, mountains and rivers, picturesque views, these and all the pleasant and inspiring scenery are manifestations of God's beauty.

E. Lovingkindness: God's arrangement and preparation of the universe for mankind, and His provision for man's every need show God's lovingkindness toward men.

F. Wisdom: the greatness, wonder, brightness, and beauty of the universe also manifest that God is a God of wisdom.

These two subjects are to make people realize the existence of God and to make them know what kind of a God this God is. According to the subjects, you are talking about the origin and the meaning of the universe, but actually you are talking about God.

Subject Three

THE CENTER OF THE UNIVERSE—MAN

Scripture: Gen. 2

I. Man is the highest one among all the creatures

First speak about who is the highest one among all creatures in the universe. Begin with the lifeless matters, then proceed to the living creatures—from vegetable life to animal life, from the lowest to the highest. Finally talk about man.

A. First say that the living creatures are higher than lifeless matter and that the conscious animal life is higher than the unconscious vegetable life. Among the animals, man is the highest. Compare the life which comes from seed, from eggs, and from birth. Compare the life which comes from a short period of pregnancy, from a long period of pregnancy, and from man's birth. From this prove that man is the highest among all creatures.

B. Then say that man's wisdom, intelligence, and behavior also prove that man is the highest creature. Tigers, leopards, and lions, however fierce they may be, cannot conquer man.

C. Finally, say that man has a spirit. The reason man has wisdom, intelligence, and good behavior is that man has a spirit. Man's spirit not only causes man to have wisdom, intelligence, and good behavior, but it is also the very organ that desires God, seeks after God, and worships God. No other creature has a spirit; therefore, no other creature can desire God or worship Him.

The proof that man has a spirit:

1. Man has a sense of guilt when he does something wrong.

2. Man has an inclination to seek after God and to worship Him.

II. Man is the center of all the creatures

It is true that in preaching the gospel you need to rely on the power of the Holy Spirit; but those who have studied the Bible all acknowledge that the Bible is very logical. Therefore, you also need to present the gospel in a logical way.

A. Based upon man being the highest creature, prove that man is the center of creation. In any organization the highest one is also its center. Man is the highest among all the creatures; therefore, man is the center of all the creatures.

B. Based on the order and the ways of God's creation, prove that man is the center of all the creatures:

1. In His creation, God created man after he had made all things.

2. The way God created man was different from the way He created other creatures. When God created the others, He just said, "Let the earth bring forth...and it was so." The Bible does not mention how He made them. But in creating man, the Bible says that first He made the body, then the spirit, and finally man became a living soul. From the way God created man, prove that man is the center of all the creatures.

III. The parts of man

Man is composed of three parts: the spirit, the soul, and the body. Man has these three parts; therefore, man has a spirit.

(*Note:* If you did not start with the universe, but with man alone, you need to speak about the origin of man first.)

A. If a man dies, we say that he is gone. The body is still there, but the spirit is gone.

B. The existence within man of an inclination to worship God is a proof that man has a spirit. With every race there is an inclination to worship God.

IV. The meaning of man (why man was created)

A. God's image: man is the image of God. How honorable this is! How can man sin and do such base things?

B. God's vessel: man is God's vessel, made to contain God. Today man always has an empty feeling because he does not have God inside of him. For instance, as a Coke bottle should be filled with Coca-cola, and an electric lamp should be filled with light, so man also should be filled with God. *This is the best way to touch people's feeling. Gospel preaching should be serious and yet relaxed.* In a simple and effective way, explain that man is for God; therefore, the meaning of man is to be for God. Actually these are two aspects of one thing, but for the listeners you need to speak from these two aspects.

V. Man's position—man's original position

A. Man was to live in the presence of God.

B. Man was over all creatures to rule them.

C. Man was sinless.

Subject Four

THE EVIL ONE OF THE UNIVERSE— THE DEVIL, SATAN

Scripture: Gen. 2, 3

I. The dark side of the universe

Disasters, disease, death, divorce, killings, murders, sufferings, wandering, smoking and drinking, gambling, whoring, corrupted hearts, disordered families, dark societies, and all kinds of corruption everywhere—these are the dark side of the universe. Originally the universe was beautiful and life was lovely. Now, however, the universe has so much darkness, misfortune, misery, and death that many even feel that living is futile; consequently, they become depressed and commit suicide. *Here is the point that can touch people the easiest.*

The ability of a gospel preacher is in portraying the real situation. Present all the real stories of human living in such a way that people will be moved and prepared to accept the Lord's salvation. Speak weightily and descriptively.

II. The source of darkness—Satan

From where did all this darkness come? Did it come from God? From men? It came neither from God nor from men but from the Devil, Satan. The Bible speaks clearly about Satan. Genesis 2 says that after man was created, God asked man to guard the garden. The reason the garden needed to be guarded was that someone was coming. In Genesis 3 that one came—the subtle one, the evil one.

He is the adversary of God. Often he transmutes himself into something that looks good and hides himself there. (Anything that looks good has Satan hidden in it.)

III. The aim of Satan (his main work)

You need to explain how Satan opposes God, how he damages God's purpose and God's work. It has been mentioned before that he is God's enemy. His aim is to gain men. You need to point out that all that men do today is not by themselves. Men cannot help themselves; they are absolutely under Satan's control. Sin, wrongdoing, and loving the world are not of men's own will. Satan gains men by means of fame, position, scholarship, money, love, and business—all the good things and bad things—so that men could not help but obey Satan. (1 John 5:19, "...the whole world lieth in the evil one.")

IV. Satan's way of working is in two main categories

A. The world.

B. Sins.

Satan gains men by means of the world and sins.

Do not present the world and sin in the way they would be presented in meetings for new beginners, but illustrate with factual stories so that the unbelievers will understand.

Subject Five

THE TRAGEDY OF THE UNIVERSE—
THE FALL OF MAN

Scripture: Gen. 3

I. Satan's temptation

In this section you need to describe the passage in Genesis 3:1-6; how Satan hid himself in a serpent and tempted man by subtle and tricky words which caused man to question God, God's heart, God's work, and God's word. All these questions were like a fog that trapped man and led him astray.

II. Man's doubt

Once man was tempted and accepted Satan's words, right away he began to doubt God, God's heart, God's work, and God's word.

III. Man was deceived

When man was deceived, Satan's temptation had succeeded.

A. Although man sinned willingly, by the choice of his free will, nevertheless, man was cheated by Satan.

B. So the New Testament says that the serpent deceived Eve (2 Cor. 11:3), that is, Satan used trickery to deceive the human race.

IV. The result of being deceived

A. There was the sense of guilt.

B. Right away man escaped from God's presence and did not dare see God.

C. Man found excuses. Indeed man had sinned, but he would not admit it.

D. Man was judged.

E. Man fell into death.

According to how Satan tempted Eve—how Eve accepted Satan's words and doubted God, God's heart, God's work, and God's words—explain how men today are still under the same deception with the same results.

THE GLAD TIDINGS OF THE UNIVERSE— THE GOSPEL

Scripture: Gen. 3:9

I. **God came to seek man**

A. After being deceived and having become fallen and guilty, man hid from God's presence. Try your best to describe that it is not that men do not know God; rather, being guilty, man would prefer that there were no God. Therefore, man would not acknowledge God nor seek Him.

B. Man hid from God's presence, but God came to seek man. Although man rebelled and would not receive God, nevertheless, God still came to seek man.

Much can be said here. God is seeking man at every time, in every place, and on many different occasions, anywhere and everywhere. Relate how God came to seek man that day to the way He comes to seek people today. *Touch people's feeling on this point.*

II. **God prepared a way for man to be saved (redemption)**

As much as we can, without contradicting spiritual truth, we should simplify spiritual terminology. For example, say "saving way" instead of "redemption."

God not only came to seek man, but He also prepared for man a saving way. Adam sinned and was condemned. He should have died, but God had a lamb killed in his stead, and God used the skin of the lamb to make a coat to cover his shame. This is salvation in type. In the New Testament time, Christ came to the earth as the Lamb of God, took upon Himself the sins of the world, and was crucified upon the cross to accomplish salvation. His blood cleanses our sins and justifies us.

III. God accepted sinners

Acceptance includes both forgiveness of sins and justification. That day God not only forgave Adam and justified him, but He also accepted him. Today God also deals with us in the same way. Forgiveness plus justification equals acceptance.

IV. God caused sinners to receive life

Adam named the woman "Eve" (meaning "the mother of all living"), thus implying that God would give life to the sinners. God not only forgives us and justifies us, but He also accepts us, and at the same time gives us life, which is regeneration.

Subject Seven

THE SAVIOR OF THE UNIVERSE—CHRIST

Scripture: Gen. 3:15

To explain that Jesus is the Savior of the universe, use these two points: "the seed of woman shall bruise the serpent's head," and "the Lamb that was slain."

I. The promise of the Savior

Describe how Adam and Eve were afraid of God after they had sinned, and how they hated the serpent, Satan. While they were in such a state of fear and hatred, God came in to give them a promise. This promise said that One would come to crush the head of the enemy they hated. This was an explicit promise. On the other hand, God killed a lamb for them, atoned for them by the shedding of the blood, and covered their shame before God. This was a figurative promise.

The explicit promise, to crush the serpent's head, deals with Satan, and the figurative promise, the blood shed for atonement, deals with man's sins before God.

II. The person of the Savior

First speak of His being born on earth as a man through a virgin; then go on to say that He was the Word becoming flesh, that He was God becoming man to be our Savior.

III. The work of the Savior

This is to speak of His death.

On one hand, He was the Mighty One. He crushed the head of Satan on the cross. He put Satan to death, and He dealt with Satan. On the other hand, He was a Lamb. He shed His blood on the cross. He washed away man's sins. He nullified the record of man's sins before God.

IV. Receiving the Savior

Just as Adam received God's promise and also received the skins for clothing, today we also should:

A. According to the words of the Bible, receive the Savior.

B. According to the work of the Savior, receive Him as Savior.

Subject Eight

THE RELATIONSHIP BETWEEN GOD AND MAN

Scripture: Gen. 2, 3

I. Man is a creature of God—showing the origin of man

A. God used the earth to form a body for man; then He breathed the breath of life into him. Today chemists can tell us that the elements of a human body are similar to the elements of the earth.

B. From the wonder of the structure of the human body, prove that man is God's creature.

II. Man is God's image—showing the dignity of man

Man's mind, wisdom, will, ideas, emotion, likes, and many other characteristics are like God's. Man's love symbolizes God's love. Point out how dignified man is to be in God's image!

III. Man is God's representative—showing the position of man

Among all the creatures, only man was to represent God to rule over everything. Even to this date, man is still in control of the whole earth. (Dr. John Sung said that before the fall man was the commander-in-chief of the navy, army, and air force.)

IV. **Man is God's vessel—showing the usefulness of man**

God's desire is to be mingled with man, to work Himself into man; so man was made for God. This is like a bulb which was made to contain electricity and shine. A bulb is a waste if it is not for the electricity to shine. Likewise, a man is a waste unless he is containing God. *With this section, it is easy to touch the feelings of the unbelievers, so you need to stress this point.* The reason men feel empty is that they will not contain God. Today men are out of place and out of use.

V. **The fellowship between God and man**

A. Man is different from all other living creatures because man has a spirit.

B. Every race worships God. Some have worshipped in a wrong way; nevertheless, their worship proves that with man there is a desire for God. Such a desire grows stronger as men grow older. Man's spirit causes man to:

1. Need God.

2. Be able to contact God. When a man touches God, right away he has fellowship with God.

VI. **The problem between God and man—showing man's sins**

In this section you need to cover four points:

A. Man fell.

B. Man sinned.

C. Man escaped from God's presence.

D. Man was condemned by God.

VII. **The salvation for man—showing man's salvation**

First speak about the Savior, then about salvation. Salvation includes:

A. Blood shed for redemption.

B. Imparting of life.

This message may be given in two days.

Subject Nine

LIFE VERSUS GOOD AND EVIL

Scripture: Gen. 2

I. Two trees

A. Mention that after God created man, He put him in front of two trees, and that He held him responsible for these two trees. Whether man would be a success or a failure, right or wrong, legal or illegal, was all dependent upon how he would deal with those two trees.

B. The tree of life.

The tree of life depicts God's life. When God made man, He gave man a life for his human existence, but God did not give him His own life. So after man was made, man had only man's life, not God's life. God intended that man would, by his own free will, choose God's life and receive His life into him. God used the tree of life to depict God's life, and God intended that man would contact the tree of life, that is, to contact God Himself.

C. The tree of the knowledge of good and evil.

Just as the tree of life depicts God's life, the tree of good and evil depicts Satan's life. God used these two trees to point out that He and Satan are opposite to one another. He wished that man would contact the tree of life and thus have a relationship with Him, and He wished that man would not contact the tree of good and evil and thus have a relationship with Satan, but He gave man a free will to choose.

II. Life is God's goal

A. God's goal for man is that man may have His life. *Emphasize this point.*

B. This life is God's life, and this life is God Himself.

C. Explain how God made man to be His vessel, so that He may pour Himself into man.

D. When man gets this life, he is up to God's standard; he is no longer empty, but is living in reality. He becomes a man of meaning.

III. Good and evil are Satan's purpose

(This point must be presented clearly; otherwise it is difficult for people with moral thinking to understand.)

A. Satan wanted to capture man, whom God had created for Himself.

B. The way Satan captured man was to cause man to pay attention to good and evil.

C. As soon as man pays attention to good and evil, he is independent of God and becomes severed from God.

D. To man there is a big difference between good and evil. All men condemn evil and justify good, but the ultimate result of either good or evil is but one: both good and evil result in independence from God and keep man from having God's life.

IV. Only life is the true goodness

A. The source of good is God Himself. You should make people realize that all the evil originated from Satan, and all genuine goodness originated from God. God is the source of all good.

B. God's true goodness is touched through God's life because God is not only good, but much more, God is life. Only when you touch God's life can you touch the true goodness.

C. Any goodness not from God and God's life is only secondary goodness, if not false. It is never the genuine goodness or the highest goodness.

This point should subdue the listeners.

V. Life is the power of goodness

A. Satan causes men to pay attention to goodness, but he would not give them the power to do good. Anyone who tries to do good outside of God and without leaning on God, only has the knowledge of good, but has no power to do it.

B. In the Chinese dictionary there are the words "virtue" and "wisdom," and even the word "wisdom-power," but not "virtue-power." This proves that the Chinese philosophers had discovered that men had the knowledge of good but lacked the power to do good.

C. This is why the more a man pays attention to good, the more he discovers the lack of power to do good. When you are sloppy, you hardly feel that you are powerless in doing good. It is when you are trying to do good that you find out that you lack the power of doing good.

D. Since God Himself is the true goodness (the highest goodness), God's power must be His life. Only when a man receives God's life can he have the real goodness and the power to do good. So if you really want to do good, you must receive the life of God.

VI. The way to receive life

A. God's life is put in Christ. *Speak more about this.*

B. Christ died to redeem us, and resurrected to release His life. Christ's death took away the problem (sins) between men and God. Unless men's sins are taken away, God (the real life) cannot get into us. Through death Christ dealt with our sins, and through resurrection Christ released His life for us to receive.

C. We must confess our sins, and repudiate our past ways and goals. In addition, there are many other evils we need to confess from our heart. We must change our mind and turn to God. As soon as we change our mind, we should pray and confess to God.

D. You must open yourself from within, and accept Christ to come into your heart, to be your living Savior.

E. Acknowledge that you have received this life because you believed. This is according to the words of the Bible (1 John 5:12-13).

This message is suitable for speaking to the more intellectual ones.

Subject Ten

"WHERE ARE YOU?"—
IN A LOST CONDITION

Scripture: Gen. 3:9; Luke 19:10; 15:3-10

Subjects 10 through 16 form a group defining the position of fallen man. They are entitled "Where Are You?" (Gen. 3:9).

I. Where did man come from?

The source of man is touched in order to bring in God, and to let men see that man came from God.

II. Who does man belong to?

Everything has an owner, and man is an important item. Then who is the owner of man? Who is your owner? From here, point out the fact that man is in a lost condition, because he looks all around and cannot find his master. Only lost articles are unable to find their owners.

III. Man is in a lost condition

The fact that man cannot find his owner proves that man is in a lost condition. Man cannot tell where he came from nor where he is going. He is like a ship which has lost its direction. Man is busy all day, but he doesn't know what he is busy for. Man is always in a hurry, but he doesn't know where he is hurrying to go. Is not this a lost condition? Use some real stories to describe how men went astray and got lost.

IV. God came to seek man

A. The Lord Jesus was God come in the flesh.

B. He is the Shepherd coming to find the lost sheep.

C. He is seeking for man through the Holy Spirit. (See Luke 15:8, the woman seeking for the lost money.)

D. The Holy Spirit moves in man through the word of the Bible. (The woman lighted a lamp.)

E. When the Holy Spirit enlightens you, you feel troubled inside. This feeling comes from the Lord Jesus enlightening you through the Holy Spirit. (The woman swept the house.) Some who are here listening to the gospel do have this troubled feeling inside because the Holy Spirit is sweeping inside of you, the Lord Jesus is seeking for you. At this point, ask anyone who has such a feeling to please stand up.

Subject Eleven

"WHERE ARE YOU?"—IN SINS

Scripture: Gen. 3:9; John 8:21, 24, 34; Rom. 7:24

Concentrate on some sins that can touch the feeling of the unbelievers. Be free to apply.

I. Lying

There are many, many kinds of lies: lying openly and secretly, deceiving with looks and deceiving with words, lying with words and with actions, lying with evil intention and with good intention, white lies and black lies, big lies and small lies, lying with hands and lying with the head, lying with true words and with false words, lying to others and lying to yourself. You deceive others and you deceive yourself. You know that there is heaven and hell, but you say that there is neither; your conscience is bothered, but you say that you are at peace.

II. Stealing

There are also many ways of stealing, including secret deals and scandals: cultured stealing, barbaric stealing, big stealing (bandits and robbers), small stealing (taking ballpoint pens, stationery, etc.).

III. Covetousness

Covetousness is without end. Someone talks about something good, and immediately you begin to think how nice it would be to have that yourself. Were there no laws to punish you and no criticism from the public to restrain you, you would have taken what you coveted.

IV. Hatred (envy)

V. Lasciviousness, adulterous thoughts

VI. Habits: dancing, movies, gambling, smoking, drinking, whoring, making evil friends

VII. How to be delivered from sins

    A. The Lord Jesus died to bear all our sins.

    B. The Lord Jesus was resurrected to set us free from the bondage of sins.

    C. We must confess all the sins we have committed, and ask for the Lord's blood to cleanse us.

    D. We must accept the Lord into us to be our life, that we may be freed from sins. Describe how Christ comes into man to become his life and enables him to be freed from sins.

Subject Twelve

"WHERE ARE YOU?"—UNDER CONDEMNATION

Scripture: Gen. 3:9

I. God governs the universe

This universe is not without a government or administration. God is the ruler of the universe.

II. Conscience governs the heart

God governs the universe, and the conscience governs our heart.

III. The condemnation of the conscience

You stole something and lied, but your conscience makes you uneasy and causes a feeling of guilt; this is the condemnation of the conscience. *Touch the feeling on this point.*

IV. God's condemnation

    A. Condemnation of the conscience proves God's condemnation.

    B. Condemnation of the conscience represents God's condemnation.

    C. Condemnation of the conscience brings in God's condemnation, therefore, whatever the conscience condemns, God also condemns.

D. God's condemnation exceeds the condemnation of the conscience.

V. God's judgment

A. Condemnation seems to follow judgment, but the Bible shows us that we are condemned first, then judged. We are not waiting to be condemned before the great white throne; rather, we are condemned first, and then we will be judged later on.

B. All those who are condemned today shall be judged before the great white throne. The fate of the judged ones will be eternal suffering in the lake of fire.

VI. How to avoid judgment

A. The Lord Jesus bore our sins and was judged for us.

B. Believe in the Lord Jesus and we shall not be condemned (John 3:18; 5:24; Heb. 9:27).

Subject Thirteen

"WHERE ARE YOU?"—UNDER WRATH

Scripture: Gen. 3:9; John 3:36; Eph. 2:3; Rom. 1:18; Rev. 14:10; Rom. 5:1

I. God's righteousness cannot tolerate sin

God's righteousness provokes God to anger, because conflict occurs as soon as God's righteousness encounters man's sins. This conflict is the wrath. A reaction takes place when two things collide. Give examples. When a cup falls and hits the ground, it will shatter. Likewise, when God's righteousness encounters man's sins, God's wrath is provoked.

II. God's righteousness keeps God from accepting man

When God first created man, God loved man the best; man was the chief delight of God's heart. But man's sins offended God's righteousness and kept God from accepting man.

III. The proof of man's conscience

Man clearly knows within himself that he has provoked

God to wrath and has become abhorred by God. All the uneasiness and condemnation of the conscience prove that God is not pleased with man. In their conscience many people are afraid of God and dare not think about Him. Many have been in terror at the time of death because they know that they must meet God, but they were afraid to see God's face. On the other hand, many Christians have passed away peacefully, with smiling faces, because they knew that they were freed from God's wrath.

IV. The proof of man's circumstances

The negative aspect of man's numerous situations and circumstances also proves that God is not pleased with man. Such things as sickness, disaster, sufferings, distress, and so on, are proof that God is not pleased with man. The crafty ones are rewarded with trickery, and the evil ones never die peacefully. The violent ones are troubled within their hearts and also in their outward circumstances. These all prove that man is under God's wrath.

V. The reason that the wrath is not yet manifested

A. God's wrath upon man is like the thunder that is about to come. John 3:36 says that God's wrath abides on him, but it has not yet erupted.

B. The reason it has not yet erupted is that God is giving you an opportunity.

C. If you would not repent at all, eventually God's wrath will erupt.

VI. How to avoid the wrath

A. The Lord Jesus has received God's wrath in our stead, because on the cross He drank the cup of bitterness, which was the cup of God's wrath (Rev. 14:10). A cup is a portion; God's wrath is the portion we deserve. The Lord Jesus took it for us, and He drank the cup of wrath in our stead.

B. If we confess our sins and accept the Lord as our Savior, we will be freed from God's wrath, we will be accepted by God, and reconciled to God.

Subject Fourteen

"WHERE ARE YOU?"—IN DEATH

Scripture: Gen. 3:9; Eph. 2:1; John 5:24-25; Rom. 5:12; Heb. 2:9; John 11:25-26

I. In sins is in death

To be in sins is to be in death, because sin brought in death. Death and sin cannot be separated. Where death is, sin is there also. And where sin is, death is there also.

II. Man is dying day by day

Man thinks that he is living day by day; actually he is dying day by day. If a man has a life span of seventy years, every year that passes is a year subtracted. This is just like a man who had seventy dollars but spent one dollar and was one dollar short. So your life is not increasing day by day, but decreasing day by day. Spend one more year, and you have one year less. Do not celebrate your birthday, because it only indicates that you are one year closer to the grave. There is an old proverb which says, "The number of the days of our life increases mercilessly only to run out." The passing of time is merciless. If you have seventy dollars, you can keep it and not spend it, but with time you have no way to keep it. Even while you are sleeping, it is slipping away. Use this kind of example to describe how men are dying day by day. Then use Ecclesiastes 12 to show that men's hands, eyes, ears, and teeth are deteriorating day by day. Men are not living but dying day by day, and at the end they are put into a coffin and buried in the ground.

III. The suffering of death

A. The suffering of old age: there is no one in their old age who does not feel the suffering of being old. The old and decrepit ones are afraid of death on the one hand, but on the other hand they wish to die. Especially those suffering from diseases such as terminal cancer have an existence little better than death, yet they are afraid of death. Old age with its deterioration is the first note of death; it is the forecast and calling card of death.

B. When death actually comes upon a man, it is especially painful. None can withhold the tears when someone passes away.

IV. **The end of death—the lake of fire**

A. First speak about hell being at the edge of the flames. There was just some baking and the rich man could not stand it (Luke 16:24).

B. Then say that suffering in the lake of fire is far worse.

V. **How to avoid death**

A. The Lord Jesus died for us, and He tasted death for us.

B. The Lord Jesus was resurrected and released His death-overcoming life.

C. When we believe in the Lord Jesus, our sins are forgiven, and the root of death is dealt with.

D. When we receive the Lord, we obtain the eternal, never-dying life.

Subject Fifteen

"WHERE ARE YOU?"—IN DARKNESS

Scripture: Gen. 3:9; Acts 26:18; John 1:5; 8:12

I. **The source of darkness is threefold: Satan, sin, and death**

A. Satan is the prince of darkness and the power of darkness.

B. Sin: a man living in sin is living in darkness. Sin causes man to be darkened. The more sins a man commits, the more he will be dull and darkened.

C. Death: the darkest one is the dead one. The ones that are in the tomb are the darkest ones; they have no light at all.

II. **The proof of darkness**

A. Man does not know the origin of the universe.

B. Man does not know where he came from.

C. Man does not know where he is going.

D. Man does not know where he is.

E. Man does not know his real situation. He is filthy, yet he has no consciousness of his filthiness.

F. Man does not know that he is wrong, yet he is really wrong. He commits sin, yet he has no consciousness of sin.

G. Man turns the truth upside down. He takes right for wrong and wrong for right.

III. The suffering of darkness

Describe the misery of a man in darkness: when a man is wrong and will not acknowledge it, he falls into darkness. In darkness man does not know where he came from or where he is going. He is like a dumb fool, very miserable. He does not know what is the right way to go on, and he does not know where to turn to get help. His living is so gloomy it seems as if the day will never break. Ask the people, "If such is your case, how can you ever find happiness?"

IV. The danger of darkness

Darkness causes you to fall into the deep pit, death, and eternal perdition.

V. How to get out of darkness

A. Christ is the light.

B. The life of Christ is the light.

C. God is light.

D. The Bible is the light.

E. So you need to receive the Bible, God, Christ, and His life. Such receiving is faith.

F. Believe in God according to the words of the Bible, confess your own sins, and receive the Lord Jesus as the Savior of your life.

Subject Sixteen

"WHERE ARE YOU?"—IN THE HAND OF SATAN

Scripture: Gen. 3:9; 1 John 5:19; Acts 26:18; John 12:31; 16:11; Eph. 2:2; Col. 1:13

I. Man is not free

Describe how man is held in the hand of Satan, subject to his slaughtering, suffering his paralyzing and killing.

A. Satan moves within man's heart and causes him to do things not of himself and beyond his own control. Explain that playing cards, adultery, and various evils are something beyond self-control. Satan uses various kinds of habits to anesthetize and ensnare man.

B. Satan has a power in man which no one can overcome. For example, dancing and drugs appear to be mere habits but they are actually the power of Satan.

II. Man's life is in Satan's hand

Describe the real situation of human living: Satan has caused man to sin, to covet fame, to steal money, to love the world, to envy others for the sake of higher position, to betray others, to scheme to destroy others' families, and to take away another's wife. Men who do these things have been deceived by Satan. Satan would first destroy men's reputation and morality and then endanger men's lives.

III. The destiny of men that are in the hand of Satan

A. Death.

B. To be the companions of Satan in the lake of fire, because the lake of fire is prepared for Satan and his subordinates. Unless you escape from the hand of Satan, you will eventually fall into the lake of fire.

IV. How to be free from Satan's hand

A. The Lord Jesus through His death on the cross has crushed the Devil who had the power of death, that is, He has judged the prince of this world, Satan.

B. If we receive the Lord Jesus as our Lord, we can overcome the power of Satan.

By repeating the question, "Where Are You?" subjects 10 through 16 continue in the theme of seeking sinners and turning them to the Lord.

Subject Seventeen

MAN'S RELIGION AND GOD'S SAVING WAY

Scripture: Gen. 4

It is not easy to give a clear picture of salvation by using the story of Cain and Abel in Genesis 4 as a gospel subject, because the main points are usually missed. However, if you use "Man's Religion and God's Saving Way" as the subject for this portion, it will be easy for you to speak, because the story of Cain speaks of man's religion, and that of Abel speaks of God's saving way.

This subject is divided into two sections. It is better to give it in two meetings.

I. **Man's religion**

A. The origin of man's religion is that it was invented by man's concept in his presumptions about God.

 1. Any human religion is invented by man.
    You should talk about the origin of each so-called religion.

 2. Man is made by God. Because man has a spirit within him, there is always within man an inclination toward worshipping God. So there is a concept of God within all men.

 3. Man has invented ways to worship God based upon this concept of God within himself, and this invention is called religion.

B. The meaning of man's religion is that it is a teaching according to something or someone that is worshipped. On one hand, you teach yourself, and on the other hand, you teach others how to worship God and behave as a man.

 1. Worship. There is always an object of worship, either a god, a person, or some thing. Among the five main religions, two worship God (Christianity and Islam), and three worship a person: Confucianism worships Confucius, Buddhism worships Siddhartha Gautama, and Taoism worships Lao-tzu.

    2. Teaching. This is to teach others, according to what you worship, how to worship God and behave as a man.

C. The central point and main emphasis of man's religion is to cultivate moral conduct by human effort.

    1. The central point of any religion is to cultivate moral conduct by human effort. In this respect Confucianism, Buddhism, Taoism and Islam are all very similar. Even today's Christianity as it is generally understood is no different.

    2. Man's religion has the hope of achieving a good result by means of human effort. All religions hold out the hope of somehow earning a future reward based on the merits of good works. The hope of all who practice cultivating moral conduct is to achieve some kind of immortality. For example, for a Buddhist, this would mean to become a Buddha.

D. Within man's religion is a hidden motivation which is a part of the Devil's scheme to damage God's plan.

    1. The central point of all religions is to cultivate moral conduct by human effort and to exhort others to do good. But God does not care for this. Many think that the central point of Christianity also is to exhort others to do good, but people must know that to do good is not God's saving way.

    2. The central point of all religions is the confusion of Satan to cover up God's saving way.

    3. All who pay attention to the central point of any religion are cheated by Satan and are damaged in relation to God's plan.

    These three points fully expose the hidden motivation of religion. Such a presentation is attractive as well as persuasive, opening up an understanding of God's salvation.

E. The destiny of those in man's religion is that they are not accepted by God, and they are fallen into sinfulness and destruction.

1. All those who rely on the central point of religion to please God are not accepted by God. We may use Cain as an example.

2. All those who rely on the central point of religion cannot have fellowship with God; instead, they are farther away from God.

3. The result is to become more and more sinful, and the end is destruction.

These three points should be based upon the story of Cain. His offering of the produce of the field to God is to cultivate moral conduct by human effort, and the result was threefold: he was not accepted by God, he was farther away from God, and later he committed murder and sins.

II. God's saving way

A. The origin of God's saving way is by God's revelation.

1. Human religion was man's invention, but God's saving way came by God's revelation. *You should repeat this until people see that religion is man's invention, but the saving way is by God's revelation.* Such a revelation is something never thought of by man. Whatever man can think of is totally a matter of religion.

2. Explain that what Abel did was not a matter of religion but something by God's revelation. You should make it clear that Cain's method or way of worshipping God came out of his own presumptions; thus it was his own invention, so that what he did was religion. What Abel did was not of his own guesswork or invention but of God's revelation, which he had learned through his parents, Adam and Eve. After Adam and Eve sinned, God killed an animal, and He clothed them with the skin of the animal. Adam and Eve must have told Abel about this. Hebrews 11 says that Abel offered up sacrifices by faith, and Romans 10 says that faith is by hearing. It can be seen that Abel's faith came by hearing from his parents, and therefore what Abel did came out of revelation.

3. The origin of religion requires no faith, but the origin of the saving way requires faith. Because religion was invented by man, you only need to guess a little. Only God's saving way is God's revelation; therefore it requires faith. Guessing will never work.

B. The meaning of God's saving way is to serve God based upon God's salvation. The meaning of religion is to belong to a sect and be taught accordingly, but the meaning of the saving way is to serve God based upon God's salvation.

   1. In the saving way, there is the experience of God's salvation.

   2. God's salvation is to cause us to serve Him. We serve Him not by a teaching, but by the salvation we experience. God's salvation is to save us to such an extent that we can serve Him.

C. The central point of God's saving way is the redemption of Christ and His salvation.

   1. Redemption. Explain how man has committed sins and how the problem of sins must be resolved. The problem of sins cannot be dealt with no matter how much man tries to cultivate moral conduct and to do good. Only by the death of Christ and His shed blood can man's sins be dealt with.

   2. Salvation. Christ is the life-giving Spirit (1 Cor. 15:45b). Once we believe in Him, His Spirit and His life will enter into us to be our power and our salvation.

   3. Compare the central points of religion and of the saving way. The central point of religion is to cultivate moral conduct and to do good, which cannot (1) resolve the problem of the sins committed in the past; (2) and much less save man from sin and enable him to overcome sin. In contrast, the central point of the saving way is Christ's redemption and salvation, by which (1) the problem of our past sins can be resolved through redemption; and (2) we are

enabled to overcome sin and to be free from sins through salvation.

D. The hidden meaning of God's saving way is the fulfillment of His plan.

God's saving way implies the fulfillment of God's plan.

1. God has His strategy and arrangement, and these make up His plan.
2. God's plan is to work Himself into man.
3. The way God works Himself into man is by His life.
4. To receive God's saving way—to believe in Christ—is to receive God's life into us.

E. The destiny of those who receive God's saving way is to be accepted by God and delivered from sin and death.

1. The redemption of Christ is by the blood of Christ; the salvation of Christ is by the life of Christ. We can be accepted by God only by having the blood and the life of Christ. Abel was accepted by God not by his own merit, but by the animal that was slain. That animal typifies Christ.
2. Being accepted by God enables us to have fellowship with God.
3. God's saving way delivers us from sin and death. Abel suffered persecution; yet he did not sin. He was killed; yet he did not perish.

Subject Eighteen

THE WAY TO ESCAPE DEATH

Scripture: Gen. 5; John 11:25, 26

I. Sin is the source of death

A. No one will escape death, because no one is sinless.
B. Give some facts to prove that sin causes death. For example, those who lose their temper very easily will surely die earlier than those who don't. Those who are given to indulgence in much eating and drinking, to fornication or to gambling, will die sooner. Sin kills men, and it was sin that brought in death.

C. Sin brought in death not only as a result of the nature of sin, but also because of the working of the law of God's righteousness. This is to say that it is not only a natural result that those who commit sins will die; but it is also the demand of God's righteousness that those who commit sins must die.

II. Everyone must die at some time

Hebrews 9:27 says, "It is reserved for men once to die."

A. Speak about the facts of death.

Genesis 5: Adam, Seth, and Enosh all died. Confucius, Buddha, your ancestors, even many of your grandparents and some of your parents have all died. One day you will also die. Can you name anyone who will not die?

B. Death is appointed to all men.

It is appointed to everyone once to die. Your destiny is death. Although you are not dead yet, an appointment with death has been made for you. You may consider that you are going in a certain direction, but whether you realize it or not, you are actually going into death; your destination is death. Perhaps it is your goal to be promoted and become rich, but do you realize that one day you will be put into a coffin? (Here you need to speak a little more about the terror of death.) No one likes to hear about death, and no one likes to mention the word *death*. Ask the listeners, "What will be *your* destiny? What will be the end of your living? Blessing, high salary, long life, money, or death? How did you feel when you saw someone in a coffin?" The day will come when you will not be able to escape death.

III. Death is the end of everything

Adam was the wisest of all mankind, wiser than any great scientist or biologist; yet one day he died and was gone. Seth feared God, but he died also. So did Enosh. Men of all occupations in all walks of life have all died. The holy and wise men, the heroes and the warriors, all have died. Many people of great reputation died of a stroke. High blood pressure is a notification that death is approaching. College professors pride themselves on their great mentalities, but should just a tiny vein in their brain break, they would die.

IV. **The way to escape death**

A. In order to escape death, you must have sin resolved first, because death came by sin.

B. You need to receive an endless life, a life that will never die.

C. Only God's life is immortal and eternal. Therefore you must have God's life so that you will never die.

D. Receive Christ and you will have this eternal life.

E. Those who receive Christ will never die. Even if their physical bodies pass through death, they will be resurrected (John 11:25, 26). Mention Enoch with the following five sub-points: (1) Enoch walked with God, (2) he was delivered from sin, (3) he had sin resolved, (4) he contacted God, and (5) he received an endless life, a life that will never die. Finally, mention that he walked with God and was delivered from sin by faith.

Subject Nineteen

THE CORRUPTION OF THE WORLD AND THE DELIVERANCE OF GOD

Scripture: Gen. 6, 7, 8

I. **The corruption of the world**

A. The cause of corruption:

1. The fall of mankind. Because of the fall of our ancestor, Adam, the entire human race has been corrupted.

2. Man's nature is corrupted. The entire human race is fallen. Many deeds of corruption among men were invented by the fallen human nature. Give some examples, such as dancing and movies. These are the invention of the fallen human nature.

B. The sphere of corruption:

1. The sphere of corruption includes everyone, every society, every group, and every family. It is difficult to find any society, group, or family free from corruption.

2. Present facts of various situations of corruption. Give examples and explain how businessmen, educators, students, doctors, nurses, and politicians are corrupt.

C. The power of corruption:

Touch their feelings on this point.

1. Explain that corruption is a tide. You may have tried to go against the tide, but you could not stand, so you joined it. When the tide comes, you have no way to withstand it. When the tide of watching a movie comes, the old and the young all go to see it, with the father, the sons, and the grandsons watching the same adulterous movie; all three generations clapping their hands together and being corrupted together. You can ask them: "Can you overcome the tide of corruption?" Try your best to find some examples to prove that men cannot overcome the tide of corruption.

2. Describe how men cannot withstand the tide. The tide is like a sweeping flood. Men are too fragile; they can only join in the same flow and be swept away. When all are lying, can you tell the truth?

If the words of the gospel are not piercing, it will be like sugar that is not sweet, vinegar that is not sour, and pepper that is not hot. So the words must be penetrating. Only the piercing words can touch men's feeling.

D. The result of corruption:

1. God's decision—God has decided to judge.

2. God's judgment. Use the judgment of the flood to explain that one day God will also judge this world,

because as the days of the flood, so shall be the days of the coming of the Son of Man (Luke 17:26).

II. God's deliverance

A. The preparation:

1. When men had become corrupted and God was determined to judge the world, He first prepared an ark for men.

2. This world is corrupt. Before God comes to judge, He first prepared Christ to be our deliverance.

3. Before the flood came, God prepared an ark for the people to enter in. Before the judgment comes, God prepared Christ, and He is waiting for men to believe and receive Him. So, deliverance is prepared by God.

B. The method:

1. The Deliverer and the delivered ones are made one. To enter into the ark is to be one with the ark. Noah's household, eight in number, deserved the judgment of the flood, but because they were united with the ark, the ark bore the judgment of the flood in their stead. Christ was made sin for us, that we might be made God's righteousness in Him. This is the union.

2. The reason the Deliverer can take the place of the delivered ones is that the delivered ones are joined with the Deliverer, for substitution is based upon union.

3. Redemption. The ark was pitched within and without with pitch. (The Hebrew word for *pitch* is the same as the word for *redemption*.) Pitch typifies redemption. When a person receives redemption, God's water of judgment cannot come upon him. The ark was pitched outside and inside as well, the pitch on the outside for dealing with God's judgment, and the pitch on the inside for peace in our conscience.

4. Deliverance. The ark not only brought redemption to those who were inside it, freeing them from God's judgment, but it also delivered them from the corrupted world and brought them to another world.

The ark rested upon the mountain of Ararat in the seventh month, the seventeenth day, which was the day of the Lord's resurrection. The ark resting on the mountain of Ararat typifies Christ in resurrection delivering the eight people, the whole household of Noah, from the corrupted world and bringing them to another world; from corruption into resurrection. The ark resting upon the mountain of Ararat typifies that we died in Christ, were resurrected, and ascended together with Him. (A mountain signifies ascension.)

C. The receiving:

1. It is not to admit. It is not enough just to admit that there is an ark, the Savior.

2. Neither is it to agree. Just to agree with the ark, to agree with Christianity, or to agree with the cross cannot save you.

3. Nor is it to merely contact. Many have encountered Christianity, but did not receive Christ. They were eventually drawn into the water.

4. It is a matter of entering in. The whole household of Noah, eight persons in all, entered into the ark. This signifies that men must enter into Christ, for the ark typifies Christ.

5. The way to enter in:

a. Entering in is a union. When the eight people entered into the ark, they were joined to the ark and united with it. Likewise, when we enter into Christ we are joined to Him and united with Him.

b. How to be joined to Christ: the problem that keeps man from being joined to Christ is sin, so you must repent and confess your sin.

c. Christ is the life-giving Spirit. When you repent and confess, you must contact Him with your human spirit.

d. Believe that when you have repented, confessed, and received Christ in this way, He will enter into you, and you are joined to Him.

Subject Twenty

GOD'S CALLING

Scripture: Gen. 12

This subject covers the calling of Abraham.

I. God's purpose in man

Do not say this too heavily. Point out that God has a purpose in man. Man is not meaningless in the universe, but the purpose of God is with him.

II. Man's fall

Do not say too much. Briefly say that man has fallen from God's purpose and has lost God's purpose.

III. Man's real situation

Using the tower of Babel as a background, tell how the people of that time lived a godless life and how they worshipped idols. Then describe how people today are living a godless life, and how they also are building a tower of Babel and a city of Babel.

IV. God's calling

A. While men were building the city and the tower of Babel, God came to call men to return to His original purpose.

B. In what way does God call? He calls by His gospel. Today the gospel preaching is God's calling.

C. How does God call?

1. He wants men to repent. To repent is to turn your heart to God. Formerly your thinking was a godless thinking, and your living was a godless living. Now you must change your mind and turn to God.

2. He wants men to believe and receive Him.

V. Answering God's call

Since you have spoken of repentance and believing in the preceding section, here you need to cover only three minor points.

A. Teach the new ones to pray and confess.

B. Help them to believe God's words.

C. Help them make the decision to live for God. (Don't consider this as something that is too deep.) There are three words which summarize a complete salvation:
1. Conviction.
2. Conversion.
3. Consecration.

In every gospel preaching you should lead the new ones to consecration. In the Old Testament picture, the people of Israel were consecrated as soon as the Passover was finished. If you have a five-day gospel conference, the last day should be used to cover the matter of consecration. This is like Peter's salvation. Peter repented and was saved, and then he left everything and followed Jesus. This is consecration.

Subject Twenty-one

THE JUDGMENT OF SODOM

Scripture: Gen. 18, 19; Matt. 11:23-24

I. The corruption of Sodom

You should touch people's feeling from the very beginning. Make it plain that the corruption of Sodom was centered in immorality, with adultery and fornication at its worst. Based on this point, describe the immoral situation in today's society, including such things as dancing, movies, nude pictures, obscene novels and photos, etc. Today's best selling books are the obscene ones. Today's world is an adulterous world. You should make mention of divorce and other abnormal relationships between men and women. Just as the corruption of Sodom in that day was centered in immorality, so also is the world today.

II. God's judgment

A. In this section make it clear that all the corruption of man is laid open before the eyes of God (Heb. 4:13). Nothing is hidden from God.

B. The corruption of mankind provoked God's righteous wrath.

C. God's wrath caused God to judge men.

D. Men's corruption is centered in immorality, and God's judgment is centered in fire. All the immoral people will be burned by fire. The same fire that burned Sodom in that day shall also burn this immoral world in a day to come. This fire is the lake of fire.

III. Deliverance in the midst of judgment

A. In this section point out that in the midst of the corrupted people there were some who feared God. In this message do not say that Lot was evil; rather, say that he was a righteous man.

B. Point out that when God executes His judgment, He also saves those who belong to Him.

C. God not only saves those who believe in Him; He is also willing to save all of the believer's relatives. Tell how Lot's wife, daughters, and sons-in-law were not willing to go out of the city, and how the angels persuaded them to go out.

IV. Men's negligence toward the gospel

A. As a basis, tell how those who heard Lot and the angels preaching the gospel thought that they were jesting and would not believe.

B. Go on to say that today people also think that we are either not serious or that we are superstitious.

C. Conclude that those who will be burned by fire will be those who heard the gospel but made light of it.

Subject Twenty-two

THE ELECTION OF GRACE

Scripture: Gen. 25:21-26; Rom. 9:10-13

Grace is the gospel. Election is also the gospel.

I. God's salvation is not of works

This gospel message is to correct men's wrong concept of placing emphasis on good works.

A. First point out that everyone has a concept that men's work counts before God, and that men's work can please God. Nearly all religions rely on works for God's reward.

B. The Bible reveals to us that God's salvation has nothing at all to do with men's works. The revelation of the Bible is contrary to men's thinking. Use the story of Jacob as an illustration. Jacob was a saved one. God had determined to grant him salvation before he was even born, much less before he could perform any works. This proves that God's salvation is not of men's works.

II. God's grace is free—Romans 4:4

A. Make it clear that grace does not require man to pay a price.

B. Make it clear that works require a price; it takes effort.

C. Works are contradictory to grace. The two do not go together. This means that it is either grace without works, or works without grace.

III. Salvation is all of grace

A. Point out that salvation is all of God's grace, which is something God freely gives to men.

B. Mention that salvation includes forgiveness, justification, obtaining life, living a holy life, inheriting a heavenly inheritance, and eternal blessings. All these are the elements of God's salvation, which God gives to men freely because of His grace.

IV. God's election

A. God's election is for God's salvation. Whoever receives God's salvation is one of God's elect. Election is the procedure, whereas salvation is the purpose. So God's election is for God's salvation.

B. Salvation is by grace, and election is also by grace. Use Jacob's story as an illustration. Jacob was saved by God, and he was elected by God. It was all of God's grace and not of his own works.

V. Receiving God's election

A. God's election is made known to us through the gospel. Through the gospel God announces to us that God has chosen us.

B. To believe the gospel is to receive the election, and to reject the gospel is to reject the election. The fact that God allows you to hear the gospel now means that God has stretched forth His hand to choose you. The question now is whether you believe the gospel or reject it.

C. To believe the gospel you must repent, confess, and receive Christ as your Savior.

D. All those who receive Christ are the elected ones, and by their receiving they become the saved ones.

Subject Twenty-three

MAN UNDER THE POWER OF SATAN

Scripture: Exo. 1—5; Acts 26:18

First use Exodus 1—5 to describe how man's life was bitter with hard labor, burning bricks, to build cities. The people were so busy that they could not hearken to the word of God. Then speak about Acts 26:18.

I. The type

Begin with the fact that the children of Israel fell into Egypt. Egypt typifies the world. The children of Israel in Egypt typify man in the world under the reign of Satan.

II. The life of the world

A. The children of Israel went down to Egypt to earn a living. They labored in Egypt making brick and building cities to earn a livelihood.

B. Today the people in the world working to earn a livelihood are under the power of Satan. Men study, practice medicine, labor, and do business all for the purpose of making a living. *You should touch their feeling on this point.*

C. *How to touch people's feeling.* For the sake of their living many people give up their morality, their reputation, and their belongings, becoming slaves of Satan. Do you think that the children of Israel made brick and built cities for the Egyptians willingly? Of course not! They were forced into these things for their living. Today likewise many people give up their reputation and do evil things, not willingly, but because they are forced to do so for their living. Don't just blame the harlots. Many people do evil things and are no better than harlots, even though others cannot tell the real situation by outward appearances. Many women get married for a living, just for their husband's money. Once their husbands become poor, they want a divorce. Why do they play the hypocrite in such a way? They do it just so that they can make a living from their husbands. It is for the sake of a living that man falls into the hands of Satan. Why have so many done all the immoral things that they knew were evil? Just to keep their livelihood. They first sold their reputation and then their soul. Some teachers do not even care for morality in their teaching; they are concerned only about their livelihood. This proves that men are forced to be under the control of Satan.

III. **The hindrance to the gospel**

A. Today the biggest hindrance to the gospel is the problem of people having to earn a living. After Moses preached the gospel to the Israelites, Pharaoh increased their tasks.

B. When people first hear the gospel, many realize that they should believe in God, but they hesitate to receive the gospel because they are too concerned about their livelihood.

C. When the gospel is preached, Satan always increases the burden and adds more sufferings to man. After the Israelites heard the gospel through Moses, Pharaoh increased their tasks and furthermore, stopped supplying the straw to them. Today, if you have heard the gospel, tomorrow you may be asked to work overtime. Satan uses such evil devices to hinder people from believing in the Lord.

D. If man accepts the words of Satan, he will think that the gospel is just a lie, just as in that day when Pharaoh said that the words of Moses were lying words.

IV. The patience of the gospel

A. Although it is so easy for man to receive the suggestions from Satan and reject the Gospel, God never gives up working on man until man receives Him. You have probably heard the gospel before. At that time Satan hindered you, and so you rejected the gospel. Perhaps two weeks later your friends invited you again to a gospel meeting. This is the God who never gives up working on you until you believe in Him.

B. During the time that God was patiently waiting for you, He would also do something through your circumstances. *Sound out more warnings in this respect.* Believe quickly, or you will suffer more. On the one hand, Satan is trying to grab you; on the other hand, God is touching you. At the same time, God may smite you through your circumstances. For instance, someone in your family may get sick, you may be out of work, or you may fail in your business.

C. Thus, many people eventually believed and received Jesus after God had worked on them, although they had been fooled by Satan's suggestions at first.

D. Since you must believe, and since eventually you will believe, why not stop your struggling and believe in Him right now?

V. The way to be saved

A. First make it clear that man has fallen under the power of Satan and cannot get out of Satan's power by himself.

B. The Lord Jesus has judged the world and destroyed Satan.

C. As soon as man repents and believes in Jesus, he is out of Satan's power and he is returned to God.

Subject Twenty-four

DETAINED BY SATAN

Scripture: Exo. 8—11

I. The type

Explain how God called the people of Israel out of Egypt, and how Pharaoh tried to detain them.

II. Serve God in Egypt

A. In the last message, Subject 23, we saw how Pharaoh did not want the people of Israel to serve God. In this message we will see how Pharaoh allowed them to worship God, but would not let them leave Egypt.

B. After hearing the gospel, many people today keep struggling until they finally begin to realize that it is hard not to believe. Then Satan would suggest, "Do not go overboard. Do not leave your attainments. Stay where you are."

C. Go on to say that nearly everyone who has received the gospel has afterward had a big change in his life and his position. Here you need to give some examples. Some had held an improper job, such as operating a casino. Once that one believed in Jesus, he knew that he had to give up that job. Another may have had a proper job. But once he believed in Jesus, his whole concept was changed. Formerly he cared only for his job and not for God; now his life is changed, and the basic principle of his behavior must also change. Formerly he was for making a living; now he is for serving God.

D. Many have realized that they had to believe in Jesus, but they hesitate to change their position. Then Satan would suggest, "Serve in Egypt! You can have both heaven in the future and your attainments in this life."

III. Don't go too far

A. In that day Pharaoh promised that the Israelites could serve God, but he would not let them go too far away from him.

B. Today many want to believe in the Lord, but Satan also suggests to them, "Don't go too far."

C. "Don't go too far" was a matter of distance in that day, but today it is a matter of situation. With many people, there is no difference between their situation before they received the Lord and afterward. For example, some gave up watching the evil movies, but they continue to watch the good ones. Others quit gambling for money, but still play poker for fun. Use some examples such as these to show that these are all Satan's suggestions.

D. The reason Satan does not want man to go too far is that he wants to be able to pull man back into the world easily at any time. Pharaoh would not let the Israelites go too far, because he wanted to grab them back at any time. If you allow yourself to continue to see the good movies, it will not be too long before you will go back to the evil ones again. In the beginning you might be playing poker just for fun, but before long you would be gambling again. Many friends would advise you, saying, "There is nothing wrong with believing in the Lord, but don't go overboard." Others might advise you, "You have worked too hard for the whole week. It would be too much for you to have nothing for your entertainment."

All these are Satan's suggestions.

IV. **The men may go, but not the little ones nor the old ones**

A. The type.

After negotiating many times, Pharaoh finally agreed to let the men go, but he would not let the young ones or the old ones go.

B. Today it is the same with many people. They would not believe until their parents are buried. In Nanking there was a college student who was very much touched by the gospel, but his mother was against his accepting the Lord. So he told the preacher that he would not believe before she dies. That preacher said to him, "What a good son you are! After you send your

parents to hell, then you will go to heaven in peace."
That student was awakened by the rebuke, and he
was saved.

C. It is also the scheme of Satan that won't let the young
ones or the old ones go. If your parents and children
all stay in Egypt, no doubt you will soon return to
Egypt yourself. Use Acts 16:31, "Believe on the Lord
Jesus, and thou shalt be saved, thou and thy house,"
to explain that with the gospel, the household is a
basic unit. Each house had to have a passover lamb.
God wants the whole household saved together.

V. **Go serve the Lord; only let your flocks and your
herds remain**

A. The type.
Then Pharaoh would let the whole household go, but
he wanted their possessions to stay.

B. Today many who believe in Jesus are doing the same
thing. They do not bring everything with them to the
Lord. Some are not able to preach such a gospel,
because they themselves still have a lot of possessions
left in Egypt.

C. The reason Satan wants men's possessions to stay in
Egypt is that he knows that where their possessions
are, there also is their heart. As long as men have
their possessions remaining in Egypt, sooner or later
they will return there themselves.

VI. **All go**

A. The type.

B. Some really bring their whole being, their whole household, and all their possessions to come and believe in
Jesus.

C. As a result, they are completely delivered out of the
power of Satan.

VII. **Smiting Pharaoh**

A. Pharaoh would not allow the Israelites to go, so God
smote Pharaoh and killed all the firstborn of the
Egyptians.

B. Your wife, friends, or teachers hindered you from believing in Jesus, so God came in to smite them.

C. Sooner or later you still have to believe in Him.

D. Since sooner or later you will have to believe, why not believe sooner, even today?

E. Those who suffer repeated smiting and still refuse to believe, not only will be bothered and have no peace, but they will also get their neighbors involved. Use the slaying of the Egyptians' firstborn in one night as an example.

F. It is better to believe in Him now.

Subject Twenty-five

THE PASSOVER

Scripture: Exo. 12

I. The position of man by birth

A. In the world. The children of Israel were born in Egypt. Every human being is born in the world.

1. All things in the world are contrary to God and against God. The world occupies mankind, which God created, in just the same way that Egypt occupied the Israelites at that time.

2. Because man has been born into the world, not only is he occupied by the world, but he also follows the world in opposing God.

B. Under the power of Satan.

1. Man is under the power of Satan just as the Israelites were under Pharaoh.

2. Exodus 12:12 says that God will smite all the gods of Egypt, which means that He will smite all the idols of Egypt. Today, people in the world are all worshipping idols and are under the power of Satan. One day God will come and judge them also.

3. Worshipping idols is the greatest sin against God, for God is a jealous God. Idol worship is just like a married woman committing adultery.

C. In sin.

    1. When the Israelites stayed in Egypt, they committed sins just as the Egyptians did.

    2. All the people in the world are committing sins. Speak about men's sins and the manner in which they are committed.

    3. For man to commit sins is to sin against God.

II. The appointed judgment

A. Judgment is appointed.

    1. Men have committed sins and have done evil things in the world; they have followed Satan and worshipped idols. God's judgment has already been appointed to men a long time ago.

    2. When the time comes, God will execute His predestinated judgment.

B. The result of judgment.

The result of judgment is death. Use Exodus 12 to explain that God's appointed judgment upon the Egyptians was that one in each house should die. Speak more about death being appointed to everyone, if time allows.

III. The way of salvation prepared by God

A. The lamb.

    1. Explain how the Israelites prepared the lamb at that time.

    2. The lamb typifies Christ.

    3. Explain how they examined the lamb. Examining the lamb is examining Christ. Those who examined Christ could not find any fault with Him.

    4. Explain how the lamb became their substitute.

B. Shedding of blood.

    1. Without the shedding of blood, there is no forgiveness of sin.

    2. When God's judgment comes only the blood can deliver man. On the day that God's judgment came to the land of Egypt, every house had to have the shed

blood. Unless you want to shed your own blood, you must have the blood of a lamb to substitute for you.

3. All the houses of Israel had the blood of the lamb to substitute for them.

4. All the houses that had the lamb as a substitute escaped death and escaped God's judgment.

C. The sign of the blood.

1. God looks only at the blood, not at man. God had the blood as the basis and as the sign.

2. Man cannot depend on his own good deeds or his own virtue to escape from God's judgment.

3. The importance of the blood. Here you can use more Scripture verses, such as the blood washes us from our sins, sins were forgiven by the blood, and we are redeemed by the blood, etc. (Eph. 1:7; Matt. 26:28; Rev. 1:5).

IV. The application of God's salvation

A. Believe.

1. In that day for the Israelites to kill the lamb was to believe the lamb. The killing was believing. At the moment we believed, we all killed the Lord Jesus on the cross. Every one that believes will have the feeling that it was my sins that had crucified my Savior on the cross. Although it was because of God's righteousness that Jesus was killed on the cross, nevertheless, in terms of our feeling, it was our sins that had crucified Him.

2. To believe is to receive.

The Israelites not only killed the lamb, but also struck the blood upon the lintel and on the two side posts. Striking the blood is receiving. There are two steps to the receiving: the first is to strike the blood, and the second is to eat the lamb. Eating the lamb is taking Christ into us as life.

B. Remission of sins.

1. The Israelites had the feast of the Passover and the feast of the Unleavened Bread at the same time.

When they ate the lamb, they also had the unleavened bread. This means that on one hand they received the Lord's life and on the other hand their sins were forgiven.

    2. The lamb should be eaten with bitter herbs. This means that with a broken and contrite heart man is willing to get rid of his sins.

C. Receive the words of God.

    1. God's saving way is prepared by God, but it was given to us through the words of God. So today when we believe in Him, we should also receive His words.

    2. Once we receive the words of God, we are saved.

    3. Once we receive the words of God, we experience the Passover. God's judgment passes over us, and we are at peace.

D. The result.

    1. Delivered from God's condemnation.

    2. Delivered from Satan's domination.

    3. Delivered from the world's occupation.

    4. Walking out of the world. When the Israelites were eating the lamb, they had to have their loins girded, shoes on their feet, and a staff in their hand. They ate in haste so that they could leave Egypt in haste.

This message may be given in two sessions.

Subject Twenty-six

THE ROCK AND THE LIVING WATER

Scripture: Exo. 17:1-6; 1 Cor. 10:4; John 4:14; 7:37-38; Rev. 22:17; Isa. 55:1

I. The wilderness of human life

This passage describes the desolation of human life.

A. First tell how the children of Israel walked in the wilderness in that day.

B. Human life itself is just a wilderness. Man's whole life is just a vast wilderness full of desolation; there is only labor and heavy burdens without rest and joy. Give a full portrait of the desolation of human life in this passage.

C. The reason human life is just a wilderness is that man is sinful and apart from God. Originally, God was the meaning of the human life, but sin separated man from God. Therefore, human life became vain and desolate, like a wilderness.

II. The thirst of human life

This passage describes the needs of human life.

A. Tell how the Israelites had no water to drink in the wilderness. They were thirsty and desperate for water to quench their thirst.

B. There is also a great need in the human life, a desperate need for a certain kind of water to quench man's thirst. Fully portray the condition of the dissatisfaction of human life. Everyone in the world, whether a farmer, soldier, laborer, business man, housewife, child, young or old, is thirsty and dissatisfied.

C. Man is thirsty because he does not have God. God is the meaning and the satisfaction of human life. Only God can quench man's thirst. A man without God cannot help but be thirsty.

III. God meeting man's needs

A. Man could not meet his needs by himself, just as the Israelites who were thirsty in the wilderness could not do anything for themselves.

B. Only God can quench man's thirst and meet man's need. It takes a work of God to quench man's thirst. To have water coming out of the rock is a miracle; human hands could never do such a thing.

C. God satisfies man through Christ. This Christ was typified by the rock in the wilderness in that day. First Corinthians 10:4 says, "That Rock was Christ." In the Bible, a rock is the symbol of solidity and dependability. The Bible shows us that Christ is as solid and dependable as a rock. Here we will not say too much about the solidity and dependability of Christ. Instead we will pay

attention to how the living water which came out of Him
can quench man's thirst. The problem in the wilderness
was not a question of solidity nor dependability, but of
thirst. Only the living water which comes out of Christ
can quench the thirst of man.

D. The living water coming out of the rock and quenching
the thirst of the Israelites typifies Christ broken on
the cross and that out of Him came the living water to
quench our thirst. The rock was solid and dependable,
yet it cracked so that water could flow out to meet the
needs of the Israelites. So also Christ was broken, and
the living water came out of Him to meet our needs.

E. The water came out of the rock after Moses had smitten
it. Moses represents the law, and his rod represents
authority. Moses' rod represents the authority of the law.
Moses' rod smiting the rock represents the authority of
the law smiting Christ so that He might be broken and
the water of life might flow out to quench man's thirst.
Man lost God because of sin. For man to receive God,
man's sins must first be judged by the authority of the
law. Christ was smitten by the law in the sinner's stead;
thus the requirements of the law were satisfied, and
now the sinners can receive the living water which came
out of Him.

F. The very water flowing out of Christ is God's life,
God's Spirit, and God Himself. Whoever this living
water flows into, God's Spirit and God Himself also
flow into him. Whosoever gets this water will be satisfied.

IV. The way of quenching man's thirst

A. The Rock is already split open, and the living water is
flowing out. The water is available for people to come
and drink.

B. Today God is calling, "Let him who is thirsty...come...
take the water of life freely" (Rev. 22:17; Isa. 55:1).

C. Drinking is receiving—receiving the water of life and
the Spirit. The Spirit is everywhere. All that man has
to do is open his heart and receive God's Spirit with

his human spirit. Whether or not man can touch God all depends upon whether or not he will drink.

D. Drinking is free. Man does not have to pay anything. There is no need of money; it is a free gift.

E. When a man opens his heart and uses his human spirit to receive the Lord Jesus as the Savior in this way, he will feel comfortable and satisfied within.

Subject Twenty-seven

THE LAW OF MOUNT SINAI

Scripture: Exo. 19

I. The nature of man

A. Man does not know himself. *This passage needs to be emphasized.*

1. On the day that the Israelites went to the lower part of Mt. Sinai, they did not know themselves.

2. Man thinks that he can do good by his own effort and that he can keep the law of God. This is just like the Israelites' answer to the Lord, "All that the Lord hath spoken we will do."

3. The fact that man thought he could do good and keep the law is a strong proof that man does not know himself.

B. The real condition of man.

1. The real condition of the Israelites was that they did a good number of things against God's covenant. God did not allow them to make idols, but they made them. They even worshipped the idols. Their real condition was totally against God's law.

2. Man thought he could do good, but actually he could not do good at all. Do you think that you can do good? Do you think that you can love your parents? As a matter of fact, you still love yourself the most. *Give some real examples of sin to touch their feeling.*

II. The manifestation of God

A. The law was given to expose the real condition of man.

1. God gave the law to man because the Israelites did not realize their real condition. God gave the law not for the Israelites to keep, but for exposing their real condition.

2. When man does not try to keep the law, he does not realize how corrupted he is. But once he tries to keep the law, he immediately discovers how powerless he is in keeping the law.

B. There is no one who has not transgressed the law.

Even before Moses brought the law back from Mount Sinai, the Israelites had already offended the law. That is why Moses cast the tables out of his hands and broke them on the way. That was a declaration that the law had been broken by the Israelites.

III. The content of the law

This part does not need to be covered in too much detail. Just pick some important points and emphasize them.

A. Combine the first few of the ten commandments and present some practical examples to explain how man has worshipped false gods.

B. Honor your father and your mother.

C. Thou shalt not kill.

D. Thou shalt not commit adultery.

E. Thou shalt not steal.

F. Thou shalt not lie.

G. Thou shalt not covet.

These items should be spoken in a very strong way, like thundering, even making the people tremble.

IV. The situation of man before the law

A. Everyone has offended the law.

B. No one can stand self-confidently before the law.

C. Man is terrified when the law is presented. Describe how the Israelites were terrified at Mt. Sinai on that day.

D. The law exposes the sins of man.

E. The law also condemns the sins of man.

V. God's saving way

A. Christ was condemned and judged in our stead. He has redeemed us from the curse of the law.

B. God wants us to receive the redemption of Christ that we may be exempt from the condemnation of the law.

Subject Twenty-eight

BEING CLEANSED FROM LEPROSY

Scripture: Lev. 14

I. Leprosy

A. Leprosy typifies man's sin.

B. Leprosy is contagious, and it is also hereditary. You have to emphasize the aspect of heredity. Sins come not only from defilement but also through heredity. No one has to learn how to commit sins. You do not have to go to school to learn to sin. Sinning came into you hereditarily just as leprosy comes into man's body by heredity.

C. Leprosy comes from within. All sins grow out from within. Use the words of Jesus concerning cleanness and uncleanness in Matthew 15:10-20. Do not think that you have no sin because you never commit any sin outwardly. Actually the sins have been hiding in you for a long time.

D. Leprosy is a kind of disease not easily cured; likewise sin is something that is not easy to get rid of.

E. None of the lepers were allowed to come to the tabernacle of the congregation to worship God; they were all fully separated from God. This means that all the sinful people have no way to be close to God.

II. The way to be cleansed—two birds

A. The meaning of the birds:

1. A bird is transcendent and spiritual.

2. The price of a bird is very small.

B. Killing the first bird and then sprinkling its blood upon the one to be cleansed typifies that Christ died for us and shed His blood to cleanse us. Once a sinner repents, his leprosy can be cleansed immediately. It is by the Lord's shed blood that man is cleansed before God.

C. The second bird typifies the resurrection of the Lord Jesus. It is by His death and the shedding of His blood that all the filth of our sins is cleansed away. But it is by His resurrection that we are delivered from the power of sin. That is why in the Old Testament time they sprinkled the living water and the blood upon the leper and the living bird. They sprinkled not only the blood, but also the living water. This means that man was cleansed by the blood on one hand, and on the other hand he also received the resurrection life of the Lord Jesus, which delivers him from the power of sin. These two birds typify the heavenly Christ who died for us and was resurrected. Now we can easily partake of Him.

III. **After being cleansed**

A. Washing the robes: dealing with the filth of the outward deeds—dealing with sins.

B. Shaving the hair: dealing with man's vain glory, strength, and ability.

C. Washing the body: a thorough cleansing and dealing with all the oldness. Now all things are new.

Subject Twenty-nine

LIFTING UP THE BRASS SERPENT

Scripture: Num. 21:4-9; John 3:14

I. **Man has sinned**

A. Firstly tell how the Israelites committed sins against God in the wilderness.

B. People in the world today are also doing evil things against God.

II. Sins brought in death

A. When the Israelites sinned, the poisonous serpents immediately came to bite them, and that bite killed them.

B. Today the people who are committing sins are also being bitten by Satan, and Satan injects the poison of death into man by his bites. The serpents represent Satan. Their biting the Israelites and putting them to death represents the fact that the one who holds the power of death has put man into death by sins. First Corinthians 15:56 says, "The sting of death is sin." Satan puts man into death by luring him to commit sins.

III. God's saving way

A. God told Moses to put a brass serpent upon a pole.

B. Moses represents the law. The brass serpent represents Christ who became flesh and died for our sins. Moses' lifting up the brass serpent upon a pole represents the fact that the law crucified Christ on the cross. Just as the brass serpent received the judgment of the law for the Israelites, so also Christ received the judgment of the law for us. Brass in the Bible represents judgment.

C. In that day it was the poisonous serpents that bit the Israelites and put them to death, and it was the brass serpent that made them alive. Both are serpents. This means that it was Satan who put men to death, and it was also Satan who was judged on the cross. Although it was Christ who was nailed upon the cross, it was actually Satan who was judged on the cross. Thus the death of Christ on the cross not only substituted for our judgment, but it also judged Satan.

IV. The way of receiving salvation

A. When the Israelites beheld the brass serpent, they were immediately made alive.

B. Today if man wants to be saved out of sins and death, he must behold the Christ who was crucified on the cross.

C. Beholding is believing and receiving. Believe Christ and receive Him as your Savior.

Subject Thirty

THE CITIES OF REFUGE

Scripture: Num. 35; Deut. 19; Josh. 20:1-6

I. It is so easy for man to sin

A. The cities of refuge were set up for those who killed any person unwittingly. (Killing unwittingly means killing ignorantly, unconsciously, or unintentionally.)

B. Today man does many things unwittingly and unconsciously offends the law in his ignorance. Some might be teaching, helping the poor, working toward a promotion, or earning money, yet unconsciously in doing these things they may be committing sins which lead to death. Give some examples to illustrate the meaning of killing unwittingly.

C. Do not think that committing sins is a light thing. Please remember that a murderer must give his life in recompense. Even though he did the killing unwittingly, he would still have to die.

II. God's saving way

A. During that time God set up six cities of refuge in Israel, three west of the Jordan River, and three east of it. (Three times two equals six. Three is the number that represents the Triune God, and two represents witness.) Three on each side of the Jordan were for the convenience of those who killed unwittingly, so that they could flee into one of them easily. If there had been only one city of refuge, it would have been more difficult for the guilty ones to reach that city.

B. The Triune God comes to the eastern world and to the western world to save people. No matter where you are today, a city of refuge is close to you, because the cities of refuge on this earth are God Himself. Whenever you discover that you deserve death, just come to this Triune God and you will be under His protection.

C. Those who fled into the city of refuge could not be

released until the death of the high priest. This typifies that we could only be released by the death of Christ. Therefore fleeing into the city of refuge is fleeing into the death of Christ. The aspect of the city of refuge shows we are escaping. The aspect of the death of Christ shows we are released. The city shows God is our escape, the death of Christ, our release.

III. The way of salvation

A. Run fast.

No doubt the city of refuge is close to you, but you have to run fast, lest the avenger catch you. Running fast is to believe quickly, or else you will have no time to flee when the avenger comes. Whatever you have done, as long as you killed others unwittingly, you have to leave that spot as quickly as possible and run into the city. Running fast is to believe the Lord quickly, for the Lord is the city of refuge.

B. Receive the death of the Lord.

Those in the cities of refuge could not be released until the death of the high priest, or the death of Christ. So you must acknowledge that the Lord has died for you.

Subject Thirty-one

THE SALVATION OF RAHAB

Scripture: Josh. 2, 6

I. The position of man since his birth

A. Rahab was born in Jericho.

B. The city of Jericho was a place which was to be destroyed. In the whole Bible Jericho typifies a cursed city that is doomed to be destroyed.

C. Since his birth, man has been under a curse and is due to be destroyed.

II. The situation of man

A. Rahab was a harlot, which means that she belonged to the lowest class of women.

B. Before God, the position of man is that of a woman.
Man should be only for God. If man were for something else, he would be like a harlot. A woman should
be only for her husband. If she loves many others
besides her husband, she is a harlot. The greatest sin
of a woman is to be a harlot.

C. The greatest sin of man is loving many things other
than God.

III. The salvation of God

A. At that time, although God was going to destroy Jericho, He extended the grace of salvation to Rahab and
her family. But His grace was conditional. Rahab had
to bind the line of scarlet thread in the window of her
house. When God was about to destroy Jericho, He
saw that mark of scarlet thread and did not destroy
Rahab nor her family.

B. Although God is going to destroy this larger Jericho
(that is, the world), He still has grace for mankind,
with the blood of Christ as the great mark. The scarlet
thread bound in the window looked like a line of
blood. The Israelites were saved by striking the blood
on the lintel. Rahab was saved by binding a scarlet
thread in the window. Both are tokens of the blood of
Christ. The mark of the blood of Christ will separate
you from the world and will save you when God
destroys the world.

C. God's saving way and God's judgment recognize only
the mark and not who a person is. Whoever has the
scarlet thread (that is, the blood of Christ) shall be
saved. Whoever does not have it shall be destroyed.

IV. The way to be saved

A. Rahab's binding of the scarlet thread in the window
was a type of our receiving the blood of Christ upon us
by faith.

B. Not only did Rahab have the scarlet thread bound in the
window, but she also stayed within the house that had
the scarlet thread. This typifies that man not only needs

to receive Christ's redemption, but he also needs to be joined to Christ. The Israelites remained inside their houses which had the passover blood on the lintel. Noah entered into the ark covered with pitch, and the whole household of Rahab hid inside the house that had the scarlet thread. All these typify that those who receive Christ need to be joined to Christ.

C. How to be joined to Christ.

Christ passed through death and resurrection and descended as the life-giving Spirit. If we will only open our heart to receive Him, we will be joined to Christ.

V. The unit of salvation

A. That day not only Rahab herself was saved; her whole household was saved.

B. The unit of salvation is not an individual person, but a household. When the Israelites ate the passover lambs, there was a lamb for each house. The ark was for the whole household of Noah. The house with the scarlet thread was also for the whole household of Rahab. In the New Testament, the salvation of Christ was also for the household. Salvation came to the house of Zaccheus. The whole household of Cornelius was saved. The whole household of the prison guard at Philippi was saved. In the future, all the saved ones will also be one large family. God doesn't save just individuals; He saves the whole household. So dear friends, if you do not believe, then all of you do not believe; or if you do believe, your whole household will believe with you.

Subject Thirty-two

MEPHIBOSHETH

Scripture: 2 Sam. 4:4; 9:1-13; 19:24-30; 21:7

This section is not only a gospel message, but also a message about loving the Lord.

I. The position of man

A. Mephibosheth was born as an enemy of David and

should have been killed by David, because the only
opponent of David on the earth was Mephibosheth's
grandfather, King Saul.

B. By birth we are enemies of God. As the king of a nation,
David represented God, who is the Lord of the universe.
Adam, the ancestor of man, was the enemy of God, just
as Mephibosheth's grandfather was the enemy of David.
We do not have to do anything against God to become
His enemy; we were born as enemies of God.

II. The condition of man

A. Mephibosheth was lame; he was unable to walk. So it
would have been very easy for David to kill him.

B. We were born as enemies of God, and every one of us
is lame. We can have no merit nor virtue, neither can
we do good. We try to obey our parents and to be good,
but we lack the power. To be lame is to be short of love,
patience, ability, etc. We are short of these things
because we are lame; we are crippled.

III. Man's feeling

A. Mephibosheth was frightened. He was afraid that David
might kill him because he was the grandson of Saul.

B. Today man's feeling toward God is just the same as
Mephibosheth's; man always thinks that God is
coming to judge him, condemn him, and put him into
hell and let him perish there.

IV. Man's action

A. Mephibosheth had no strength in his legs, but he
could still escape from David.

B. Man has no strength to do good, yet he has strength to
run away from God. Even after man has received God,
he may still try to escape from God.

V. God's seeking

A. David was seeking for someone left of the house of
Saul. Mephibosheth misunderstood David's intention
and thought that David was seeking revenge, not realizing that David just wanted to show his kindness to
him.

B. Man misunderstands God and thinks that God is coming to judge. Man does not realize that God wants to show His love. God asks whether there is still someone left of the house of Adam. God came not for revenge, but to show mercy to the man represented by Mephibosheth. While David was seeking for Mephibosheth, Mephibosheth was running away from David. Man also runs away from the very God who is seeking for him. The reason God seeks for man is that He loves him and wants to show His love for him.

VI. **God's salvation**

A. Because of the covenant he had made with Jonathan, David preserved Mephibosheth's life and restored to him all his inheritance. David even dined with him at the same table and they were joyful together.

B. All this typifies that God, because of the covenant He made with Christ, saves us from perishing, restores to us all the heritage which we lost in Adam, and also allows us to eat and be joyful with Him.

VII. **The way to receive this salvation**

A. Mephibosheth did not have to do anything. He simply received all the grace freely bestowed upon him by David.

B. Today we also receive God's salvation freely. God bestows His grace upon us only because of the covenant He has made with Christ.

C. After Mephibosheth received grace from David, he only looked at the riches on David's table; he never again looked at his two lame legs underneath the table. In the same way, after we have been saved, we should only look upon God's grace and not look at our own situation. Whenever we look at ourselves, we discover that we are lame and we become discouraged. Anyone who still looks at his own lame condition does not really understand his salvation.

VIII. **The security of salvation**

A. David was to deliver seven men of the sons of Saul to the

Gibeonites, but David spared Mephibosheth because of
the oath he made with Jonathan (2 Sam. 21:6-7). This
speaks of the security of salvation. Once a man is saved,
he shall be saved forever.

B. Because of the New Covenant which God made with
Christ, God can never deliver us unto death again.

Subject Thirty-three

HOW LONG WILL YOU HESITATE
BETWEEN TWO OPINIONS?

Scripture: 1 Kings 18:21

I. **The two sides in the universe**

A. Explain that in the universe there is God, and there is
also Satan. God and Satan are the two sides or two
sources in the universe. On God's side there is light,
good, heaven, life, etc. On Satan's side there is darkness, evil, hell, death, etc.

B. Because of the two sides or two sources in the universe, man has two possible choices: he may choose to
follow God, which means to choose light, a good life,
and heaven; or he may choose to follow Satan, which
means to choose darkness, evil, death, and hell.

II. **The conflict within man**

A. Because man has two possible choices, he has a conflict within him. On the one hand he is inclined
toward light, but on the other hand he is drawn
toward darkness. He likes good, but he also has an
appetite for evil. He desires life, but he also bends
toward death. He wants heaven, but he cannot stay
away from hell. Here we may give some examples to
describe the condition within man.

B. Then explain that the conflict within man is a battle
between God and Satan. Whenever man inwardly bends
toward light, toward good, and toward life, that is the
Spirit of God working inside of him to gain him. Whenever man inwardly bends toward darkness, evil, and

death, that is Satan's evil spirit working inside of him to gain him.

III. Man's indecision toward the gospel

Now we may draw people's attention to the gospel.

A. Many people have heard the gospel, agreed with it, acknowledged it, and even almost believed it. But because they were still fond of darkness, evil, death, and the things of the flesh, they were not able to make a final decision.

B. The desire to believe is the working of the Holy Spirit. But indecision is the hindering of the evil spirit. At this point we should describe the feeling of the moving of the Holy Spirit and the feeling of indecision.

IV. The urging of the Holy Spirit

A. You are hearing the gospel today because of the reminding and urging of the Holy Spirit. The Holy Spirit not only urges you during the gospel meeting, but also often urges you in private. Nevertheless, the strongest urging is in the gospel meeting.

B. Listen to the urging voice of the Holy Spirit saying, "How long will you remain in indecision?" Now you must check with yourself. If the gospel is not worthy of being believed, you should refuse it right away. If hell is the place you would like to go, you should go right ahead. If God ought not to be accepted, you should put Him aside. Obviously, you know that you should choose good and life; yet you would not give up darkness, evil, and death! How long will you falter between two opinions?

V. The way of decision

A. It is easy to make a decision.

B. The faster you decide, the easier it will be.

C. Therefore, you should make a decision right now. Ask all those who want to make a decision to please stand up. Saying it in this way makes it sound very easy to stand up. To stand up is to make a decision.

Subject Thirty-four

THE HEALING OF NAAMAN THE LEPER

Scripture: 2 Kings 5

I. Naaman's position

A. Naaman was a commander of the army, a man in a high position.

B. Today in society there are many people with high positions.

II. Naaman's condition

In preaching the gospel we can never stay away from position and condition.

A. Though he was a commander in a high position, Naaman was full of leprosy. He was a mighty man of valor, but he was a leper.

B. Today many people, even though they are in high positions, are full of sin and evil. Leprosy keeps man from coming near to God. In like manner, sin cuts off the fellowship or communication between man and God.

III. Naaman heard the gospel

A. Through a little maid from the land of Israel, Naaman heard that in Israel there was a prophet, Elisha, who could cure him of his leprosy. This was good news of great joy. This was the gospel!

B. Today there are many little Christian maids at the side of people in high positions. They are their maids or waitresses. They are the ones to whom people do not pay much attention, but they bring them the gospel. They tell them that there is a Savior who can save them, One who can take away all of their sins.

IV. The Savior's way of salvation

A. The way Elisha healed Naaman was to tell him to go and wash in the Jordan River seven times.

B. At that time the savior was Elisha the prophet. Elisha typifies Christ. The way of salvation at that time was to wash seven times in the river Jordan. This typifies that the only way of being cleansed is to enter into the death of Christ. The Savior sent by God is Christ, and the way of salvation prepared by God is the death of Christ. For your sin to be taken away and for your leprosy to be cleansed, you have to accept the death of Christ.

V. The way to be cured

A. You must give up the world's method of being cured.

When Naaman heard that he had to go and wash in the Jordan River in the land of Israel, he was angry and demanded, "Are not the rivers of Damascus better than all the waters of Israel? Are there not rivers outside Israel?" But eventually he had to go to Israel's Jordan River to be cured. The rivers of Damascus, the ways of religion, must be given up. Only by receiving Christ, including receiving the death of Christ, can anyone be cured.

B. You must be humble.

Because of his pride, Naaman nearly lost the opportunity of being cured.

C. You must believe the word of the Lord.

Naaman was cured because he believed the word of Elisha. Likewise, if a sinner wants to be saved today, he must believe the word of the Lord Jesus. The Lord said, "He that believes and is baptized shall be saved." Therefore you must believe and be baptized.

D. You must receive the Lord's death and be buried into the water.

Naaman dipped seven times in the river Jordan, which typifies: (1) receiving the death of Christ, and (2) being united with Christ. As Naaman believed the word of Elisha in his day and washed seven times in the river Jordan, so today we must likewise believe the word of the Lord and be buried.

VI. The result of salvation

A. When Naaman came up from the river Jordan, his flesh was restored like the flesh of a little child.

B. The moment we believe in the Lord and receive the second birth, immediately the expression of that new life will be seen.

C. Since the old life was buried into the water of baptism (the Jordan River), we ought to live the new life as soon as we come up from that water.

Subject Thirty-five

THE REDEEMER

Scripture: Job 19:25

I. Man's position

A. Man is born a sinner.

B. Because man is born a sinner, therefore he ought to die.

II. Man's situation

A. Man is sinful and is condemned.

B. Man commits sins and cannot redeem himself.

Points I and II tell us that man needs a redeemer.

III. Man's need

A. Man needs redemption.

The universe is not without an owner. It is ruled by God, who controls the universe with His rules. God's rules are God's laws. God's law is righteous. He cannot regard a sinful man as sinless. Man has sin and is condemned under the law. Therefore sinful man needs redemption. A price must be paid to fulfill the demand of the law and to redeem man from the condemnation of the law.

B. Man needs salvation.

To redeem man from the condemnation of the law is redemption. To save man from the bondage of sin is salvation. Redemption can only free man from the condemnation of the law, but it cannot free man from the power of sin. It cannot prevent man from sinning again. Therefore, after redemption we still need salvation.

C. The difference between redemption and salvation.

  1. Redemption requires the payment of a price. Because of the law, the sinner has to pay a price for redemption.

  2. Salvation requires power. Because of the forces of sin and evil, the sinner needs the power to be saved.

IV. The Redeemer

A. Jesus Christ is the Redeemer whom God has prepared for men. Here we should say something about the Lord as a person. The Lord is God become flesh, God revealed in the flesh, to be our Redeemer.

B. The Lord Jesus shed His blood on the cross to bear our sins. He fulfilled the requirement of the law and redeemed us sinners from the condemnation of the law.

C. The Lord rose from the dead that He might be able to give life to His believing ones. This life is the mighty power of resurrection which comes into man and becomes the power to save man from the forces of sin and evil. Points B and C show us that the Lord has accomplished both redemption and salvation to meet man's need of redemption and salvation.

V. How to receive this Redeemer

A. We have to admit that we are sinners, under condemnation and under the power of sin as well.

B. We have to repent and confess our sins.

C. We have to believe and receive Jesus Christ as our Redeemer and Savior.

D. We must believe that we are redeemed and saved according to the word of the Bible.

Subject Thirty-six

THE WAY TO OBTAIN PEACE AND BLESSING

Scripture: Job 22:21-30

I. The meaning of peace and blessing

A. Peace is the rest and satisfaction within.

B. Blessing is the happiness and hope within. Happiness is for the present and hope is for eternity. If anyone has this blessing within, he is happy at the present and has hope for the future. Explain that some people may have fame, wealth, and high position today, but they do not have real peace and blessing within.

II. The source of peace and blessing

A. The source of peace and blessing is God. Man has been created for God. Only when he has received God is there the inward peace and satisfaction. Only when he has God as his life is it possible for him to have peace today and hope for the future.

B. The reason man does not have such peace and blessing within is that he has lost God.

III. The way to obtain peace and blessing

A. Man lost his inner peace and blessing because he committed sins and was separated from God.

B. To regain the peace and blessing, man must receive God. To receive God, man must return to God and depart from sin. *Emphasize the words in the book of Job:* "Acquaint now thyself with him, and be at peace: thereby good shall come unto thee...If thou return to the Almighty, thou shalt be built up, if thou shalt put away unrighteousness far from thy tents." To return to the Almighty is to come back to God; to put away iniquity is to depart from sin.

C. Accept the word of God and receive God according to His word. Explain that once a man receives the word of God, he has eternal life, forgiveness of sins, justification, and all other blessings.

D. Have delight in God and treasure Him:

Verse 26: "Then shalt thou delight thyself in the Almighty, and shalt lift up thy face unto God."

Verses 24-25: "Lay thou thy treasure in the dust,...and the Almighty will be thy treasure, and precious silver unto thee."

Describe man's real situation: how he loves his children, money, education, position, etc. Yet, eventually these things only hurt him. For example, if you love money, one day the bank may become insolvent; if you love your children, they may disappoint you.

E. Pray to God. He will hear you if you pray. Confess your sins before Him, ask for His forgiveness and cleansing, and sincerely receive the Lord Jesus as your Savior.

IV. The result

A. The man who accepts the word of God, has delight in God, treasures Him, and prays, will be able to know God, and peace and blessing will come upon him.

B. He will have light, and the light will shine upon his ways. From this time on, there will be light in his life. He will behave in light, and he will have a way to go on.

C. He will be saved.

D. He will be exalted. A person who has accepted God is higher than other people, and he will become higher and higher until he reaches the New Jerusalem.

Subject Thirty-seven

THOSE WHO CHOOSE ANOTHER GOD

Scripture: Psa. 16:4

This is to explain the difference between the true God and false gods.

I. **There is a God in the universe: there must be a God in the universe**

II. **There is only one God**

III. **God's name is JEHOVAH**

Explain the meaning of the name Jehovah. God is the I AM. God is the One Who is, and Who was, and Who is to come (Rev. 1:4).

IV. **All other gods are not God**

Explain this point clearly with abundant materials to prove the point.

V. Those who choose another god

A. Those who choose another god worship idols.

B. The result of idol worship is the multiplication of sorrows.

Use a lot of examples to describe the sorrowful conditions of the people who worship idols.

VI. Cast off idols and return to God

A. Explain that men should worship the Lord of the heavens and the earth.

B. This Lord of the heavens and the earth became flesh, and His name is Jesus Christ.

C. Today, if a man returns to God, he must return to the Lord Jesus.

VII. How to turn to the Lord ·

A. Sin separates man from God and leads him to go astray to worship false gods.

B. Therefore, man must confess his sins and repent.

C. He must accept the redemption of Jesus Christ and receive Him as the Savior.

D. He must destroy the idols.

Subject Thirty-eight

THE SUFFERING UPON THE CROSS

Scripture: Psa. 22:1, 14-18

I. The cause of the suffering upon the cross

A. Man sinned.

B. God is righteous.

C. God is also love.

These three things produced the suffering on the cross. If you put these three things together, there must be the cross. The principle of the gospel is very consistent with logic and legal principles. If a gospel preacher understands logic and legal principles, he can preach the gospel in a thorough way.

II. The meaning of the suffering upon the cross

A. During the time of the Roman Empire, crucifixion was the most cruel capital punishment in existence. In world history there has never been, in any democratic country, any capital punishment to compare with crucifixion. Only the Roman Empire, two thousand years ago, had adopted such a cruel capital punishment.

B. In Old Testament times, God had prophesied that the Savior would be punished with a kind of punishment similar to crucifixion. Give some examples from the Old Testament: (1) He that is hanged is accursed. (2) The serpent of brass which was put upon a pole is the same as the Son of Man being lifted up on the cross. (3) A passover lamb was slaughtered by nailing its two front feet on a horizontal piece of wood, and binding its two rear feet on a vertical piece of wood. This picture clearly signifies the crucifixion.

C. The suffering of crucifixion is beyond description. The two hands are nailed to a horizontal piece of wood, and the two feet are laid upon each other and nailed to a vertical piece of wood. The weight of the whole body hangs down, so that the muscles are stretched and the bones are out of joint, until the breathing out of the last breath.

III. The crucified One

Explain that the crucified One to whom we refer is Christ.

A. Every one being crucified is being executed.

B. Christ's crucifixion was His being put to death for us sinners.

C. Because we had sinned, and because God is both righteousness and love, Christ had to be crucified for us.

D. Christ bore our sins on the cross; therefore He said, "My God, my God, why hast thou forsaken me?" God forsook Christ because Christ was bearing our sins. Christ is the beloved of God, and He obeys God's will; therefore God should be with Him all the time. When

Christ was on the earth, He said that God was with Him. But when He was on the cross, God forsook Him. This is the evidence that He was bearing our sins.

IV. The suffering upon the cross

A. He was poured out like water. According to Psalm 22, while His body was hanging down, He was like water poured out.

B. All His bones were out of joint. While the body was hanging down, each and every bone was out of joint.

C. His heart was like melted wax. Because the fierce fire of God was burning upon Him, inside of Him it was like melted wax.

D. "My strength is dried up like a potsherd." This is the losing of strength, or the exhaustion of strength. The suffering of exhaustion is very difficult to describe. On the cross, Christ was totally and completely exhausted, even to the extent that there was no moisture left in His body. Yet He was still alive and suffering. Up to this day no one has been able to imagine what a suffering the Lord experienced on the cross.

E. "My tongue cleaveth to my jaws."

F. "Thou hast brought me into the dust of death." He endured the taste of death, and death had buried Him.

G. "Dogs have compassed me: a company of evil-doers have enclosed me."

H. "They pierced my hands and my feet." The Lord's hands and feet were nailed to the cross.

I. "I may count all my bones; they look and stare upon me."

J. "They part my garments among them, and upon my vesture do they cast lots."

V. The reaction to the cross

A. For generations many people have repented and turned to the Lord by hearing about the suffering of Christ upon the cross.

B. We hope the message of the cross will also touch our hearts today.

C. Everyone who has been touched by the suffering of the cross should confess his sins and receive the crucified Christ as his Savior.

Subject Thirty-nine

THE BLESSEDNESS OF HAVING SINS FORGIVEN

Scripture: Psa. 32:1-7

I. Man has sinned

A. Make it clear, in principle, that every man has sinned, and every man has offended God.

B. We may pick up four of five items of practical sins in detail, such as stealing, lying, covetousness, lust, etc., to describe the situation.

II. The necessity of confession

A. Man must confess that he has sinned in the eyes of God.

B. We must pray and confess our sin before God. Quote verses 3 and 5 of Psalm 32.

C. We should follow the inner feelings when we confess our sins, confessing them item by item.

III. The promise of forgiveness

A. Forgiveness of sins is based upon the death of the Lord Jesus and the shedding of His blood. The reason God can forgive man's sins is that the Lord Jesus has died and has shed His blood for man and has eliminated man's sins.

B. The promise of forgiveness of sin is given in the Bible. After God resolved our sins through the Lord Jesus, He clearly told us through the Bible to believe, and we shall receive the forgiveness of sins. This promise is the gospel.

C. Only believe the word of the Bible, and you will obtain the promise of the forgiveness of sins. Once you believe, you receive the pardon; you will have no condemnation but rather, justification.

IV. The blessedness of having sins forgiven

A. When God forgives men's sins, He not only covers and pardons our sins, but He also blots them out, just as though man had never sinned. That is why Psalm 32 says, "Blessed is the man unto whom the Lord imputeth not iniquity." In God's eyes, all that have been forgiven by Him are the same as those who have never sinned.

B. A man whose sin is forgiven will always have peace in his heart. All the heavy burdens are taken away.

C. Obtaining the joy of salvation: a man whose sins are forgiven shall always flow out songs of deliverance (Psa. 32:7).

Subject Forty

THE DREADFULNESS OF SIN

Scripture: Psa. 40:12

I. Calamities of the human life

A. Our human life is full of calamities. No one in this world has been without tragedy. The older you are, the more evils you have experienced.

B. Give practical examples of calamities. Choose the examples according to the audience.

II. The cause of calamities

A. Calamities are a result of sin. The reason there are calamities in this world is because of the existence of sin.

B. Speaking in a practical way, man experiences these evils because he has sinned. This needs to be explained in a substantiating way. For example, someone did a certain wicked deed and was elated because no one knew about it. But suddenly, some disaster came upon him, such as a terrible disease, his son may have died, or he may become blind, etc. Sin always causes man to suffer evil. Although we cannot say that all the calamities will be realized today, nevertheless, sins eventually always provoke calamities.

III. Sins take hold of a man

A. If you commit a sin, you are planting a cause. A cause leads to an effect. It does not matter what kind of sin you have committed. All sins are a kind of cause. Therefore, there must be an effect.

B. This effect is that sin will take hold of you. You may be able to forget your sin, but your sin will never forget you. It will follow you forever.

C. The sins that have been following you sometimes overtake you at the present time; otherwise they will take hold of you in eternity. If they overtake you today, the consequence will be calamity. If they take hold of you in eternity, the result will be destruction. *We should use suitable stories to emphasize this point.*

IV. The way to escape from sins

A. If you want to escape from your sins, you must acknowledge them. When you confess that you have sinned, you will realize how numerous your sins are. The Psalmist said, "They are more than the hairs of my head."

B. You should be terrified by iniquities. When I remember my sins, as the Psalmist says, "My heart fails me."

C. You must repent with a broken and contrite heart.

D. You must pray and confess your sins.

E. You must accept the Lord Jesus as your Savior.

Subject Forty-one

VANITY, VANITY, VANITY

Scripture: Eccl. 1:2; 12:1-8

The best way to present this is according to the order mentioned in hymn #1080 in *Hymns.*

I. All things in the human life are vanity

II. Knowledge is vanity

The more knowledge you have, the more grief you have.

The people who commit suicide are mostly those who are intellectual.

III. Worldly enjoyment is vanity

This includes all worldly enjoyment. Solomon was king in Jerusalem. He built palaces to live in. His clothing and his diet were the best. He enjoyed everything the world had to offer, but at the very end he said, "Vanity of vanities." This included his wives, concubines, children, and everything.

IV. Careers are vanity

Your career causes you to overwork and exhaust yourself, and it leaves you weary and sleepless during the night. And it will all be over when you die.

V. Position is vanity

Position includes a good reputation and honor.

VI. Turn to the Lord while you are young

The Book of Ecclesiastes was not written to old people, but it was written by an old man to young people. No elderly person needs to listen to a message about vanity, because all elderly ones have already known vanity. Only young people dream golden dreams. Therefore the aged Solomon said, "Remember now thy Creator in the days of thy youth," so that you will not be sorry when you get old. Now let us look at some of the pitiful conditions of an aged person. Use Ecclesiastes 12:1-8.

A. There is no pleasure. When a person is seventy or eighty years old, death is so close. There is no more pleasure.

B. The sun, the light, the moon, and the stars are darkened. In man's old age, nothing is bright. Because the eyes of the aged are dimmed, they cannot see things clearly. The sun, the moon, and the stars are darkened to them.

C. The clouds return after the rain. It is noisy while the rain is falling, but when the rain stops it becomes quiet. Some people were very busy while they were managing a factory or serving as administrator of a school, but after all the troublesome work, the clouds returned. The ones who have battled in the business world one day get old. The clouds return after the rain.

D. The keepers of the house tremble. The body is the house referred to here, and the keepers of the house are the hands and feet. The hands and feet of an aged person tremble, and the older he gets, the worse the trembling becomes.

E. The strong men are bent: the back becomes bent.

F. The grinders cease because they are few. The teeth are all gone, and even dentures will not work.

G. Those that look through the windows are dimmed. The windows of a man are his eyes. Now the eyes are dimmed.

H. The doors on the street are shut. The ears become deaf, and no sound can get in.

I. The sound of the grinding is low. Even the chewing sound of his own mouth he cannot hear. What a deafness!

J. One rises up at the voice of a bird. The older ones cannot sleep well during the night. The older one gets, the harder it is to have a good night's sleep.

K. All the daughters of song are brought low. The voice becomes low and hoarse.

L. They are afraid of what is high. Aged ones are afraid of high places.

M. Terrors are on the way. They are afraid of walking on the street.

N. The almond tree blossoms. The hair becomes white, as the white blossoms of the almond tree.

O. The grasshopper shall be a burden. They are without any strength at all.

P. Desire fails. They cannot have interest in anything.

Q. Man goes to his eternal home: he dies.

R. The mourners going about the streets are a funeral procession.

S. The silver cord is loosed: in the tomb the spine will become disconnected.

T. The golden bowl is broken. When it is buried in the grave, the skull is broken.

U. The pitcher is broken at the fountain: the nose will collapse.

V. The wheel is broken at the cistern. The cistern represents man's eye, and the wheel represents the eyeball. Both of them will perish in the grave.

W. The dust returns to the earth: the dead body becomes dust.

VII. We must repent, confess our sins, and receive the Lord

Subject Forty-two

THOUGH AS SCARLET, WHITE AS SNOW

Scripture: Isa. 1:18

I. Sins are like scarlet

A. All men have sin.

B. All the sins of men are deep and serious.

C. The sins of men are deep and serious to such an extent that they are like scarlet, which is a very bright red color that draws people's attention. Many people's sins are also like this; they are so deep and serious that they draw people's attention.

D. The color red represents God's condemnation. The color that symbolizes godliness is blue. Red is the color that symbolizes something satanic. In the Scriptures, red is the color of blood, which is the color of death. Therefore, when the Bible says that your sins are as scarlet, it not only refers to how deeply serious your sins are, but it also signifies that sins are hated by God and ought to be terminated.

II. They shall be as white as snow

A. Snow white is a kind of natural white, rather than an artificial or a manufactured white.

B. How can sins become as white as snow? They can become white only by the cleansing of the blood. The blood is red, and by using red to eliminate red, it becomes snow white. If you look at a piece of red paper through a red glass, the red paper becomes white.

C. The blood of the Lord can wash sins away and make them pure white because the blood of the Lord satisfies the righteous requirement of God.

III. The way to become pure white

A. You must confess that you are a sinner.

B. You must repent and confess your sins.

C. You must believe that Christ has shed His blood and borne your sins on the cross.

D. You must receive Christ as your Savior.

E. You must believe what is written in Isaiah 1:18, because the Lord has said, "Though your sins be as scarlet, they shall be as white as snow."

Subject Forty-three

THE WONDERFUL SAVIOR

Scripture: Isa. 9:6

I. The prophecies concerning the Savior

Before the Savior came into this world, there were many prophecies concerning Him written in the Scriptures. The most numerous and clear prophecies concerning the Savior are found in the book of Isaiah. The most clear verse is Isaiah 9:6.

II. The position of the Savior

A. Whatever job a person has, there must be a position for that job.

B. The Scriptures speak of the person or the position of the Savior.

C. The person of the Savior has two aspects. On one hand, He is a child born, who was given to us. On the other hand, He is the Almighty God. When He was on the earth, He was like the Almighty God. He brought things which had no being into being, and he caused the stormy sea to be still. On one hand, He was the Son; on the other hand, He was the eternal Father. In coming to this world in time, He is the Son. Before He came into the world, He was the eternal Father. The Father is the source, and the Son is the revelation of the Father. God the Father came into time to be the Son. This is the wonderful Savior.

D. Because He is not only the child but also the Almighty God, He is wonderful! He is the Son, and He is also the Father. He is in time, but He is also in eternity.

III. What the Savior is to us

A. He is the Counselor. The Almighty God is our Counselor.

    1. This Counselor councils you in how to do things and provides solutions to your problems.

    2. He is a wonderful Savior. No matter what difficulty you have, He always has a way to solve your problem for you. When you have sinned, He has shed His blood for you to redeem you from sin. If you are sick, He is able to heal you. When you are laboring, He will bear the burden for you. You have no way to heaven, but He is the way. If you have lost your money, or if you have lost your son, He is able to find them and bring them back to you. Whatever problems you may have, He will solve them for you. You should give a lot of examples.

B. He is the Prince of Peace; the eternal Father becomes the Prince of Peace. After men have sinned, they have no peace with God and no peace with men. Whether it is a case of husbands and wives, schoolmates, doctors and nurses, or teachers and students, they all have no peace among them. But this wonderful Savior is the Prince of Peace. Once you have received Him, everything is in peace. We have to find many examples to prove this point. This is the good news of the gospel. The gospel is not just a high and deep doctrine, but it is the Lord's way to solve the practical needs of man.

IV. The way to receive the Savior

A. You must confess you are a sinner.

B. You have to believe that the Savior is both God and Man.

C. You have to believe that the Savior died for you.

D. You have to believe and receive Him as your Savior.

Subject Forty-four

LOOK UNTO GOD

Scripture: Isa. 45:22

I. Man is separated from God

A. Because man fell, he is separated from God.

B. To be separated from God means that man turns away from God, and forsakes Him, and then loses God's presence.

II. Man looks at things lower than himself

A. When man forsakes God, his heart turns toward things other than God. These things include parents, wife, children, possessions, money, and job or profession. In conclusion, whatever is outside of God are things.

B. When men turn to things, they pay their attention to them, and their hearts turn from God to things. All things are outside of God, and they are lower than man. Therefore, when man pays attention to things, he looks downward.

III. The anguish of man's separation from God

A. Outside of God, all things are death. All the anguish is a sign of death. All the anguish of man's life firstly shows that he is separated from God.

B. In addition, the anguish foretells man's death.

IV. God is man's salvation

A. Man has only one need—man needs God. All man's difficulties are due to the lack of God.

B. Man's salvation is in God.

C. God is waiting for man to receive Him.

V. The way to obtain salvation

A. To obtain salvation is to accept God, because God is our salvation.

B. God firstly was crucified on the cross for us. Secondly, He resurrected and ascended. Thirdly, today He is in the heavens waiting for men to accept Him as their Savior.

C. When man accepts God, he must look up unto God. He must look up unto the God who died on the cross, look up unto the God who ascended, look up unto the God who sits in the heavenlies to be our Savior. No matter whether we speak of His death, His resurrection, or His sitting in the heavenlies, He is always above us. It is just the opposite of all the things outside of God. They are all beneath us. Therefore, when we accept Him, we must look up unto Him.

VI. The result of looking up

A. Sins are forgiven.

B. We receive God as our life.

C. We are saved from all anguish, including sin, death, judgment, and hell.

Subject Forty-five

LOVE SO EXCELLING

Scripture: Isa. 49:15

I. The source of man

A. God compares the relationship between a mother and her nursing child to the relationship between God and man.

B. A child comes out of the mother; the mother is the source of the child. Therefore, the meaning of this verse is that we human beings have come out of God, and God is the source of man.

II. What God is to man

A. What God is to man can be compared to what a mother is to a child.

B. The whole relationship of a mother to her nursing child is love. Likewise, the whole relationship of God to man is also love.

C. Men have a wrong concept concerning the relationship of God to man, and we need to correct that wrong concept according to the two points just mentioned. People think that God is severely strict toward men, just like a judge. But in reality, God is like a loving mother to man.

III. The love of God is so excelling

A. There is no problem with the *nature* of a mother's love, but there is a limitation of *power* with a mother's love. There is a limitation of a mother's ability to carry out what the mother's love is longing for.

B. In nature, the love of God is like a mother's love, but with the love of God the power is unlimited. Many a time a mother's love would not be able to help, whereas, wherever God's love is, there is also the power to fulfill all that God's love longs for.

C. Furthermore, the love of God not only excels the love of a mother in power and strength, but the nature of the love of God also excels the nature of a mother's love. As a matter of fact, a mother's love is limited. Even though a woman can scarcely forget her nursing child, yet there is still the possibility that she could forget. That is why it says here, "Yea, they may forget, yet will I not forget thee." This is not a matter of power, but a matter of the heart. A mother's loving heart may be limited, but the love of God is forever unlimited. That is why the heart of God can never forget us.

IV. The manifestation of God's love

A. God's love is manifested through nature. Although there are numerous calamities in the universe, and nature also has its dark side, yet nature is still a blessing to man, positive, and bright. This is the manifestation of God's love through nature.

B. The principle is the same in man's experiences. Although each of us has experienced a lot of suffering and many a misfortune in our lives, nevertheless, speaking in principle, we also have a lot of happiness and goodness and blessing in our lives.

Points A and B on the one hand will eliminate men's concept that the universe is dark and evil, and on the other hand they will remove people's concept that they are unfortunate. Principally, man's life is good and happy. The blessings and happiness prove to us the love of God toward men.

C. God's love is manifested through God's redemption. The most obvious manifestation of God's love is the sending of His Son to accomplish redemption for man.

This is the center of this gospel message. In explaining the accomplishment of the Lord's redemption, stress and expound how the Lord became flesh, accomplished redemption, and shed His blood for man.

D. God's love is manifested through the gospel. Because God loves us, He not only accomplished redemption for us, but also arranged our environment and sent someone to bring the gospel of redemption to us. We never had any intention of hearing God's gospel or of listening to it. We were like a ship floating on the sea which happened to bump into someone who was preaching the gospel. This is the manifestation of God's love.

V. How to receive God's love

A. Acknowledge that God has something to do with you.

B. Acknowledge that you need God's love. *We should touch people's feeling.* Explain how warm a thing love is. Men need the warmth of love the most. But none of the worldly loves can be warm enough to meet man's need. Only the love of God has the real warmth.

C. Confess that you have been ungrateful toward God. God has loved us so much, but we have come short of Him.

From the four points under item IV we see how ungrateful we have been toward God. Do not talk about theology too much; rather, speak from the aspect of love.

D. Accept the love of the cross. The love of the cross is the highest manifestation of God's love. If you want to receive the love of God, you must accept the love of the cross.

Subject Forty-six

THE SAVIOR PREPARED BY GOD

Scripture: Isa. 53

I. God prepared a Savior for man

A. Man did not seek God's salvation; it was God who came to save man.

B. When God wanted to save man, He had to prepare a Savior for him.

C. The reason God had to prepare a Savior for man is that God is righteous. His love caused Him to come to save man. His righteousness required that He prepare a Savior for him.

II. The person of the Savior

A. The Savior is the arm of God. The arm refers to power and strength. Therefore, the arm of the Lord is the power of God. The power of God is just God Himself. God, when manifesting Himself to be our saving power, is our Savior.

B. The Savior is God revealed to be our saving power; yet He came as a poor man. Therefore Isaiah 53:2 says, "He grew up before him as a tender plant, and as a root out of dry ground." This refers to the fact that the Lord was brought up in a poor family. He is the Almighty God, but He became a poor man. Because He was poor and like a root out of dry ground, He had no form nor comeliness. There is no beauty that we should desire Him. Chapter 52 of this book tells us that His appearance was so marred, more than any man, and His form more than the sons of men. Today all the so-called pictures of Jesus are unscriptural. They all portray Him as One who is so desirable. But the Jesus of that time had no beauty that men should desire Him.

III. The Savior's sufferings

A. He was a man of sorrows. We should quote all the verses in Isaiah 53. A very special term is used in Isaiah 53:3, "a man of sorrows."

B. His whole life, from the manger to the cross, was full of sorrows. He was born in sorrow and suffered continually until He was finally laid to rest in the tomb. This is to speak of His sufferings from the manger to the cross. Hymn #628 can be used as a reference.

C. The sufferings during His lifetime came from three directions: from man, from God, and from Satan. What came from man was the suffering of persecutions. What came from Satan was the suffering of attacks. What came from God was the suffering of punishment.

IV. The Savior's bearing of sins

A. The righteousness of God requires that God judge man's sins.

B. God put all the sins of mankind upon the Savior. Quote verse 6: "The Lord hath laid on him the iniquity of us all."

C. Because God laid all the iniquities of mankind on the Savior, the judgments of God toward men were also inflicted upon the Savior's body.

D. Because God judged this Savior who bore our sins, He was bruised.

E. There is the evidence of bearing sin: "He was numbered with the transgressors." This shows us that God

looked at Him at that time as He would look at a
sinner, because He was bearing our sins.

V. The Savior's accomplishment

The Savior has fully accomplished His saving work and
has become a perfect Savior.

A. The Savior has borne our sins to satisfy the righteous
requirement of God. Therefore, the situation at the
time of His burial was different from the situation at
the time of His death. While He was dying, He was
numbered with the transgressors; but when He was
buried, He was put into a rich man's tomb, because he
had satisfied the righteous requirement of God.

B. God raised Him from the dead. This resurrection is
what is spoken of in Isaiah 53:10, "He shall see his
seed, he shall prolong his days, and the pleasure
of the Lord shall prosper in his hand." Because He
has resurrected from the dead, He can be the Savior
in resurrection, and He can accomplish that which is
pleasing to God. Therefore it is also said in verse 11,
"He shall see the travail of his soul, and shall be satisfied."

C. In His resurrection He has gained, together with God,
all the people which should be saved. Verse 12 says,
"Therefore will I divide him a portion with the great,
and he shall divide the spoil with the strong." The
Great is God; the Strong is also God. He resurrected
from the dead and enjoys the result of salvation with
God. This result is to recapture people from the hand
of Satan.

D. Because of His resurrection and ascension, He causes
so many people to obtain His salvation, and to be justified because of Him.

VI. How to accept the Savior

A. The way to accept is to believe. In the very beginning
of this chapter it says, "Who hath *believed* our message?"

B. To believe is to receive with your heart and your

spirit. Not only acknowledge Him as your Savior, but also open your heart to receive Him as your Savior.

C. According to Romans 10:13, the believers must call, and calling includes the confessing of sins: "Whosoever shall call upon the name of the Lord shall be saved."

Subject Forty-seven

THE SAVIOR'S BEARING OF OUR SINS

Scripture: Isa. 53:5-6, 10, 12

I. Man has gone astray. "All we like sheep have gone astray; we have turned every one to his own way."

A. All men in the world are sheep in the hand of God.

B. But man has turned to his own way. Use examples to show that men live on this earth and do things according to their own will.

C. Because man has turned to his own way, he has committed all kinds of transgressions and iniquities in the sight of God.

II. God's judgment

A. God's righteousness requires God to judge man.

B. God's love causes God to save man.

C. Therefore, God caused the Savior to bear our sins and to be judged in our stead.

D. The way God judged the Savior on the cross was to put the Savior to death; He wounded and bruised the Savior so that He tasted death for us.

III. The Savior's bearing of our sins

A. Not only was the Savior who was nailed on the cross persecuted by men, but moreover, He was chastised and punished by God.

B. The fact that the Savior was persecuted by men is a proof that men are against God. The fact that the Savior was punished by God proves that God saves man.

C. The reason God punished the Savior was that God laid on Him the iniquity of us all. Therefore, during the latter part of His crucifixion, God had to forsake Him. He cried out, "My God, my God, why hast thou forsaken me?" God had forsaken Him because of sin. The Savior had no sin, so God ought not to forsake Him. But He was bearing the sins of men; therefore God did forsake Him. If the Lord were only suffering the persecution of men, then God should be with Him all the more, just as in the case of a martyr like Stephen, who was full of the presence of God during the time of martyrdom. Therefore, the fact that the Savior was forsaken proves that He was not a martyr but a sin-bearing One.

IV. **How to accept the Savior**

  A. Return from the path of error. You must confess that you are a lost sheep, and turn back from the way of error.

  B. Repent. To turn back is an outward action, but to repent is an inward change. To turn back is to say that my way is wrong. But to repent is to say that my being is wrong. To turn back is to say that the direction of my life is wrong, but to repent is to say that my living is wrong.

  C. Confess your sins. Since God has laid your sins upon the Savior and let Him bear them for you, therefore you must confess all your sins.

  D. Believe in the Savior, receive the Savior into your heart, and take Him as your Savior.

  This message could be very powerful, if inspired. It is practical and sound in truth as well.

Subject Forty-eight

THERE IS NO PEACE TO THE WICKED

Scripture: Isa. 57:20-21

When we preach the gospel, we have to be careful in choosing words and topics. Try not to close people's hearts the moment you open your mouth.

I. **Everything in the universe has a law**

  A. Use enough examples to let people see that everything in the universe has a law. Not only do the stars have their laws, but in the existence of all living creatures there are laws. Try not to give too many examples, but use just enough to prove that everything in the universe has a law.

B. If any kind of living thing that exists in the universe follows its own law, then it will be at peace. If it goes against the law, then it will have no rest.

What we have said so far is to lay the foundation.

II. The law of human life

A. The law of human life is based upon the relationship between God and man.

No doubt when we preach the gospel we must rely upon the Holy Spirit, but we also have to catch people's thought. Because there are many in the meeting with well-trained minds, the thoughts of the one who preaches should not be lacking in refinement.

B. God is very orderly. Therefore the human life planned by God is also very orderly. Expound this point.

C. The order which God has set up for man's life is good, bright, righteous, kind, and upright. These five points should be explained in detail, from both the positive and the negative sides. For example, the opposite of good is evil, and everything which is not orderly is evil.

III. The abnormality of human life

A. The order which God has set up for man's life is almost entirely contradicted by man. God ordered that man's life should be good, bright, righteous, kind, and upright. But in reality man is evil, dark, jealous, hateful, unrighteous, and crooked. Describe the negative side.

B. Because man's life is so abnormal and contrary to the order set up by God, his life is full of evil.

C. The evil of man's life is his rebellion against God's law. Take for example: stealing, not loving his wife, having envy against his classmates, disrespect toward his parents, not loving his colleagues, not helping a person who is suffering, and having no sympathy toward a poor beggar. All of these are against God's law.

When we preach, we must touch people's feeling. If

you want to hit someone, you should hit him hard. Hit him
all over until he is very sensitive; then he will be saved.

D. The evil in human life causes life to be out of balance.
Therefore, the human life becomes a life without peace.
Since it is out of balance, the human life is restless.

IV. **Life's restlessness**

A. The restlessness of life is manifested in man's conscience. When man goes against the good laws of God, there is the restless feeling of condemnation in his conscience. When a man steals, his conscience jumps up and down. If you have done something wrong or have lied, you would tremble, if someone should point at you. This is why a lie detector can test the inner situation of a person. The Chinese have a saying in the same principle, "discern a person according to his expressions."

B. The restlessness of a person's heart. If you spend money which you earned by your own labor and hard work, you feel an inner calm and a sweet sense within. But if you spend money which has been stolen from others, you will feel uneasy. Another example: if you use your money to support and honor your parents, your heart feels peaceful. But if you keep the money for your own luxury or to spend on other women behind your wife's back, then your heart will be uneasy. The whole reason men feel uneasy and have a sense of fear is that they have contradicted God's laws.

C. The restlessness in the environment. After a short time, anything stolen may be exposed. Even if they are not exposed, a few days later you may have a car accident, or you may meet a pickpocket, or you may hit someone riding a bicycle. For three months you have tried your best to embezzle in your office or business to get two thousand dollars. Then you fell down and had to stay in the hospital, and the hospital bill was three thousand dollars. These are examples of the restlessness in the environment.

D. These three points of restlessness are all caused by man's disobedience of God's law. The restlessness is God's reprimand. It is like a train. If it is derailed, something is out of order. God's laws are like the rails. If the conscience is restless that is your warning telling you to repent.

E. God's laws are meant to bring you to repentance. If you do not obey, in the future you will fall into the lake of everlasting fire. You will have no peace forever. Therefore God said, "There is no peace to the wicked." The life of the wicked is like the tossing sea. Its waters toss up mire and dirt.

Use some examples to describe how peaceful it is whenever anyone honors his parents or gets along well with his neighbors, and how restless it is otherwise. Explain from both the negative and the positive sides.

V. **The way of peace for man's life**

A. Explain that in our life, the source of peace is God. Just as God is the source of good and light, He is also the source of peace. When a man has God, he has peace. If he does not have God, he has no peace. Therefore, if you want to have peace, you must turn back to God and receive God, because God is the way to have peace.

B. Repent and forsake evil. Evil makes a man restless. But God gives men peace. Therefore, to obtain peace we must forsake evil and turn back to God.

C. Receive the Lord Jesus as your Savior of peace. The Lord Jesus shed His blood on the cross to solve the problem of man's sin before God, to accomplish eternal peace, and to reconcile men to God. The salvation and redemption of the Lord Jesus will give men peace. For this reason you must receive this Savior as your Savior.

D. Many people have accepted the Savior. They not only have the peace within, but also have a peaceful environment without.

Subject Forty-nine

MAN'S CONDITION—FOUR COMPARISONS

Scripture: Isa. 64:6

I. **Man is like an unclean thing**

In the Hebrew language, the unclean person is called the unclean thing.

A. Man's nature is filthy.

B. Man's heart is filthy.

C. Man's thought is filthy.

D. Man's behavior is filthy.

E. Man's whole being is filthy.

Therefore, it says here that man is like an unclean thing. Although you may consider yourself a moral man, you should check whether your mind is really clean or not. A tiny spot of black makes an entire white shirt dirty. Any dirty spot also makes your behavior unclean.

II. Man's righteousness is like filthy rags

A. Man is filthy. Although man's righteousness is good in one sense, it is still filthy. Nothing clean can come out of uncleanness. If you hold a piece of candy with a dirty hand, the candy will be dirty also. Although you give alms to the poor and honor your parents, all these good deeds and efforts are defiled because your being is filthy. You consider yourself a humble person; yet you condemn others. You love one man; yet you hate another. You honor your parents; yet you condemn others who dishonor their parents. Since your righteousness is mixed with filthiness, though you are a gentleman, you are filthy.

B. Therefore it says here in the Bible that all of our righteousnesses are like filthy rags. Your righteousnesses are not only filthy but also like rags. How can we make clothes out of rags to cover our bodies? Adam sewed leaves together, but his shame could not be covered by his own effort. Therefore, God came in and clothed him. You honor your parents; but you also lose your temper. How many holes you have in your righteousness! So, friend, although you are a righteous person, your righteousness still means nothing because it is filthy and like rags. *Emphasize the point of man's righteousness being like rags. A good presentation of the gospel conquers a self-righteous person.*

III. Man fades like a leaf

It is very meaningful that God brought in the word *fading* here. Leaves fade under the breeze of autumn; then the wind takes them away.

A. All self-righteous men are those who will never receive nourishment deep within. The harder they try to do something, the faster they fade away, and the less water they have. This water is just God and God's grace. You consider yourself a righteous man, but deep within, you lack God and God's grace.

B. Man fades away because he is cut off from God.

C. Man is cut off from God because of sin, but he is cut off further from God because of his self-righteousness. Man's sin separates him from God. However, man doesn't confess the sin that he has, and he considers himself to be self-righteous. This self-righteousness separates man further from God.

D. Since man is cut off from God, he has lost all of his supply and nourishment. Therefore, man fades away.

IV. Man's iniquities are like the wind, blowing man away

A. Since man has faded, he can be easily taken away.

B. The iniquities not only cause man to fade away, but have also taken man away from God. Iniquities separate man from God, bring judgment to man, separate man from God's supply, and bring God's anger upon man.

C. Man sinned and gave up God. It would have still been tolerable to God if man had confessed his sins. However, because of self-righteousness, man could never confess his sins. Therefore, man was separated further from God. Man was further dried up. The judgment that sin brought in eventually blows man away.

V. Conclusion—the way for man to be saved

A. Man must humble himself, not only to confess that he has sinned and sinned against God, but also to confess the self-righteousness which cannot stand before God. In

God's presence our own righteousness is filthy and like rags.

B. Man must repent and turn to God to receive God's supply.

C. Man must receive the Lord Jesus as the Savior of righteousness. The Lord bore our sin on the cross so that we may be justified before God. He has also entered into us to become our righteousness.

Subject Fifty

TWO EVILS

Scripture: Jer. 2:13

I. Forsaking God

A. God is everything to human life. God is also the full supply for man's need.

B. God is the fountain of living waters to man. A fountain is the source of water supply. Water is something for quenching thirst. This is to say that God can satisfy all of man's thirst, because God is the fountain of living waters.

C. Man has forsaken God, who is the fountain of living waters.

D. Man's forsaking God is not only a loss, but also a sin. It is like children forsaking their parents. Therefore, God said here, "My people have committed two evils." The first evil is forsaking God.

E. Man's forsaking God is a loss and a sin as well, so two things result from this: suffering and condemnation. Suffering means there is no peace in the outward circumstances. Condemnation means there is no peace within our hearts. Since forsaking God is a loss and causes suffering, there will be no peace in the outward circumstances. Since forsaking God causes condemnation, there will be no peace, but suffering in our hearts.

II. Man devising his own way—"hewed them out cisterns"

A. All those who have forsaken God want to do something in their own way.

B. God is the fountain of living water, supplying water to men. Man's own efforts are broken cisterns from which water is leaking out.

C. Give practical examples to show in what things God is the fountain of living waters and human effort is the broken cisterns.

  1. The precious blood that God shed for us on the cross has become the fountain of living waters to cleanse away our sin. Islam and Buddhism teach people to establish their own merit, to cultivate morality, and to make up for their shortcomings by good works. All of these are broken cisterns.

  2. The life that God has released is the fountain of living waters. This life can give people strength to do good. However, if men depend upon their own strength, the more they try, the more they will fail. This is just a broken cistern.

  3. Human life is hungry, thirsty, and never satisfied. Only God's living water can satisfy man. To try to quench thirst by man's own methods, knowledge, and ability is a broken cistern.

  4. Conclusion: Man devising his own way is not dependable.

III. The way of salvation

A. Drop your own way, as the Samaritan woman who left her waterpot.

B. Turn to God, that is, turn from your own way to God.

C. Repent and confess your sin.

D. Believe and receive Christ as your own Savior, because God in Christ is your Savior today.

Subject Fifty-one

WHEN WILL YOU BE SAVED?—DO NOT DELAY

Scripture: Jer. 8:7, 20

I. The meaning of being saved

A. Man is sinful and dead.

B. To be saved is to be forgiven of sins and receive God's life.

C. To be saved also means to be delivered from sins, the world, and death.

II. The importance of being saved

A. Man is under condemnation.

B. There is the possibility that a man could perish at any time, because there is the possibility that he could encounter death at any time.

These two points show that man is already under condemnation. Before man's death, however, God still gives man opportunities to be saved from perishing eternally.

III. Salvation is related to time

A. Time provides opportunities for people to be saved. Time is the opportunity. All opportunities are in time. Losing time is losing the opportunity. This is why men always try to make use of time in whatever they are doing.

B. When time is past, there will be no more opportunity. *This point should be stressed.* Here, apply the verse, "The harvest is past, the summer is ended, and we are not saved." The time for harvest is past, the summer is over, but we are not yet saved; nevertheless there is still time, still an opportunity left—now. If we let it go by, no one can say whether this opportunity will come again.

C. It should be concluded that salvation must be in time. To be saved is not in eternity, although it is for eternity. Salvation must be in time. This time is this present life. This present life may be finished at any time. Give some examples and stories. Some who heard the gospel but did not believe it right away were killed in car accidents on their way home. Use some examples to prove that man's life may be finished at any time in this world. When time is past, eternity will come. Therefore, you must believe Him today. Sing verse 3 of hymn #1043 in *Hymns.*

IV. Grasp this opportunity

A. Emphasize that the opportunity is now. After this moment, there may be no more opportunities.

B. To grasp the opportunity is to grasp this moment. Those who want to grasp the opportunity must grasp this moment right now.

C. Ask those who want to grasp this opportunity right now, to please stand up. Sing the chorus of hymn #1042, "Why not now? Why not now?"

Subject Fifty-two

IT IS IMPOSSIBLE FOR THE EVIL NATURE TO BE CHANGED

Scripture: Jer. 13:23

I. The explanation of man's nature—good or evil

A. Through the generations, there have been two schools of thought concerning man's nature. Some say that man's nature is good (Mencius' school), but some say that it is evil (Shun's school).

B. The self-evidence of man's nature.

We must ask ourselves whether our own nature is good or evil.

C. From our own nature we can see that, although we sometimes have the desire and intention to do good, most of the time our desire to do evil is much stronger.

D. Man's good intentions come from God's creation. Man's evil nature comes from Satan's corruption. Here we have to expound man's fall. Many famous scholars in past history found that man's nature consists of both good and evil. The reason is that by God's creation, man has a good element within, and through man's fall and corruption, man has an evil element within.

II. Man's actual condition

A. Although man's nature contains both a good and an

evil element, the good has been corrupted by the evil; thus the evil element has become dominant.

B. Therefore man's actual condition is that the evil nature overcomes the good nature. It does not mean that man does not have a good nature, but that his good nature is a defeated one. Give some facts to prove this. For example: in your heart you have a desire to respect your parents, yet you scold them; you have a desire to be honest, yet you cheat; deep inside you do not want to gamble, but you still go on gambling; you want to break your ties with your evil friends, but you still live a life of sin with them. This is man's actual condition.

III. Can the evil nature be changed?

This paragraph speaks of man's way.

A. All people in past generations, whether they regarded man's nature as good or as evil, insisted upon changing men. Islam, Buddhism, Chinese philosophy, Confucianism, and those Christians who do not really know the way of the Lord, all insisted upon changing men.

B. Actually, man's evil nature cannot be changed. Man can change the outward behavior, but he cannot change the nature. Man can change the deed, but he cannot change the disposition. If the change of behavior is not false, it is at best only superficial. Only the change in nature is a real change. But the evil nature can never be changed, so man has never had a real and thorough change.

C. Conclusion: it is impossible for man to change his nature.

IV. God's saving way

A. God's way to save is not to change but to replace. It is not to change the old, but to replace it with the new; not to change the old nature, but to replace it with a new nature.

B. God's saving way is by regeneration. Regeneration gives you God's life.

V. The way to be regenerated

A. Acknowledge that you have an evil nature that is stronger than your good intentions.

B. Acknowledge that you cannot change your evil nature.

C. Receive the Lord Jesus as the Savior of life. The Lord Jesus is the incarnation of God Himself. God's life is in Him. To receive Him is to receive God's life.

Subject Fifty-three

THE DECEITFULNESS OF THE HEART

Scripture: Jer. 17:9-10

I. The source of deceit

A. At the beginning the heart was not deceitful, but honest and good, because it was made by God.

B. The heart became deceitful later on.

C. Because of man's contact with Satan, the heart became deceitful. Hence, the source of man's deceit is Satan. "When he speaks a lie, he speaks out of his own self; for he is a liar, and the father of it" (John 8:44). To lie is to be deceitful.

II. The condition of deceit

A. Man's deceit is from deep inside the heart.

B. Man was born with deceit; there is no need to learn to be deceitful.

C. Use some practical examples of man's deceitfulness to describe man's actual condition: how people deceive their parents, wives, children, teachers, classmates, colleagues, and friends, etc.

This is the most important section of this subject.

III. The extent of deceit

A. The heart is more deceitful than anything else. Among all things, the heart is the most deceitful. All other things added together cannot be compared with the deceitfulness of man's heart.

B. The heart is exceedingly corrupt. In the original, the words "exceedingly corrupt" mean that the heart is so deceitful that it is beyond remedy and can never be cured. It is like a bad potato that begins rotting from the center until it reaches the outside and is beyond remedy.

C. The heart is so corrupt that you cannot know it your-self. Only God knows it.

IV. The result of deceit

A. Every deceitful man is recompensed according to his deceit. The Bible says that God will deal perversely with the perverse. The one who deceives others even-tually hurts himself. The result of being deceitful is to be recompensed with deceit. No one who has suc-ceeded through deceit can last long; rather, the deceit will only destroy that one's business and family.

B. Deceit causes man to perish. The recompense of deceit is in this present age, whereas perishing is eternal. Revelation 21:8 says that all liars shall have their part in the lake of fire.

Points such as this should be repeated.

V. How to put off deceit

A. Good intentions are useless. It is useless to decide not to deceive.

B. Self-improvement is useless. Trying to change your-self so that you are not deceitful is useless.

C. Your life must be changed and replaced with a non-deceiving life.

VI. How to receive this non-deceiving life

Point to the way of salvation:

A. The non-deceiving life is God's life.

B. To receive God's life, you need to confess your sins, especially the sin of deceit, and repent.

C. Believe that Jesus Christ is the Son of God, and receive Him as your Savior, because God's life is in Him.

Subject Fifty-four
TWO WAYS

Scripture: Jer. 21:8

I. Man's opportunity

A. Man's opportunity comes from God.

B. God has set two ways before man: the way of life and the way of death.

C. In the beginning, after God made man, He put man in front of life (the tree of life) and death (the tree of the knowledge of good and evil).

D. God let man choose life or death. Both ways are opportunities given by God. The choice and the decision are up to man.

II. Man's free will to choose

A. God set two ways before man because God gave man a free will.

B. The fact that man is given a free will is a proof that God honors man, and also that man is the highest creature.

C. God let man choose either life or death according to man's free will.

III. The results of these two ways

A. The way of life leads to eternal life, which includes God's life, the eternal peace and blessing, and the heavenly joy.

B. The way of death leads to eternal death, which includes the elements of Satan, eternal suffering, and punishment in the lake of fire.

IV. How to choose the way of life

A. Acknowledge that you are already on the way of death—the way you have been treading is a way of death.

B. Turn from the way of death.

C. Repent and confess your sins.

D. Believe that Christ is the life and the way. Only He can give man life, and only He can lead man to the way of life.

Subject Fifty-five

GOD CAME AS MAN'S RIGHTEOUSNESS— THE LORD OUR RIGHTEOUSNESS

Scripture: Jer. 23:5-6

I. God came as a man

A. Point out that the "Righteous Branch" mentioned in Jeremiah 23:5-6 signifies the Lord Jesus incarnated in the flesh to be the Son of Man.

B. This Branch of David is Jesus Christ, who is God coming as a man.

II. The only righteous man

A. All of Adam's descendants are unrighteous. Neither Adam nor any of his descendants are in one accord with God.

B. Only the Branch of David is called a Righteous Branch by God. In the New Testament He is called "The righteous One." Only Jesus Christ is righteous among men and before God. His nature and His behavior are in one accord with God.

III. The union of Christ and man

A. Christ is the very God become flesh to unite with man. He put on human nature and became one with man.

B. He was made sin in man's behalf on the cross. Man is unrighteous. Man is sinful. When He became one with man, He was made sin, and as sin He was judged on the cross.

C. He resurrected from the dead and released His life to man so that man can be one with Him.

IV. Christ has become the righteousness of man

A. Before God, man is sinful and Christ is righteous.

B. Christ resurrected that man might have His life, which is just Christ Himself.

C. Christ Himself is righteousness. Hence, if a man receives Christ, he receives Christ as his righteousness. The one who receives Him receives righteousness, and this righteousness is Christ Himself.

D. Christ becomes man's righteousness not only that man may be justified, but also that man may become righteous. Justification is a matter of outward position. Righteousness is a matter of inward reality.

E. To receive Christ as our life is to let Christ become our righteousness. Hence, this righteousness is something living. It not only gives us the position of being justified, but also implants within us a righteous life to live out righteousness.

V. How to receive Christ as righteousness

A. Confess that you yourself are unrighteous.

B. Receive Christ as the Savior of righteousness. He is the One without sin. He bears our sin and enters into us to become our righteousness.

Subject Fifty-six

TURN, TURN; WHY WILL YOU DIE?

Scripture: Ezek. 33:11

I. Man is on the pathway of death

A. The fall of the first ancestor of mankind brought man to the way of death. Since that time, the entire human race has been on the pathway of death.

B. As soon as a man is born, he is on the way of death. Hence, man's life, from beginning to end, is on the pathway of death.

C. Death means: to depart from God, turn your back on God, be inclined to sin and evildoing, and yet have no feeling. Even if there is some feeling, it will be too feeble to stop you from what you are doing. This is the meaning of death, and these are also the conditions of death.

D. Give practical examples to prove that man has forsaken God, has been committing sins, and how he is walking on the pathway of death.

II. The result of walking on the way of death

A. Death comes from sin. Death also leads to judgment and hell. These four things are mutually related: sin, death, judgment, and hell. Sin brings in death, and death brings in judgment and hell. If a man is walking on the pathway of death, he will eventually be led to judgment and hell.

B. There is a death waiting for everyone who is walking on the pathway of death, and this death will be a final verdict, forever.

III. The call of God's love

A. God loves man. *Repeat this point.*

Although man is not thinking about God, God is thinking of man. Man forgets God, but God remembers man.

B. God's love causes Him to call those who are walking on the pathway of death. You have totally forgotten about God, but today He is calling you: "Turn, turn; why will you die?" I believe the gospel that I am preaching today is God's calling of love. Maybe you have heard it and still do not want to turn; nevertheless it will stay in your ears. When you are walking in darkness, doing evil things, dancing, playing cards, or even trying to commit suicide, He will be calling you: "Turn, turn; why will you die?"

C. This calling will continue throughout your lifetime, until you receive Him. Maybe at the time you are about to die, He will still be calling you: "Turn, turn; why will you die?" He may call you for ten or twenty years. If you still do not receive Him, even at the time you are about to die, He will be calling: "Turn, turn; why will you die?" No one can estimate the result of gospel preaching. You and I are just sowing the seeds. Only God knows its result. While you are getting married or celebrating your birthday, He will be calling you: "Turn, turn; why will you die?" Gospel preaching should not be too gentle. The more you are released, the easier it will be for the Holy Spirit to work. If you are nice and gentle, no one will be saved.

IV. How to turn

A. Receive God's call of love.

B. Repent and confess your sins.

C. Pray right now. Those who want to pray, stand up right now.

D. When you pray, receive Jesus as your Savior.

These points are the strategy and the tactic to defeat Satan. This point is the dividing line between heaven and hell. In preaching the gospel, just as in cooking, you must be skillful. Many who have heard have become indifferent, because you have spoiled them. Please take note that it is easier for those who are hearing the gospel for the first time to be saved.

Subject Fifty-seven

GOD'S SAVING WAY

Scripture: Ezek. 36:25-28

I. Cleansing—to solve the problem of our deeds

A. Man became filthy because of sin. There are two aspects of man's sin: the shortage of morality toward man, which is the filthiness of our conduct, and the shortage of worship toward God, which is the filthiness of idol worship. Since man's conduct is filthy, it needs to be cleansed.

B. God caused the Lord Jesus to shed His blood on the cross to cleanse away the sins of those who believe into Him.

C. When we believe into the Lord, God will use the blood of the Lord Jesus to cleanse away all our filthiness. *Stress strongly that when we believe into the Lord, God uses the blood of the Lord Jesus to cleanse away the filthiness of our conscience.*

II. Renewing—to solve the problem of our nature

A. Because of sin, our hearts became corrupted and our spirits became deadened. The heart and the spirit are important elements of man's being. Once sin entered into man, man's nature was corrupted, and his spirit was deadened. The preceding paragraph speaks of man's conduct, which is filthy and needs to be cleansed. This paragraph speaks of man's nature which is corrupted and deadened and needs to be renewed. Renewing is for resolving the corruption of man's nature, and cleansing is for resolving the filthiness of his conduct.

B. When we believe into Him, God renews our corrupted heart and makes it a new heart. Man's corrupted heart is evil. Worse than that, it is hardened toward God. As to morality, it is evil; as to God, it is hardened. Hence, it says in Ezekiel that our heart was a stony heart, as hard as a rock. When God saves us, He softens our stony heart and thus renews our heart.

C. When we believe into the Lord, God not only renews our heart but also renews our spirit. The religions of the world and the philosophy of men can never cleanse the conduct, much less renew the disposition. The heart is man's loving organ. Man's likes, his delights, and his willingness are functions of the heart. Because of the fall, our heart was hardened toward God. It did not love God, did not want God, and had no delight in God; on the contrary, it was full of hatred and rebellion toward God, and it turned away from God and rejected Him. When God saved us, He softened our stony hearts and caused us to turn back to Him. Nevertheless, the heart does not have the ability to have fellowship with God, although it may have the desire to do so. The spirit is the organ for fellowship with God. It is the spirit that can contact God and have fellowship with Him. So when God saved us, He not only renewed our heart but also renewed our spirit. The renewed heart enables us to desire God, love Him, and have delight in Him. The renewed spirit enables us to be near Him and contact Him. The renewed spirit is a spirit which has been made alive. Because of the fall, our spirit was deadened toward God and lost its function toward God. When God renewed our spirit, He made our spirit alive again and restored its function. Our heart used to be hardened toward God, but the renewed heart softened us so that we could turn toward God. This is like the blind eyes and the deaf ears. Because they have lost their functions, they are deadened. However, if the eyes are opened and the ears can hear again, they are renewed.

III. The giving of the Spirit

A. Although we have covered the matter of our conduct being cleansed and our disposition being renewed, we have not yet covered the matter of receiving God's life.

B. When God saves us, He not only cleanses our conduct and renews our disposition, but also gives us His own Spirit. He puts the Spirit inside of us so that we may contact Him and be mingled with Him. Formerly, God and man were not mingled together and could not make contact. But now man can contact God and be mingled with Him.

C. God's Spirit is God's life. Once God's Spirit gets in, His life also gets in, and we are regenerated. Regeneration is to be born again, to be born of God, to receive another life besides man's natural life. Once we are regenerated, we have God's disposition, and we become the children of God. When God's life, which is God Himself, gets into us, God and man are mingled together.

IV. The result

A. Our conduct is cleansed. Our disposition is renewed. We have God's life and God's disposition. God Himself also lives in our spirit.

B. Therefore, we can be God's children, and God can be our God. This means that we can serve God. He cleanses our filthiness so that we may be justified and accepted by God. He renews our disposition and softens our hearts so that we may turn to God and love God. At the same time, God's Spirit also lives in us to enable us to know God and contact Him. Hence, we can be God's children, and God can be our God.

Subject Fifty-eight

THOU ART WEIGHED IN THE BALANCES, AND ART FOUND WANTING

Scripture: Dan. 5:27

I. It is not man's responsibility to evaluate himself

A. Everyone has his own evaluation of himself. King Belshazzar had his own evaluation of himself; likewise, we each have such an evaluation of ourselves.

B. Man's own evaluations are too high. King Belshazzar evaluated himself as a high and honorable king. Many people consider themselves better than others. Everyone considers himself a fine gentleman. There is not one who is not self-righteous and self-justifying.

C. Man's evaluation of himself is inaccurate. King Belshazzar rated himself as an honorable king, but God said, "Thou art weighed in the balances, and art found wanting." He was short of something. You may consider yourself a fine gentleman, but you may actually be quite poor.

D. Man is not qualified to evaluate himself, because man is not Lord of the universe. The Lord of the universe is God. When a citizen who is accused of some wrongdoing claims that he is innocent, it means nothing unless he is acquitted by the court. Likewise, it is not up to man to evaluate himself.

II. Man's evaluation is up to God

A. God is the Lord of the universe. God is the ruler of the universe.

B. God rules the universe according to His laws, not allowing things to happen in a random way in the universe. Give examples to prove this point.

C. God evaluates man according to His laws, which are the balances.

D. The balances are made up of the ten commandments. There is no need to talk about all of the ten commandments. Just choose three or four to weigh them, and that will be sufficient. If you are put on the balances, you are immediately exposed. Some examples are: (1) dishonoring your parents, (2) committing fornication, (3) stealing, and (4) lying. "Thou art weighed in the balances, and art found wanting."

E. Man's conscience is also a balance. You may claim that you are a certain kind of person, but you are only pretending; your conscience protests within you.

F. Furthermore, the coming judgment will be a real balance. In the gospel today we are putting forth the balance. If you do not take heed, even if you ignore the condemnation of your conscience, there will be no escape for you when the final balance, the judgment, comes.

III. The result of God's evaluation

A. The result of God's evaluation is that all men are condemned. There is not one weighed in God's balance who is not found guilty.

B. Following the condemnation will be perishing, which includes death and hell.

IV. How to meet God's evaluation

A. By his own conduct no one can be justified by God. This is to say that no one's conduct can measure up to God's standard. Once you have been evaluated by God, you are through. Once you have been weighed in His balances, you are completely finished.

B. This is why God sent the Lord Jesus to accomplish redemption and to bear our sins.

C. To meet God's evaluation, we must confess our shortages before God. Do not be self-righteous any more.

D. Receive the Lord Jesus and His redemption so that you may obtain God's justification.

Subject Fifty-nine

PREPARE TO MEET THY GOD

Scripture: Amos 4:12

I. The relationship between God and man

A. God is the creator of man, and God is man's ruler.

B. We live and move in Him, and we shall be judged by God. This paragraph is to show that our living is related to God.

II. Man shall meet God

A. Today man doesn't feel that he is related to God. You should portray man's condition of dumbness and dullness toward God. Man is insensitive to God and does not care for God.

B. Each one will have to leave this world one day. When a man dies, his present life is finished, and eternity begins. When a man enters eternity, he shall meet God.

III. God's judgment

A. When a man meets God, he shall be judged by God.

B. God's judgment is according to a man's work.

C. No man's work can meet the standard of God's judgment.

D. Hence, the result of God's judgment is that man will be condemned to perish.

IV. How to prepare to meet God

A. Repent and turn to God.

B. Confess and forsake your sins.

C. Believe and receive Christ and His redemption.

D. Serve God.

Subject Sixty

THE FOUNTAIN OF CLEANSING

Scripture: Zech. 13:1

I. Man's sins

A. From the time of Adam's fall until now, the human race has been in sins and evildoings.

B. Point out the fact that man is born in iniquity. Give examples to prove that man is born in sin. There is no need to teach a person to commit sin, because sin grows out of man's corrupt nature.

C. Also point out in a solid way the fact that man commits

sins. Bring out a few things to prove the point, such as lying, stealing, covetousness, and craftiness.

II. God's righteousness

A. God's righteousness causes Him to judge the sin of man.

B. According to God's righteousness, all men are under God's condemnation, and all should perish in the lake of fire.

III. God's love

A. God's righteousness causes Him to condemn men, but God's love causes Him to come to save men.

B. God's love prepares the way of salvation for men. Expound these two points.

IV. God's saving way

A. God is both righteous and loving. These two aspects caused God to accomplish a saving way for us. This saving way not only fulfills the purpose of His love, but also meets His righteous requirements.

B. God caused the Lord Jesus to shed His blood on the cross in order that He might redeem us from our sins. Such a redemption shows God's love on one hand and God's righteousness on the other. Because God loves us, He gave His Son for us. Because God is righteous, He required the sacrifice of His Son in our stead.

C. The Son of God shed His blood on the cross for our redemption. This blood became the fountain of cleansing. This blood not only cleanses away our sins and evildoings according to God's righteousness, but also causes us to realize God's love, so that we will no longer partake of such evil-doings.

Repeat this point.

V. How to be cleansed from sins

A. Confess that you are sinful.

B. Receive the Lord Jesus and the redemption of His cross.

Part II
New Testament
Subjects

Subject Sixty-one

JESUS IS THE SAVIOR

Scripture: Matt. 1:21, 23

I. Who Jesus is

Prove that Jesus is God.

A. Who did the ancient people say that Jesus was?

The Jews said that Jesus was a carpenter from Nazareth. Others said that He was one of the prophets, and still others said that He was a holy man or a religious revolutionary. In other words, they all considered that He was no more than an ordinary man.

B. Who does the Bible say Jesus is?

Chapter one of Matthew points out that Jesus had two names, Jesus and Immanuel (which is, God with us). According to this name (Immanuel), we know that the Lord Jesus is God with man. Jesus is God.

C. The facts prove who the Lord Jesus is.

Church history over the past two thousand years has proved that Jesus is an extraordinary person. There is an extraordinary power in the Christian faith and its gospel has produced an extraordinary effect. This extraordinary One is God Himself.

This point should be emphasized.

II. Jesus is God coming as the Savior

A. Jesus means Jehovah the Savior. "Je" means Jehovah. When Jesus was born, an angel declared that His name should be called Jesus, which means Jehovah the Savior.

B. Jehovah is God.

He is God incarnated to be the Savior; therefore, this Savior is God become man. He is God as well as man. As God He is able to accomplish salvation for man; as man He can become the substitute for all men.

III. How did Jesus become man's Savior?

A. Jesus was crucified. Describe how He bore our sins, shed His blood for us, and suffered God's righteous judgment. Thus, He solved the problem of our sins.

B. He was resurrected from the dead and ascended to the heavens to be the Almighty Savior for all mankind.

C. As the Spirit, He entered into man to become man's living Savior, that man might be set free from sin. He was crucified and shed His blood to wash away all man's sins. He entered into us as the Spirit that we might be delivered from the power of sin and from our sinful living.

D. By His death and resurrection and His descending as the Life-giving Spirit, He is able to save men from sins. Sin has its punishment, its power, and its living. The shedding of the blood of the Lord Jesus makes it possible for man to be free from sin's punishment. The resurrection of the Lord Jesus and His descending as the Spirit enable man to be delivered from the power of sin and from sinful living. Therefore, He is able to save us out of our sins.

IV. How can man receive Jesus as Savior?

A. By confessing that we were born in sin, brought up in sin, have lived in sin, and were also under the condemnation of sin.

B. By repenting and confessing our sins.

C. By confessing that the Lord Jesus died for our sins, that He was resurrected, and that He ascended to the heavens.

D. By receiving the Lord Jesus as our Savior.

Subject Sixty-two

A PORTRAIT OF THIS GENERATION

Scripture: Matt. 11:16-19

I. This generation is like children at play

A. In the eyes of the Lord, all our life is like child's play.

B. Although all is but children's play to the Lord, yet men look at this generation as something great. These two are in contrast.

C. Because men's viewpoint of this generation and the Lord's viewpoint are different, the emphasis is also different. Men of this generation stress today's living and neglect the consequence in the future, but the Lord Jesus disregards today's living and takes it as child's play. He cares for the consequence in the future.

This section should be strongly emphasized. This is the only place in the whole Bible where it is mentioned that the life of this generation is but child's play.

II. The wailing of the gospel

A. Because the Lord disregards the life of this generation and cares much for the future consequence, He preached the gospel to men. The gospel turns men's attention from this generation to the future. In other words, the gospel changes men's viewpoint from this generation to the future.

B. When a man only pays attention to the life of this generation, he does not realize that there is any problem with his morality. When a man pays attention to the future, his conscience is activated and he immediately realizes that he is sinful.

C. So the Lord's gospel is to wail, because: (1) men are sinful, but they are not conscious of their sinfulness, and (2) they are on the way to destruction, yet do not know it. Hence, the Lord's gospel is to wail so that men may be made aware and that they would repent.

III. The piping of the gospel

A. On the negative side, the gospel is to wail and to cause men to repent. On the positive side, it is the piping to cause men to rejoice. If the gospel is only the negative wailing and not the positive piping, the glad tidings would have become bad news. The reason that the gospel is glad tidings is because its wailing is for the piping.

B. The gospel piping is the good tidings of great joy proclaiming to us that our Lord Jesus is our Savior who takes away our sins, delivers us from perishing, and gives us eternal life. All these should cause us to rejoice. Such a proclamation really sounds like music.

IV. Men's reactions

A. Men do not understand the wailing of the Lord Jesus and take it as something crazy; they think that He was out of His mind. Some heard the believers testifying about this sin, that sin, and many other sins, and they said, "These people must be crazy. They must be out of their minds." What they did not know was that this is the wailing. Had they seen the terror of man's perishing, they would have sorrowfully repented and would have not lived such a life in a stupor of carefree indulgence.

B. Men do not accept the gospel piping, and they consider it ridiculous and wasteful. The Lord Jesus piped to them, yet they said that the Lord Jesus was a gluttonous man and a winebibber. Men of this generation also criticize the joyful life of Christians. Christians often meet together and praise God. Those of this generation do not accept the music of Christians' piping, and they say, "They are just wasting their time. Why do they go to the meetings instead of studying hard? Why don't they take care of their business rather than listening to the messages?" They think that the Christians' meeting, listening to messages, and prayers are altogether wasteful.

V. The choice of the wise

A. The general reaction of men who reject the gospel is foolish. Here you should argue the reactions of the two points mentioned earlier. Make it clear to them: because men are sinful and shall perish, shouldn't we wail? On the other hand, because Jesus shed His blood and gives life, shouldn't we pipe?

B. Conclude that there should be a wise decision: to stress the future but not this generation; to choose Christ and not the pleasure of sins. I should lament when the gospel is being wailed, and I should dance when the gospel is being piped. With a sorrowful and contrite heart I should echo the gospel's wailing, and with joy and rejoicing I should echo the gospel's piping.

C. The result of the wise choice is first the lamenting and then the dancing. First comes the sorrow, but the end is rejoicing.

Subject Sixty-three
COME TO THE REST

Scripture: Matt. 11:28

I. The labor of the human life

A. Man's whole life is a labor. *Point out strongly the various kinds of man's laborings.* For example, how laborious it is from grade school to college! There are different kinds of laboring in all occupations: teachers, farmers, workers, and merchants.

B. Not only is man's laboring something laborious, but it is also a suffering. When there is laboring, there is also suffering. Point out the feeling of suffering: the laboring and suffering of students, businessmen, teachers and workers. *Point out the suffering of man to touch people's feeling.*

II. The heavy burden of the human life

A. Man's laboring and suffering is his heavy burden. Laboring is a heavy burden, and so is suffering. Point out real examples of the heavy burden of those who are parents, children, husbands, wives, employers, managers, bosses, servants, employees, maids, rich, poor, students, learned, and unlearned.

B. Besides the heavy burden of laboring and suffering, there is the heavy burden of sin. The heavy burden of laboring and suffering is physical, emotional, and psychological. The heavy burden of sin is a matter of the conscience.

Touch the feeling of man's conscience. When a man is committing sins and doing evil, his conscience is bearing a heavy burden. He feels bound up and condemned.

The heavy burden of laboring and suffering is related to the matter of man's living. The heavy burden of sin is related to the matter of morality. There is a heavy burden and demand in man's daily living on his morality, on his emotions, on his physical body, on his psychological being, and on his conscience.

III. A resting place

A. Man himself has no rest. No matter how he may try, he cannot find rest, nor can he put off the heavy burden of laboring, suffering, and sin.

B. Man needs rest and salvation.

C. All the philosophers and founders of religious movements only increase man's heavy burden. They cannot reduce man's suffering; therefore, they are not man's salvation, because they cannot cause man to find rest.

D. Only Christ can save man from his heavy burden of sin, laboring, and suffering. Therefore, He alone can give man rest. He is the place of rest. This is why He calls man to come to Him to find rest.

IV. How Christ gives man rest

A. He takes away man's sin. Here, point out the redemption of the cross, how the Lord was crucified and shed His blood to cleanse man's conscience and to take away man's heavy burden of sin.

B. He gives man His life to be man's strength and to meet man's need.

C. His life saves man from inordinant living. Man thus finds rest. In others words: (1) His shed blood cleanses man's conscience and washes away man's sins; (2) His life gives us strength and meets our daily needs; and (3) His life also saves us from inordinant living.

V. How to receive the rest of Christ

A. Come unto Me. *Stress the word "Come."* "Come to me all who labor and are burdened, and I will give you rest." Come unto Jesus. Come to where Jesus is.

B. Surrender yourself, your sins, and all you have to Christ. Commit your life and all your being to Christ.

C. Accept Christ and His salvation.

Subject Sixty-four
WHO IS JESUS?

Scripture: Matt. 16:13-17

The Lord Jesus and His disciples discussed one subject in these verses: "Who do men say that the Son of man is?...Who do you say that I am?" This was mentioned in Subject 61, but was not a complete message. Now, we make it a full subject. This subject is more difficult to preach.

I. Who did the Jews say that Jesus was?

A. Those who opposed Him said that Jesus was a carpenter from Nazareth, the son of Joseph; they said that He was only a man.

B. Those who favored Him said that He was one of the prophets, like Elijah, Jeremiah, or John the Baptist.

II. Who did the Gentiles say that He was?

A. The Gentiles of the past generations said that He was a religious revolutionary or a noble philosopher.

B. Others said that He was a servant who sacrificed Himself. To summarize, men have said that Jesus was one of four things: (1) a religious revolutionist, (2) a noble philosopher, (3) a noble moralist, or (4) a sacrificial servant.

III. Who does He Himself say that He is?

A. He said that He is the Son of God.

B. He accepts man's worship as God. He told people that He was the Son of God. The Son of God is God. Therefore, He accepts man's worship to Him as God.

C. His doings substantiated His words. His word says that He is the Son of God. He called not being as being; He commanded the storm and the waves, and they were calm. He healed the sick, He cast out demons, and He gave life to the dead. All these proved His words.

IV. Who does the Bible say that He is?

A. The Old Testament says that He is God. In Isaiah 7:14 He is called Immanuel. Isaiah 9:6 says that a child is born, and His name shall be called the Mighty God. Micah 5:2 says, "Out of thee shall one come forth unto me that is to be ruler in Israel; whose goings forth are from of old, from everlasting."

B. The New Testament tells us more clearly that He is God, the Son of God (John 10:30; 3:16).

V. Who does history say that He is?

A. The two thousand year history of the Christian faith proves that He is an extraordinary One. History reveals to us that no matter how people on this earth have opposed Him, He has always been victorious.

B. The fact of today's continued evangelism proves that He is God.

VI. The fruits of the gospel prove that He is God

A. Man receives inner peace whenever he accepts Jesus. Because He is God, He can forgive man's sins and give peace to man's conscience.

B. When man accepts Jesus as Savior, his life is changed. From deep within to his outward living, there is a great change. This wonderful change proves that Jesus is God.

C. Many believers had sicknesses which were healed when they called upon the name of the Lord. This also proves that He is God.

VII. What shall we do with Him?

A. Turn to Him and repent.

B. Accept Him; believe in Him.

C. Follow Him, that is, serve Him.

Subject Sixty-five

THE VALUE OF THE SOUL

Scripture: Matt. 16:26

I. Life makes man valuable

A. Man is the highest creature in the universe. Why? It is because man possesses a life which surpasses every other created life.

B. The human life, a life that surpasses the life of all other creatures, is commonly known as the soul. Man is precious because he has a soul, a human life. The difference between man and all other creatures is that man is the only one who has a soul.

C. Show how real the soul is and speak of its nature. Use examples to demonstrate that the soul is real. For example, the conscience is a proof of the existence of the soul. Describe how man's conscience condemns him when he does wrong. Prove the existence of the soul by using love as an example. Love is something that cannot be seen, but there is no question that love exists. Lastly, show that the soul is intangible, spiritual, and inward.

II. The value of life

A. The one thing that man neglects most in himself is his own life. Some may think that they are taking good care of their life, but they are actually only taking care of their physical bodies, not their life. Today people only care for their physical bodies. Their caring for "life" is only caring for bodily health. Others care for the education of their mentality. This education is only for their mentality, their psychological faculty. Although man cares for his body and his mind, he neglects his real life, which is his soul.

B. According to the appraisal of the Lord Jesus, the life, or the soul, which man neglects is more valuable than the whole world. The total wealth of the whole world cannot be compared with the value of one soul. Quote Matthew 16:26: "For what shall man be profited if he

should gain the whole world, but forfeit his soul-life?"
Nothing in the whole universe can be compared with
the life of man's soul.

III. How man can lose the life of his soul

A. Man loses the life of his soul due to his negligence.
Man cares only for the body and his mentality, and he
neglects life. This causes him to lose the life of his soul.

B. Man loses his soul also because he cares too much for
the material things. Because he cares for the body and
the mind, he gives his full attention to the material
things which the body and the mind require. Because
he cares for the material things, he neglects the soul.
So man forfeits his life simply because of material
things. Man pays his soul for wealth, advancement,
savings, knowledge, position, fame, and riches. This is
what the Lord Jesus meant when he said a man gains
the whole world, and forfeits his soul-life.

IV. How man's soul can be saved

A. Explain that he must despise the material things,
that is, he must despise this age, and the needs of the
body and the mind.

B. He must then treasure his soul and the future. Just as
the body and the mind are related to this age, so the
soul is related to the future.

C. Receive the Lord Jesus as the Savior. Only He is the
Savior of our soul. He can forgive our sins, and He can
cause man's soul to be saved, because He can give
eternal life to man.

Subject Sixty-six

THE QUESTION OF QUESTIONS

Scripture: Matt. 21:23-27; 22:15-22, 23-33, 34-40, 41-46

In the first passage, the chief priests and elders came to ask
Jesus, "By what authority are you doing these things?"
In return, Jesus asked them this question: "The baptism of
John, whence was it? From heaven or from men?" In the

second passage, the Pharisees and Herodians asked the Lord, "Is it lawful to give tribute to Caesar, or not?" But Jesus asked, "Whose is this image and inscription?" In the third passage, the Sadducees asked about the resurrection. Jesus said, "In the resurrection they neither marry nor are given in marriage." In the fourth passage, the lawyer asked, "Which is the great commandment in the law?" The Lord Jesus said, "You shall love the Lord your God with all your heart, and with all your soul, and with all your mind...You shall love your neighbor as yourself." In the last passage, the Lord Jesus asked, "What do you think concerning the Christ? Whose Son is He?" Eventually they were not able to answer Him. Matthew 21 and 22 record how Jesus, the last week in Jerusalem, was questioned by different classes of society, and how He answered all four of their questions. At the end, Jesus asked them a question. The question Jesus asked is the question of questions.

I. The question of religion

A. The chief priests and the elders were religious people asking a religious question.

B. They asked about the source of authority. This is a matter of the ultimate authority of religion. It is also a matter of the orthodoxy or unorthodoxy of the religion.

C. In return the Lord asked where the baptism of John came from. During that time, the multitude acknowledged that John's baptism came from God. The Lord was very wise: if they admitted that John was sent from God, they should also admit that the Lord Jesus was from God.

D. This forced them to lie. They said that they did not know. The Lord Jesus said, "Neither tell I you." You should stress this point heavily, and place the blame on many religious people: pastors, elders, monks, priests, and nuns for telling lies to cover their consciences. Although they knew clearly, yet they said that they did not know. Although they studied religion daily, yet they told lies. Therefore do not believe what such ones say and do not be cheated by them.

II. The political question

    A. The question of taxation asked by the Pharisees and Herodians was a political question. The Pharisees were the patriotic ones. The Herodians were the Jewish rebels who helped the Romans rule the Jews. Ordinarily, these two groups were opposed to each other and would never cooperate. Yet surprisingly, on that day they united together to oppose the Lord Jesus.

    B. If the Lord Jesus said to pay the tax, the whole Jewish people would all be stirred up to oppose Him as a Jewish rebel. If the Lord said not to pay the tax, the Herodians would surely say that the Lord was against the Romans. Therefore, no matter what the Lord would say—to pay the tax or not to pay the tax—neither answer would be right.

    C. The Lord Jesus answered by asking them to show Him a coin from their pocket. Note that *they* had money to pay the tax; yet the Lord Jesus had no money in His pocket. Then He asked them, "Whose is this image and inscription?" They said, "Caesar's." The Lord said, "Pay then what is Caesar's to Caesar, and what is God's to God." Thus the Lord Jesus solved their political problem.

III. The question of faith, or of believing

    A. The Sadducees, the unbelieving ones, said that there were no angels, no demons, and no resurrection. They were just like the modernists of today.

    B. Their question was about the resurrection.

    C. But Jesus answered and said unto them, "God is the God of Abraham, and the God of Isaac, and the God of Jacob. God is not the God of the dead, but of the living." This proved that Abraham, Isaac and Jacob will all be resurrected from death. Therefore, there must be a resurrection.

IV. The question of Bible interpretation

    A. The lawyers were not like the lawyers of today. All they did was to interpret the Old Testament. What they asked was related to Bible interpretation.

B. They asked which commandment of the law is the greatest and most important.

C. The Lord's answer concerning the law was love toward God, love with three *all's*.

D. These four classes of people surrounded the Lord Jesus. The Lord Jesus was troubled from four directions. These were the leaders of all classes attacking Him, but the Lord Jesus solved all their questions completely.

V. The question of questions

In return, the Lord asked them the question of questions.

A. These four questions represent the questions of all human society. The questions of all the friends among the listeners are not beyond the scope of these four questions. The first two questions were asked by unbelievers. The last two questions were asked by the seeking ones.

B. What do you think of Christ?

The previous four questions of religion, politics, faith and Bible interpretation cannot save people. Only by knowing Christ is man able to be saved. What do you think of Christ?

C. Who is Christ?

Outwardly, He was the son of David. In reality, He is the Lord of David. Outwardly, He seems to be only a man; in reality He is both God and man.

D. In the day that the four questions were raised up, everyone was clear about the questions. But the question of Christ was neglected; therefore, they could not answer this question. Who is Christ? They did not know. Today among the listeners there may be some who are like them. They do not know who Christ is. *Here strongly emphasize that Christ is God as well as man.*

VI. What should you do with Christ?

A. Confess that He is God incarnated to become man, to be man's Savior.

B. With a humble heart, receive Him to be your Savior.

Subject Sixty-seven

THE BLOOD OF THE COVENANT

Scripture: Matt. 26:28

This gospel message is suitable for the intellectual.

I. The problem between man and God

A. Due to man's sin, man is not right with God.

B. Man lost God because of his sin, and man also lost all the blessings given by God.

C. Man's sin also caused him to come under the judgment of God.

II. The Lord Jesus accomplished redemption for man

A. The Lord Jesus died on the cross to accomplish man's redemption according to the requirement of the righteousness of God.

B. The redeeming blood takes away man's sins before God.

C. The blood of the Lord Jesus reconciles man to God.

D. The blood of the Lord Jesus brought man back to God and recovered God's blessing upon man.

III. The blood of the covenant

A. The blood which the Lord Jesus shed on the cross not only paid the price of redemption, but also was the seal of the covenant.

B. In the age of grace, God not only accomplished redemption for us, but also made a covenant with us. In this covenant, He promised to forgive our sins and restore our relationship with God, so that man might be able to receive all the blessings given by Him.

C. The blood of the Lord Jesus is the price and the seal of this covenant.

D. When we receive the blood of the Lord Jesus, we receive the price of the redemption of sins and receive the seal of this covenant. Therefore, when we receive the blood, our sins are forgiven, and we also have the seal of forgiveness.

IV. How to receive the blood of Christ

A. Confess that you are sinful and that you are not right with God.

B. Confess that the shedding of the blood of Christ on the cross is for your redemption.

C. Receive Christ and His redemption.

Subject Sixty-eight

THE EFFECTIVENESS OF THE LORD'S DEATH

Scripture: Matt. 27:45-54

I. Why did the Lord Jesus die?

A. The Lord Jesus died to bear our sins and to satisfy the requirement of God's righteousness.

B. During His crucifixion, there was darkness in heaven and on earth for three hours. This darkness symbolized sin. During that time, God gathered together all the sins of man and put them on Him. This was the time God judged sin in the universe. That was why there was darkness in heaven and on earth.

C. Because He had taken up man's sins at that moment, God forsook Him. God judged Him as if He were a sinner. That was why He cried, "My God, My God, why have You forsaken Me?"

II. The effectiveness of the Lord's death

A. The Lord Jesus bore our sins and died to satisfy the requirement of God's righteousness.

B. Because the death of the Lord has fulfilled the righteous requirements of God, his death has several obvious effects.

C. The first effect was that the barrier between man and God was removed. As soon as the Lord Jesus died, the veil in the temple was rent from top to bottom. The veil in the temple was the barrier between man and God.

D. The second effect is to quench the thirst of man. The moment He died, the rock was smitten. According to the record in the Old Testament, when the rock was smitten, there was living water flowing out to quench man's thirst. The rock is something dry; it cannot issue water, and it cannot quench man's thirst. Because of the death of the Lord Jesus, the Rock has been smitten, and the living water can flow out to quench man's thirst.

E. The third effect is to remove the power of death. When the Lord Jesus died, some graves were opened. The grave was the power of death which had man bound within. After the Lord's death, the Lord's people came out from the power of death.

F. The Lord's death solved the problem between man and God, the problem of man himself, and the problem between man and Satan. To God, the rent veil solved the problem between man and God; the barrier was removed. To man, the smitten rock solved man's own problem; his thirst was quenched. To the devil, the opened graves solved the problem between man and Satan; the power of death was broken.

III. **How to obtain the effectiveness of the Lord's death**

A. There is a barrier between you and God. That barrier is sin. Therefore sin must be confessed.

B. Confess that your life is a life of thirst; you are not satisfied.

C. Confess that you are under Satan's power of death. Man is in the process of dying daily and is on the way to death.

D. Then confess that Christ died for you.

E. Receive Christ and His salvation.

Subject Sixty-nine

THE SALVATION OF THE PARALYZED MAN

Scripture: Mark 2:1-12

The following points are concerning the selection of materials for gospel preaching:

1. When you choose this passage for a gospel message, never emphasize that this is a case of a paralyzed man being healed, because people might misunderstand that this is just a sickness that was healed and not realize that it is a matter of a soul being saved.

2. Do not go to the book of Matthew to find a story of healing for preaching the gospel, because that book shows us that the Lord Jesus is the King expressing authority, rather than one ministering to man. The narrative in Matthew does not fit as gospel material. Therefore, when you want to use the miracles performed by the Lord Jesus as gospel material, take the text from the book of Mark. When you are preaching the gospel of life, take the text from the book of John. When you are preaching the gospel of forgiveness of sin, Luke is the book.

3. Outwardly speaking, the miracles in the four Gospels show that the Lord healed the physical body. In reality, the Lord saved the person. Therefore, all the miracles in the gospels should be considered as symbols of salvation.

4. When you use the gospels of Luke and Mark, the more simple and common the title, the better it is. Your presentation should also be simple and easily understood. When you use the gospel of John, the title and the presentation should be deeper, because it is a matter of life.

I. Man was born paralyzed, "sick of the palsy"

In the gospels, the sickness of the physical body symbolizes the sickness of life. Therefore, this paralysis means the paralysis of human life.

A. Before God, man can do nothing. As to pleasing God or obeying the will of God and doing good, man is just like one paralyzed, without any strength.

B. Give an example of the paralyzed condition of man in the matter of doing good. He knows that he should do good, yet he just cannot do it. He knows that he should be kind and live righteously, yet he is not able to be kind or live righteously. *Touch people's feeling at the very beginning.*

II. Then Jesus came

A. In the second chapter of Mark Jesus went into Capernaum which was a slum area of Galilee filled with paralyzed people. The place where man lives is just like a slum area for paralyzed people.

B. When Jesus entered into Capernaum, He came not openly in the street, but into a house. Christianity is such a house. The denominations—Presbyterian, Baptist, etc.—are such houses. Even the homes of believers may be such houses.

III. Come to Jesus

A. Jesus came to save us; yet we still need to go to Him. Although He came into the house, yet He was surrounded by the house. We need to break through this house to come close to Him.

B. Anyone that comes to Jesus needs to break through His surroundings. What was it that surrounded Jesus? It was the house where He was. The Christians in Christianity are the surroundings of Jesus. Although in Christianity there is some measure of Christ, yet the organization and the Christians themselves have completely imprisoned Him. If you blame them in this way, the listeners will surely agree with you. They have never respected the organization of Christianity, nor the Christians with their so-called Christian families. If you point out these things and preach in this way, the listeners will surely agree with you, and the gospel meeting will be opened up. People will get saved. You should know people's psychology when you are preaching. Do not think people will not be convinced, when you are condemning Christian organizations and nominal Christians in this way. Sometimes it is really convincing. For example, in China, Dr. John Sung strongly condemned the Western missionaries when he was preaching; yet the missionaries were helped while the listeners were saved. For he condemned the sins, but he did not condemn the sinning ones. Christ is confined by the house—by many Christian schools, Christian hospitals, and Christian homes. Although Christ may be in them, they have confined Christ so that man can hardly approach Him.

C. The way to break through:

1. You need transcendency. They climbed over the roof top of the house which surrounded Jesus. This was the same as Zaccheus, who climbed the sycamore tree. You need to transcend over the house of Christianity, the Christian organizations, the Christian works, and even Christians themselves.

2. You need to tear down the roof top. Tear through the Christian organizations and you will see Jesus.

D. You need to present yourself and your condition before Jesus. This is what the paralyzed one did in presenting himself on his bed in front of Jesus. If you want to come to Jesus, you should do the same.

E. Anything you do to come to Jesus should be done in faith.

IV. **The Lord's salvation**

A. The paralyzed one only knows the result of being paralyzed, but does not know the cause of his condition. We only know we should do good, but have no strength to do good. As far as doing good is concerned, man is paralyzed. Yet we do not know the cause of being paralyzed.

B. The paralyzed one does not know the cause of being paralyzed, yet the Lord knows the cause. When the paralyzed one came to the Lord for healing, the Lord did not heal his sickness first; rather, He said, "Your sins are forgiven," because the cause of being paralyzed was sin. Therefore, friends, if you do not want to be paralyzed in your human living, you have to solve the problem of sin.

C. The healing of the paralyzed man was based on the forgiveness of sins. Our salvation is also based on the forgiveness of sins. *You need to touch people's feeling on this point.* Do you not feel guilty in your conscience? Do you not feel that you are sinful? You should not consider your own ability in doing good; rather, you should pay attention to the cause of not being able to do good. Therefore, you should take care of the problem of the forgiveness of sins.

D. Only God can forgive man's sins. Because the Lord Jesus is God, He can forgive man's sins. At that time Jesus said, "Your sins are forgiven," and they all murmured. Today, although there is some measure of Christ in Christianity, however, many still do not know that Christ can forgive sins, so even their own sins have not been forgiven. Here you should condemn the pastors and elders in Christianity. They are the scribes daily preaching from the Bible; yet they do not know that the Lord can forgive sins. Even their own sins have not been forgiven.

E. The proof of the forgiveness of sins is that the paralyzed man rose up, took up his bed, and walked out. Once a man receives the Lord, his paralyzed condition is healed and he can rise up and walk. Formerly, it was the bed that held him; now he can take up his bed and walk. Once he followed his bed; now his bed follows him. In Jesus, nothing is impossible. Which is easier, to forgive sins or tell the paralyzed one to rise up and walk? In the Lord all things are easy. But the scribes murmured and said, "It is too hard to forgive sins. Who has the authority to forgive man's sins?" Actually, to tell the man to take up his bed and walk is even harder. If you tell him to take up his bed and walk, he cannot rise and walk. What shall you do?

V. The results of being saved

A. The man not only had his sins forgiven, but also rose up and walked. Once a man comes to the Lord Jesus and is saved, he not only has peace within, but also has the outward strength to walk.

B. Once a man comes to the Lord Jesus and is saved, he can glorify God.

Subject Seventy

JESUS CAME NOT TO CALL THE RIGHTEOUS

Scripture: Mark 2:13-18

I. Jesus came to the seashore

A. Man's life is on the seashore. The sea is not a good thing; rather, the sea is the depth of sins. All that is against God is in the sea. For instance, the demon-possessed herd of swine rushed into the sea. The sea is the nest where the demons make their dwelling place. Movie houses and dancing halls are all seas.

B. Jesus came to the custom house. The custom house is the place where money is handled, where money is the center of everything. At the movie houses, the dancing halls, the sporting events, the markets, money is the center of conversation. Those who count the money, who handle the money, are all publicans.

II. Jesus came to call the sinners

Stress that He did not come to call the righteous, and at the same time quote the words of the Lord Jesus.

A. When Jesus came to the custom house, He met the publicans. During that time the publicans were the most despised people. Money was everything to them, and justice was nothing. They sacrificed morality, reputation, justice, background, personality, everything, all for money.

B. Today, Jesus is calling the sinners. Jesus never met the good people. Most of those He met were publicans. Are there any good people in the movie theaters and the dancing halls? Can those who sacrifice morality and reputation for money be good people? Jesus came to call such publicans.

Repeat that He came not to call the righteous. Quote verse 17.

III. The murmuring of the self-righteous

A. During that time, the Pharisees were questioning within themselves. The Pharisees were the false moralists, the false gentlemen. They had the outward appearance of doing good, yet they did not have the reality of doing good. They questioned why Jesus became the friend of sinners.

B. In today's society there are Pharisees. Outwardly, they are cultured gentlemen; inwardly, they are robbers and prostitutes. They look down on the gospel of the Christian faith. They think that only the thieves and sinners need the gospel. They consider themselves gentlemen who do not need the gospel. *At this point, strongly condemn these false gentlemen.*

IV. The joy of sinners

A. Jesus came to the place where the sinners were. He brought glad tidings and joy.

B. Jesus is willing to be with sinners. This is the joy of sinners.

C. Where Jesus is, there is joy.

D. Whoever responds to the call of Jesus will have joy. Give the example of the tax collector, Levi. When he responded to the call of Jesus, right away he prepared a feast in his house. Preparing a feast is a matter of happiness.

V. What happened to the sinners who were called?

A. They were freed from the old ways of living; that is, they were freed from their former living. Levi had been a tax collector. When he responded to the Lord's calling, he immediately left the tax office. He would no longer live a life of sacrificing his life and his reputation for money.

B. They followed Jesus. When a man is freed from his old ways of living, he immediately follows Jesus and becomes a fully saved person.

Subject Seventy-one

THE PARABLE OF THE SOWER

Scripture: Mark 4:1-20

I. The sower

A. The sower is the Lord Jesus. The sowing is to sow the

seed of life into the field that it may grow something living. The Lord Jesus is such a sower.

B. The Lord Jesus came to the earth to sow the life of God into man, that the life of God may grow in man.

II. The seed

A. The seed that the Lord Jesus sowed was the life of God.

B. The life of God is in the word of the Lord. The words that the Lord Jesus spoke or preached are the seed of life.

III. The field

A. The Lord sows the seed of life into the heart of man. Therefore, man's heart becomes the field for the seed of life.

B. There are four kinds of soil.

IV. The wayside heart

A. The first heart is the heart of the wayside. The Lord said that some seed fell on the wayside. The wayside is the shoulder of the way where man walks. Although you may say that it is the way, and perhaps it even looks like the way, yet it is not really the way, it is beside the way. Although it is not the real way, because it is the soil beside the way, it is trodden by man. Therefore, it becomes hardened and the seed cannot easily be grown in it.

B. Many hearts are like the wayside with many things passing through. The soil is continually trodden down by the traffic of all these things. Therefore, man's heart becomes hardened toward the word of God.

C. Because of the hardness of the soil of the wayside, the seed cannot be sown into it. The birds come to eat it up. When anyone is deeply involved with the things of the world, the soil of his heart is hardened. The words of the gospel cannot penetrate deeply into his heart. The birds, which represent Satan, come to eat the seed of the gospel.

V. The stony heart

A. The stony heart is the ground with soil on the surface and rocks underneath.

B. Some listen to the word of the Lord, but they only hear it superficially; deep inside of them are the hidden rocks. The rocks are sins, the world, friendship, fame, etc. They are not willing to give up these things.

C. Those who have believed only superficially stumble when the trials come. They are like seedlings in shallow soil that withered away by the scorching of the sun.

VI. The thorny heart

A. Although there are no rocks in the thorny heart, yet there are other things growing there. The earthly cares, the deceitfulness of riches, and other lusts are the thorns.

B. Today there are also some who accept the words of the Lord, yet their hearts have not been freed from the cares of this life, the deceitfulness of riches, and other lusts.

C. After a man has heard the word, the word of God inside him does not result in much growth when it encounters the thorns.

VII. The heart with the good soil

A. The good soil is not the wayside soil, nor the rocky soil, nor the soil with thorns.

B. This soil does not have the traffic of people and worldly things. It is not shallow, does not have hidden sins and love of the world. It is not thorny, does not have the anxiety of the world, the deceitfulness of riches and the desire for other lusts. This heart is good soil.

C. When anyone with such a heart with good soil accepts the word of the Lord, the result is the fruit bearing of the Lord's life, some thirtyfold, some sixtyfold, and some a hundredfold.

VIII. How to have a heart with good soil

A. Do not allow your heart to be trodden by the traffic of people and worldly things; keep your heart from being too close to these things.

B. Get rid of the hidden sins and the worldly love in your heart.

Give examples to expose their hearts.

C. Get rid of the anxiety of the deceitfulness of riches, and the lusts for other things.

D. Receive the word of the Lord with a good heart. The word of the Lord is also the life of the Lord.

Subject Seventy-two

THE SALVATION
OF THE DEMON-POSSESSED MAN

Scripture: Mark 5:1-20

I. Jesus came to the seashore

(Same as Section I, Subject 70.)

A. The human life is like the seashore. The sea is the depth of sins. All that is against God is in the sea. For example, the demon-possessed herd of swine rushed into the sea. The sea is the very nest of demons. The theaters and the dancing halls are the sea.

B. Jesus came to the place where the demon-possessed person was.

II. The demon-possessed man

A. The people on the seashore are the demon-possessed ones. To meet a demon-possessed person, you need to go to the seashore.

B. What is a demon-possessed person? He is one who is not free, who cannot control himself, who is controlled by a force outside of himself. For example, some may be controlled by drugs, by gambling, by movies, by dancing, by smoking, by their temper, by their fashionable clothing, or by reading novels. When the demon-ruled person becomes obsessed with these things, he does not care about anything else. Give examples to show that those who are obsessed in this way are the demon-possessed ones.

C. The demon-possessed ones live in the graveyard. Graveyards are the dwelling places for the dead, and they are full of darkness and death. Those who are possessed by the movies, dancing, and drinking live in the graveyard. Is it not true that the movie theaters, dancing halls, casinos, bars and houses of prostitution are the graveyards?

D. The life of one who is demon-possessed is not subject to any other ruling, and is insane. Governmental laws, school regulations and home discipline cannot guard such a one. Even an iron chain cannot subdue him.

E. The proof that one is demon-possessed:

  1. There is shouting, crying, and disorder.

  2. Such a one bruises himself. All those possessed by demons have no self-control. They shout and cry in an unreasonable way, and they cannot keep silent. They torture themselves and hurt their own bodies. They damage their own reputation, their position, and their family name.

III. Meeting Jesus

A. Jesus came to the seashore where the demon-possessed man was; therefore, it was easy for the demon-possessed one to meet Jesus.

B. When he met Jesus, he reacted by asking Jesus, "What have you to do with me?" Whoever says that he has nothing to do with Jesus is a demon-possessed person. Perhaps there are some in our midst who say that you have nothing to do with Jesus. If this is the case, this proves that you are demon-possessed.

IV. Jesus casting out the demon

A. The demon-possessed man said that he had nothing to do with Jesus and did not want Jesus to ask him any questions, but Jesus insisted on questioning him.

B. The more you say that you have nothing to do with Jesus, the more He would like to question you.

C. The questioning of Jesus is your salvation.

D. The salvation of Jesus frees you from a force that is outside of you.

E. When the Lord Jesus cast out the demons, the demons got into a herd of swine. The swine represent the filthiest ones among all people. The habits that the Lord cast out of you went into the filthiest people in the society. They became more deeply possessed by the demons. Perhaps, among your colleagues and classmates, there is a herd of swine. If you should leave them, they may fall more deeply into sin than ever.

V. The result of the casting out of the demons

A. The man was sitting down. The demon-possessed person cannot stand still. If he does not go to Las Vegas, he will find a worse place. If he is not in a theater, he will be in a bar. But now the one who used to be like that is calmed down.

B. He put on clothing. Formerly he did not care for his shamefulness, his reputation, his personality or his nakedness; now he is conscious of his shame, and he puts on clothing.

C. His understanding began to be restored. Formerly he was obsessed, as one who was living foolishly; now he understands.

D. He testified for the Lord. The Lord asked him to go home to his relatives and friends to tell them what a great thing the Lord had done for him and how merciful He was with him. That man went home and proclaimed what a great thing the Lord had done for him.

Note:

When you are using the stories in the Gospels as materials for gospel preaching, never try to be nice or gentle. Dr. John Sung was the wildest gospel preacher in the last two or three centuries. You cannot be nice about hitting a man. There are all kinds of people among the audience.

The gospel causes man to be saved. The words don't have to be profound. Something like, "Do not look at others, I'm talking about you," is good enough to save people.

The gospel must be powerful. You must pick up the stories in the Gospels. Indeed, out of the sixty-six books of the entire Bible, the first four books of the New Testament are called the Gospels. We should often exercise ourselves into the Gospel stories until we are crystal clear within. You must be able to pick up any subject, such as the thorns, weeds, or robbers, etc., and speak right away. To be powerful, you should apply the Gospels in a living way, not like telling a story. Gospel preaching will be ineffective if it is merely a telling of stories. Preach to the point with life, with facts, and inspirit, and the gospel will be effective.

Subject Seventy-three

THE SALVATION OF TWO DIFFICULT CASES

Scripture: Mark 5:21-43

The outstanding feature in this passage of the Bible is that the two women who were healed were related to the number twelve. The older one had been sick for twelve years, and the younger one was twelve years old. The older woman had the sickness from the time the young girl was born. Thus the Holy Spirit signifies here that both had the same problem. The two were one. At first it was the father of the young girl seeking for healing, and then on the way the older woman came also seeking healing. At the time the older one was healed, the younger one was also healed.

I. Jesus came to the seashore

Stories such as this one as mentioned in the Gospel of Mark almost always occurred at the seashore. (See Section I of Subject 70 regarding the seashore.)

A. Petitioned by others. The girl was in serious sickness, and her father petitioned the Lord Jesus for her.

B. Petitioned for one's self. The older woman came to petition the Lord for herself. This point is to explain that both the older and the younger women refer to the same sinner. The reason is that the older woman began to have her sickness when the girl was born. The older woman had been sick for twelve years when the girl was twelve. So the two are actually one. The Holy Spirit put them together to show that they refer to one person: on one hand it is others who petition for you, and on the other hand you petition for yourself.

C. You must break through the crowd. Today in the midst of the crowd there are many Christians, as well as many who listen to the gospel. All are crowding Jesus and surrounding Him. If you want the Lord Jesus, you must break through the crowd.

D. You need to touch Jesus. Repeat the difference between crowding Jesus and touching Him. To touch is to contact. To crowd Jesus is to be close to Him without making contact with Him. Today even many pastors and Christian leaders are not contacting Jesus; they are only crowding Him.

E. Here there is something quite hard to explain, and that is the matter of touching Jesus' garment. Strictly speaking, she did not contact Jesus Himself directly; she only touched Jesus' garment.

  1. A garment is something to hide a person within. Today when you touch a person who is clothed, you can only touch his clothing.

  2. The spiritual meaning of the garment refers to man's work. So when the woman touched the Lord, although you might say that she touched the Lord, strictly speaking she was touching the Lord's garment. To touch the Lord's garment is to touch the Lord's work. The stories in the Gospels can be considered as the Lord's work, because all these stories contain what the Lord has done. When you touch these stories, you touch Jesus. It is enough to touch the Lord's garment; you do not need to touch the Lord Himself directly.

Just touch what the Lord has done and you will be healed. Just touch these stories and you will be saved.

II. The two women symbolize one person

A. Man's position before God is a woman's position.

B. The two women here actually symbolize one person. The reasons:

1. Their problems involved twelve years.

2. The Scripture put them together in the same passage.

C. The young girl was sick, at the point of death. The scripture does not mention what kind of sickness she had. If the two women refer to one person, then the sickness is the issuing of blood. This is to tell us that man has the problem of issuing blood. Blood issuing is something leaking from within a person. Whatever comes out of a man is no good. Blood issuing is a deadly sickness. One who is recovered from the issuing of blood is one who is brought back to life from the point of death.

III. The saving power

A. Point out that the saving power is the Lord's saving, not man's improvement in behavior. The teaching and the help of men are altogether useless. The physicians symbolize men's help and teaching. The fact that she "spent all that she had" means that she paid the full price to improve her behavior, but the end result was "suffering many things," and nothing helped her a bit. The philosophers are physicians. Your parents and teachers are physicians, but they are of no help to you.

B. The saving power is supernatural. When the woman touched the Lord, right away a supernatural power came out of the Lord's body. To receive the Lord and be saved is not that you just receive some message, but that a supernatural power, which is the power of God, comes upon you and causes you to be saved.

C. The saving power depends upon your touching Jesus. You do not have to see Jesus with your own eyes; neither do you have to touch Him with your own hands. Just touch what He has done, and you will be healed. To touch how He was incarnated in the flesh, how He was crucified on the cross for you, and how He resurrected from the dead is to touch what He has done, and is to touch His garment. Just touch His garment, and you will be saved.

IV. The result of salvation

A. Delivered from sin. The two women symbolize one person healed from the issuing of blood, which means delivered from sin. The issuing of blood means that man is born in sin, and what comes out of a man is nothing but sins. Now because of touching Christ, a power comes out of Christ, and causes us to be delivered from sin.

B. Made alive. The young girl was made alive after the older woman was healed. This symbolizes that after we are delivered from sin, we are made alive.

Note:

You may insert "People's mocking" into this message, depending upon the time allowable, to say that when you believe in the Lord Jesus, the people will come and laugh at you.

Subject Seventy-four

SHEEP WITHOUT A SHEPHERD

Scripture: Mark 6:32-44

I. The wilderness of human living

A. This passage records that Jesus came to the wilderness. The wilderness signifies the desolation of human living. The wilderness is the place for the lost and wandering sheep. It is also the place for the hungry ones who cannot find satisfaction. The wilderness is not related to sin, but is related to desolation.

B. Describe how the desolation of human living is like the wilderness. All things of human living are tasteless. Solomon said, "Vanity of vanities, all is vanity." He also said all things under the sun are like chasing the wind and grasping a shadow. Here you need to make all the things of the world sound so desolate, and make home, school and business sound meaningless and empty.

II. The wandering of human living

A. Point out that in the eyes of God men are His sheep. Man did not come into being by himself, but he came from God and belongs to God. All of man's living comes out of God. So men are God's flock, and God is a God who created men and who cares for men.

B. When man lost God, he became a "sheep without a shepherd" just like a sheep who lost its shepherd.

C. Because man lost God, man's living became a wandering, without a master. There is a saying, "Everything has its own master." Where is your master? You cannot tell. You have no master. When you are sick, there is no one to comfort you. When a tragedy overtakes you, there is no one to rescue you. All of this is true because you are a sheep without a shepherd and without a master. This section is to speak about the situation of the wandering of human living.

D. Because you are a person without a master, your living has no purpose, and you are just wandering around in the wilderness.

III. The vanity of human living

A. Those who were with Jesus in that day were like sheep without a shepherd on one hand, and were hungry on the other hand. They were not only wandering in the wilderness, but also empty and dissatisfied.

B. Today's human living is in wandering and dissatisfaction, lacking food for satisfying the hunger. Human living is dissatisfied because of the lack of food. There is nothing that can substitute for food. You might have fame, position, etc., but you are still empty and dissatisfied.

C. In the wilderness you cannot find food. You have no food, and you have nowhere to buy food. *You should stress the point that in the wilderness of human living, you have no way to satisfy yourself.* Even if you paid a great price, you would still be dissatisfied. People like the monks, nuns, and those who strive to cultivate their morality all end up dissatisfied, empty, and having nothing to fill themselves up with.

IV. Then Jesus came

A. That day the Lord Jesus came to the wilderness, the place of the desolation of human living. You need to portray how into such a big wilderness there came the Savior.

B. Seeing the multitude of the hungry ones, Jesus was moved and had compassion for them.

C. Jesus fed them. This feeding was miraculous, because the bread was not purchased and had not been brought along with them, but it was supplied by the Lord. This supplying was done through a supernatural power; only Jesus can supply the bread. In the wilderness of human living, there is nothing to satisfy man; only Jesus can supply the bread.

D. Jesus became the good shepherd. Inasmuch as He had satisfied men and made them His sheep, He is responsible for all their lives. Formerly you had no one to lead you. Now that you are saved, Jesus will lead you, and He will become the good shepherd of all your life.

V. How to be saved

A. Receive Jesus. To receive is to eat. The fact that they received the bread into them means that they received Jesus by faith.

B. Jesus is the bread of life, and needs to be received by us. Jesus is also the good shepherd, and needs us to follow Him. To receive the bread solves the problem of the vanity and emptiness of human living; to follow the shepherd solves the problem of the wandering of human living. As soon as our vanity, emptiness, and wandering are over, the wilderness is past.

VI. The result of receiving

A. Fed. Jesus is the bread of life, causing us to be fed and satisfied.

B. Led. Jesus is the good shepherd who can lead us. Feeding solves the problem of emptiness, and leading solves the problem of wandering.

Subject Seventy-five

THE FILTHINESS OF THE HEART

Scripture: Mark 7:1-23

This is a very good gospel subject, but it is one that is not so easy to begin, because you cannot start with the filthiness of the heart. The Bible first presented a story to illustrate the point; then it goes on to say that such filthiness is not from without but from within.

I. The filthiness of human living

A. The whole world is filthy. It is filthy materially and morally. Go and take a walk in the street, and your whole being will be filthy.

B. The filthiness of the world symbolizes the fact that the whole human living is filthy. Any activity in the human living causes you to be defiled. The Jews followed the tradition of washing their hands and feet, because both the hands and the feet are the members related to man's activities, the points of contacting things. This is to say that whenever you move and touch something, you are liable to be defiled. Not only is doing evil things filthy, but even honoring your parents is also filthy, because man also has pride and self-glory growing within him when he is honoring his parents. When you are not doing anything the filthiness does not show. Once you do something, the filthiness shows right away. There is no need to mention that it is filthy to do evil things with your hands and feet; even doing good things is filthy. Of course it is filthy to pick up dung with your hands, but even if you are holding some clean things, it is still filthy. A man lying in bed for three days, doing nothing, will smell bad if he does not take a bath. Move, and you are filthy; be still, and you are filthy just the same. You need to speak to such an extent that you leave no escape for them.

II. Man's effort to be cleansed

A. In that day the Jews had to wash their hands and feet whenever they did something because they were defiled by their doing.

B. Today people are just like the Jews, only paying attention to the outward washing, and trying to make themselves clean by human effort. The washing of the hands signifies innocence, that you will no longer do evil things. Some who used to dance, watch movies and gamble now have washed their hands and have quit doing these things. Man's way is to wash his hands.

C. All of man's effort is outward. You need to speak in a serious way that all man's efforts are merely washing the outward things.

III. The source of man's filthiness

A. Man's filthiness shows on the outside, but the source of his filthiness is not outside of him.

B. The source of man's filthiness is in the heart. You need to quote the words of the Lord Jesus, "There is nothing from without the man, that going into him can defile him; but the things which proceed out of the man, are those that defile the man."

C. So just to cleanse the outside is useless. You must deal from within.

IV. The content of man's filthiness

Pick three or four items out of the thirteen mentioned in this passage of the Scripture and hit them. It would take a special conference to cover all thirteen items in detail: Evil thoughts, fornications, thefts, murders, adulteries, covetings, wickednesses, deceit, lasciviousness, an evil eye, railing, pride, and foolishness. Before you speak, you should prepare yourself thoroughly on these items. You should speak to such an extent that people dare not lift up their heads. For instance, when you are talking about the evil thoughts, you should say that you may seem to honor your parents outwardly, but within your heart you wish that they would die soon. Allow the heavenly x-ray to manifest the real situation of man.

V. **God's saving way of cleansing**

   A. Man washes the outside, but God deals with the heart.

   B. The way God deals with the heart is by regeneration.

      1. He makes our deadened spirit alive. The dead people are the most filthy ones. If you really want to escape the filthiness and want to be made alive, you must have life.

      2. He renews our heart.

      3. He makes us partakers of God's divine life and nature.

   C. God's saving way of cleansing includes two aspects: outwardly, God uses the blood to cleanse the filthiness of our outward behavior; and inwardly God regenerates us to resolve the filthiness within us.

VI. **How to be cleansed**

   A. Confess that you are filthy within and without.

   B. Receive the Lord as your Savior. As soon as you receive the Lord as your Savior, the Lord's blood cleanses the filthiness of your outward behavior, and at the same time the Lord's Spirit regenerates you, and resolves the filthy thoughts within you.

Subject Seventy-six

THE SAVING FAITH (THE CANAANITE WOMAN)

Scripture: Matt. 15:21-28; Mark 7:24-30

(The record in Mark is not as detailed as that in Matthew.)

I. **Jesus came to the Gentiles**

A. Tyre and Sidon are cities of the Gentiles. When Jesus came to these places, He came to the Gentiles.

B. Today the gospel of Jesus is being preached here. This is Jesus coming to this place.

II. Man possessed by demons

A. When Jesus came to Tyre and Sidon, there came a woman crying to Him, "My daughter is badly demon-possessed." The asking one was a woman, and the demon-possessed one was also a woman.

B. Woman represents the position of man before God. Man before God is a woman.

C. The fact that the daughter of a woman was possessed by a demon symbolizes the fact that all the ones born of women are possessed by demons.

D. Use some examples to show the meaning of being demon-possessed: some are possessed by the demons of movies, some of dancing, fornication, gambling, drinking, etc. Speak about the situation of man being possessed by demons.

III. Man's position before God

A. After the woman's request, the Lord said, "It is not good to take the children's bread and throw it to the dogs." Do not interpret this portion of the scripture to say that the Jews are the children, and that the Gentiles are the dogs; that Jesus came as the bread to the Jews, and that we are the dogs, having no part in the bread. Don't talk about these things, or else it will be complicated.

B. Today the condition of men before God is like that of the dogs.

C. Why in the eyes of God are we like the dogs? *Dog* is a descriptive term, speaking of the filthiness of our condition. Dogs like to feed on dirty things, such as dung. The condition of man before God is just like that of the dogs. Man will not come to the meeting hall where there are plenty of empty seats; instead, he would rather sell the shirt off his back to buy a ticket to some evil event, even waiting in a long line where people are standing shoulder to shoulder. Let me ask you: are you a sheep or a dog? Are you dirty or are you clean?

IV. God's portion for man

A. Although man is like a dog before God, God still gives man a portion, which is the crumbs fallen from the table.

B. Although you cannot quite see Jesus today, the gospel, nevertheless, is put before you. When you receive this gospel, which is like the crumbs, it is good enough to cause you to be saved. You do not have to see Jesus completely. You do not have to climb up to the table because you have already fallen under the table. Yes, the bread is on the table, but there are also the crumbs underneath. Although man in his fallen condition is not worthy to come up to the table as the children, nevertheless you can be saved just by receiving the crumbs under the table.

V. How to be saved

A. Confess your condition. When that woman heard the Lord calling her a dog, she did not deny it. She acknowledged that her position was that of a dog.

B. Lay hold on the Lord according to the Lord's word. The word *dog* came out of the mouth of the Lord, and the woman laid hold of that word, *dog,* and she was saved. Today, out of the mouth of the Lord comes not the word *dog,* but, "He that believes has eternal life." If you would only lay hold of the word of the Lord, you will be saved.

C. The faith that saves comes from laying hold of the word of the Lord. To believe is not only to agree or to understand, but to lay hold of the words spoken by the Lord. If you lay hold of a check for a thousand dollars, you get a thousand dollars. Today the Lord is spreading the gospel before you by means of His words, and these words are the check. Lay hold of His words, and you will be saved.

Subject Seventy-seven

THE BLIND MAN RECEIVES SIGHT

Scripture: Mark 8:22-26; 10:46-52

Put the two blind men in chapters 8 and 10 together.

I. Man's loss of sight

A. In both Bethsaida and Jericho, Jesus met blind men. This proves that there are blind ones everywhere.

B. Men are born blind because they do not know the meaning of human living, and they are not clear about God and the things of God. So spiritually speaking, man is blind. *Stress the point of spiritual blindness.*

II. Jesus came into the midst of men

A. These two portions record that Jesus came to the places of the blind men. This proves that where the blind men are, there Jesus comes. Bethsaida means the house of fishing. It was a place of fish. This means that Bethsaida is close to the seashore. The seashore is a place of sins. Jericho was a cursed city. This means that wherever the blind men are is a cursed place. From the meaning of these two places, it can be seen that man is born blind because man has sinned and is under a curse.

B. Jesus comes to the place where we are, the cursed place. Today the gospel is being preached to this place, which means that Jesus is coming to this place. Jesus comes to the sinful and cursed place.

III. Come to Jesus

A. Some who came to Jesus were brought by others. The blind man of Bethsaida was brought to Jesus by others. This means that the one who came to Jesus was brought in by his relatives and friends. He needed others to bring him in because he could not see the way. Maybe some among you have been brought in by your relatives and friends.

B. Some heard of His fame and came by themselves; they heard the name of Jesus of Nazareth and came. The

blind man of Jericho heard the name of Jesus of Nazareth and came by himself. Some among you came by
yourselves, because you had heard the gospel before.

C. Whether you are brought in by others or you come by
yourself, the principle is the same. You need to touch
Jesus.

IV. The Lord's saving way

A. The blind man of Bethsaida was brought out of the village by the Lord. This means that he was brought out
of the sinful environment. The village was the place
where the sinful ones were concentrated. Maybe the
movie theater, the dancing hall, or the gambling table is
your village. You are living in the village of sins. Now
that you have come to the Lord, the first step the Lord
takes is to lead you out of the village. You cannot stay in
the movie theater, or the Lord will not save you.

B. Jesus spit on his eyes. The spittle came out of the
mouth of the Lord, which signifies: (1) the word of the
Lord, and (2) the Spirit of the Lord. On the evening of
the Lord's resurrection, the Lord breathed upon the
disciples, and said, "Receive the Holy Spirit." To
recover your eyesight, you must receive the words of
the Lord, which are the Lord's life and Spirit. The
Lord's life and His Spirit are all in the Lord's words.
When the words of the Lord get into you, your eyes
are opened, and you can see again.

C. The Lord laid hands on the blind man of Bethsaida. The
laying on of hands means uniting as one. This means
that the Lord comes to you and becomes one with you.
The Lord must come into you and be mingled as one
with you before your eyesight can be recovered.

D. When the Lord laid hands on the blind man of
Bethsaida the first time, the blind man's eyes were
half-opened. He could see, but things were not too
clear, so he beheld men as trees. So the Lord laid His
hands on him the second time. This is to give more
room to the Lord and to have a further union with the
Lord. Hence his vision became clear.

E. The Lord commanded him to go home, but not to go back into the village. This village is your movie theater, dancing hall, or the gambling table, etc. If you go back there, you will be blind again.

These five points are related to the blind man of Bethsaida, concerning the aspect of sin. He was blind because of his sin, so when his sight was recovered, it was necessary for him to leave Bethsaida, the place of sins.

F. The way the Lord healed the blind man of Jericho was by calling him. When the blind man of Jericho heard the name of Jesus and came, he did not expect the Lord to know him, neither did he know that the Lord would save him. He considered himself a pitiful blind man and thought the Lord would never notice him or care for him. Yet unexpectedly the Lord Jesus came and called him cordially. Jericho was a cursed place. Man under a curse thought that he had been forsaken by God; yet the Lord came. This demonstrates that God does not forsake the cursed ones.

G. When the blind man of Jericho heard the calling of the Lord, he cast away his garment. This garment was a garment of begging, which means that the work of the cursed ones cannot make men alive; man must rely on someone's mercy. Now that this one has come to Jesus and has heard Jesus' calling, he no longer needs his own torn garment. So he casts away the garment of Jericho—the effort of man to achieve righteousness— which was cursed. The blind man of Bethsaida had to go out of the village, out of the place of sin and evil doings. The blind man of Jericho had to cast away his garment, cast away his tattered behavior.

H. The one who casts away his garment is the one who gives up his own work. As soon as he cast away his garment and asked the Lord, he was healed. In this respect there is no need for the laying on of hands. Simply by giving up his own work and asking the Lord for sight, he proved his faith. Hence the Lord said, "Thy faith hath made thee whole."

V. After being saved

A. After the blind man of Bethsaida was saved, he no longer went back to the village, the place of sins.

B. After the blind man of Jericho was saved, he followed Jesus.

C. Once man's spiritual eyes have been opened, right away he knows that he is in a sinful place, that the former living was sinful, and therefore he would not go back any more. Meanwhile, he also sees that only Jesus can be his guide, so he follows Jesus.

Subject Seventy-eight

"HIMSELF HE CANNOT SAVE"

Scripture: Mark 15:22-39

I. Jesus was crucified on the cross

A. First describe how men brought the Lord Jesus to Golgotha and crucified Him on the cross.

B. When Jesus was crucified on the cross, He was treated like a prisoner, because He was crucified with two others who were robbers. He was placed among the transgressors.

C. According to the mocking cries of men, He should never have been crucified, and being on the cross He should have been able to save Himself.

II. The reasons for the crucifixion of Jesus

A. Before Jesus was crucified on the cross, He was examined three times by the Jews according to God's law, and then examined again three times by the Romans according to men's law; yet they could find no fault at all with Jesus. So the Lord Jesus was not crucified because He had sin.

B. Although the Lord Jesus was sinless and did not deserve the death penalty, yet for the sake of jealousy, people still used an excuse to sentence Him to death. Such jealousy can be considered the reason for the crucifixion of the Lord Jesus on man's side. Because men were jealous of Him, therefore they crucified Him on the cross.

C. The reason for the Lord's crucifixion on man's side is very light compared to the reason on God's side. On God's side, it was because God put all of our sins upon the Lord Jesus and caused Him to bear those sins for us. Thus, the main reason for the crucifixion of the Lord Jesus was to bear the burden of sins for us.

III. The setting of Jesus' crucifixion

A. The setting of Jesus' crucifixion included both the natural and the supernatural aspects:

1. The natural aspect was an act of men. Men set up a wooden cross, nailed the hands and feet of Jesus to the cross, and then parted His garments, which meant that they stripped Him naked. They put Him to shame publicly, shook their heads, and mocked Him.

2. The supernatural aspect was an act of God. God caused the whole earth to be darkened, which was not an act of men, but of God. When the Lord Jesus gave up His breath, the veil of the temple was rent in two from the top to the bottom. This was also an act of God.

B. The setting of men's act occupied the first half of the Lord's crucifixion, which covered the period from nine in the morning until noon.

C. The setting of God's act occupied the second half of the Lord's crucifixion, which covered the period from noon until three in the afternoon, when the whole earth was darkened.

D. The setting of men's act depicts the killing of Jesus by human hands; the setting of God's act depicts the judgment upon Jesus by God. During the second half of the Lord's crucifixion, the whole earth was darkened. Darkness is the symbol of sin. When Jesus died, the veil of the temple was rent from the top to the bottom. The veil represents the barrier between man and God because of sin. The fact that the earth was darkened and the veil rent was a proof that God was judging the Lord Jesus, because at that time the Lord Jesus became man's sin-bearer.

IV. Jesus could not save Himself

A. If Jesus had only been killed by men, He could have saved Himself. He was capable of saving Himself. For thirty-three years on earth, many had attempted to kill Him, but He escaped them. It was very easy for Him to save Himself.

B. He did not save Himself but rather on the cross He was mocked and killed by men. Furthermore, He was forsaken and judged by God because He was bearing man's sins. If He had saved Himself, our sin problem would never have been resolved.

C. Because He would not save Himself, we are saved.

D. By not saving Himself, He became our substitute and became our Savior.

V. The attitude we should have toward Jesus

A. We should appreciate the fact that He suffered persecution and endured crucifixion for us.

B. But just to appreciate His sufferings could not save us. That is not enough to cause us to be saved.

C. We must thank Him for not saving Himself. We must thank Him for becoming our substitute to bear our sins, thus being judged by God's righteousness.

D. Whoever thanks Him and treats Him in this way is a believer, one saved by Him.

Subject Seventy-nine

THE DAYSPRING OF MERCY

Scripture: Luke 1:76-79

I. Human living is in darkness

A. In the Bible darkness symbolizes sins. So man living in darkness is living in sins.

B. Sin brings in the shadow of death. Although sin is not

death, it is at least the shadow of death. So men living in sins are living under the shadow of death. This is why Luke says, "them that sit in darkness and the shadow of death."

II. God's mercy toward men

A. According to the condition of men living in sins, God should deal with men according to His righteousness. But God's heart causes Him to be merciful toward men. Mercy is something within God's heart. According to God's procedure and His laws, God should deal with us in righteousness. But not only does God have His procedure and His laws; He also has a heart, and it is His heart that causes Him to deal with us in mercy.

B. Mercy reaches farther than grace; mercy reaches even to the unworthy ones. Grace is freely given, but it is given only to those who are worthy. If God had only grace and not mercy, all of us who are living in sins would be unworthy of His grace. But thank God, He is also merciful. Our position before God today is like that of a beggar needing God's mercy. To give something freely to someone who deserves it is grace; to give something to a beggar is mercy.

C. God's mercy causes the dayspring to shine upon us. The dayspring signifies the end of darkness, and the dawn of the day. This is to say that whoever has God's mercy upon him has his darkness ended. So God's mercy is not only the light, but also the sunshine of the dawn. Friends, maybe today God's dayspring is shining upon you, to end your darkness, and to bring light into your life.

III. Christ is the sunshine of the dayspring

A. God's mercy is to send Christ as our Savior.

B. We are living in darkness and under the shadow of death. Christ comes to meet our need, to cause our darkness to vanish, and to chase away the shadow of death. It is the business of the sunshine to cause darkness to vanish. Christ is the sunshine of the dayspring to us.

C. When Christ comes upon someone, the most obvious work is to make that one bright inside. Everyone who meets Christ right away feels that he sees light. Everyone who hears the gospel of Christ instantly feels that he is bright inside. Everyone who meets Christ instantly feels that his life has come to the daylight, and that he has come out of darkness.

D. Darkness is sins; sunshine is Christ. When a man meets Christ, he is sure to be delivered from sins, that is, from the shadow of death. The shining of Christ causes man to be delivered from sin and death.

IV. The result of being enlightened by Christ

A. The Bible says that evildoers have no rest in them. When a man sins, his conscience is troubled, and there is no peace between man and God; even there is no peace with the environment. Furthermore, there will be the eternal unrest in hell. Here you need to give some examples to illustrate how, after a person committed a certain sin, there was the unrest in his conscience and in his family.

B. Since Christ's enlightenment causes us to see light, it also causes us to be delivered from the causes of unrest and the elements of unrest. All the unrest comes from sins, darkness, and the shadow of death. Since Christ's shining causes us to be delivered from these things, we are delivered from the causes of unrest and its elements.

C. So Christ's shining guides our feet into the way of peace. Those who are in darkness are walking in the way of sins and living a life of unrest. As soon as we receive Christ's salvation and Christ shines upon us, we have peace in our conscience, peace with our environment, harmony with God, and are at peace constantly.

V. What should we do with Christ?

A. Do not reject His shining. It is God's mercy reaching to you that you are hearing this gospel message today. So friends, do not reject the shining of Christ.

B. Humble yourself and receive Christ as your Savior.

Subject Eighty

GOOD TIDINGS OF GREAT JOY

Scripture: Luke 2:8-14

I. The birth of the Savior

Do not just tell the story, or you will lose the power of the Holy Spirit.

A. The Savior was born in Bethlehem. When He was born, there were shepherds in the field keeping watch over their flock by night. Suddenly an angel came to announce to them the glad tidings that a Savior was born to men. This section covers the scene of His birth.

B. Those who heard the glad tidings were in the field, and it was at night. The place was out in the field, the time was at night, and the work was shepherding. All these are meaningful as symbols. The field symbolizes the wilderness of human living; the night symbolizes the darkness of human living; the shepherding symbolizes the need of the men in the dark field for shepherding. *These three points need to be described emphatically.* The announcement of the Savior's birth to the shepherds by an angel symbolizes the fact that a Savior was born for the people in the dark field.

C. The birth of the Savior was for all nations. The Savior was born in Bethlehem of Judea, but He was not only for the Jews, but for all the nations as well.

II. The meaning of the Savior's birth

A. The angel said that He was born to be the Savior of all nations. So His birth is for the salvation of all nations.

B. The angel said that His birth was to give peace on earth among men, that is to say that He came as the Savior of men, that men may have peace.

C. The angel also said, "Glory to God in the highest," that is to say that the Savior was born not only that men may have peace, but also that God may be glorified.

D. Peace and glory explain the meaning of the salvation of the Savior. Peace is toward men, and glory is toward God. Peace is to get rid of sins, sufferings, and death. Glory is to manifest God's life, nature, and work. The Savior comes to save men, so that on one hand men may be delivered from sins, and on the other hand men may have the life of God. To be delivered from sins is a matter of peace for men; to have God's life is a matter of glory to God.

III. The good tidings of great joy

A. Man is born in sin, without peace.

B. Man is waiting for death. Death belongs to Satan. Man waiting for death means that man is waiting for the destiny of Satan. In this there is no glory, because glory belongs to God.

C. The Savior comes to give peace to men, that men may be delivered from sins. Also, He comes that God may be glorified, by man having God's life and thus being delivered from the death of Satan. So His birth is good tidings of great joy to us, the sinners.

IV. How we should receive the Savior

A. Confess that we are in sin, waiting for death, without peace, and deserving eternal shame.

B. Receive this Savior as our Savior who came to save us from sins and to give us God's life. He delivers us from sins that we may have peace, and He gives us life that God may be glorified.

Subject Eighty-one

THE LORD'S GRACIOUS WORDS

Scripture: Luke 4:16-22

I. Good tidings to the poor

A. Men are born poor. This poverty does not refer to the lack of possessions, but to the lack of God's presence, the lack of God's blessing, the lack of life and peace, and the lack of eternal life. So in the Lord's eyes, men are absolutely poor, without anything.

B. The first item of the Lord's gracious words tells us that good tidings are to be preached to the poor. The Lord's gospel causes us to have God and all the blessings of God, to have life and peace, and to enjoy eternal life.

II. Release to the captives

A. Men are born captives. Men's forefathers were captured by Satan. Being born of the captured forefathers, men are captives by birth, having no freedom. Many things do not depend upon man himself, because upon man and within man there is another power controlling and reigning over him. For instance, a man may not like to have the habits of fornication and gambling, but he cannot control them.

B. The Lord's gracious words tell us that we, the captives, can be released. The Lord Jesus is the Son of God; He has been manifested to destroy the works of the Devil. On the cross He has already destroyed the Devil who has the power of death. So today He can dispel the power of the Devil from men, and release men from the power of the Devil. For example, if someone was captured by a bandit, you would need someone with a greater power to conquer the bandit in order to release the captured one.

III. Recovering of sight to the blind

A. Man is born blind, not knowing God, not knowing the origin of the universe, not knowing the meaning of human life, not knowing the destiny of man, and not knowing the snares of the Devil. All these items of "not knowing" prove that man is born blind.

B. The Lord's gracious words tell us that the blind recover their sight. This is because the Lord is light. He is the One who can shine upon the eyes of man's heart. This enables man to know God and know the origin of the universe, to have a full understanding of the meaning of human life and the destiny of man. Thus, man is also able to recognize the snares and deceit of Satan, the Devil.

IV. Liberty to the oppressed

A. Men are born oppressed. Men are not only captives
   in Satan's hands, but also are oppressed. Men's oppressions include the oppression that comes from physical
   burdens, such as the burdens of family, business, education, and sickness. Men's oppressions also include
   psychological oppressions which come from dissatisfaction of the heart, restlessness, unhappiness, uneasiness,
   and bondage. All of these are psychological burdens.
   Some people may have no physical burdens. They may
   have abundance in their living, good physical health,
   and their business, profession or education may all be
   very smooth. But they still have psychological burdens.
   Then there may be some who have no physical or psychological burdens, but instead feel guilty in their
   consciences and are afraid of death, hell, and God's judgment. They are afraid of God examining their living.
   These are burdens of the conscience. Thus, no one is free
   from oppression.

B. The Lord's gracious words tell us that the oppressed
   may be set free. The Lord can free us from our physical burdens. He can heal our sickness and bear the
   burden of all our weaknesses and sufferings. So He
   says, "Come unto me, all ye that are heavy laden, and
   I will give you rest." The Lord can satisfy our psychological need and rid us of all psychological oppression.
   Much more Christ can bear the burden of the punishment for sin and the burden of the conscience, so that
   men no longer need to be oppressed in the conscience.
   Many who were afraid of the punishment for sin and
   were afraid of hell had peace in their conscience as
   soon as they received the Lord.

V. The acceptable year of the Lord

A. Since the day man sinned, the whole life of the entire
   human race has been miserable and disastrous, having no peace, no joy, no freedom, and no light. Man's
   condition is described by the four points previously mentioned: poor, in captivity, blind, and oppressed.

B. The Lord's gracious words tell us that now is the acceptable year. Since the coming of the Lord, a new era has started in human history. When Adam fell, human history entered the age of misery. When Christ came, an age of joy began in human history.

C. This happy and blissful age is the acceptable year of the Lord. Adam's sin caused God to forsake man and to condemn man. But when Christ came, His redemption caused God not only to forgive man, but also on the positive side, to accept man. Acceptance includes: reconciliation between man and God, resolving the problem that formerly existed between man and God, and God being pleased with man.

D. Conclusion:

The Lord's gracious words give us six items: (1) the gospel's good tidings, (2) release, (3) sight, (4) liberty, (5) the acceptable year, and (6) God's acceptance.

VI. How to receive the Lord's gracious words

A. Confess our condition according to the Lord's word. This is to confess that we are poor, in captivity, blind, oppressed, and miserable.

B. Believe the words of the Lord. Believe the gospel, and what the gospel will bring to us: release, sight, liberty, the acceptable year, and God's acceptance. To believe is to receive according to the Lord's words. Repeat the words in Luke 4:18-19. Believe whatever the Lord says.

This message may be presented in six meetings. Each item is good enough for a single message.

Subject Eighty-two

THE SALVATION OF PETER

Scripture: Luke 5:1-11

I. Jesus came

A. Jesus came to the Lake of Gennesaret. A lake is a little sea. Gennesaret is called a sea in other verses. So Jesus came to the sea, which is a place of sin. Peter did not have a problem of sin on big issues, but on small issues. If he went to dances or to the movies, he was not that enthusiastic about dances or movies. Going to movies in a big city is like a sea; in a small town, a lake. A real enthusiast is a sea; a casual participant is a lake. Gambling on a large scale is a sea; gambling on a small scale is a lake.

B. People pressed on Jesus. When Jesus came to the lake, which is the place of sin, people pressed on Him to hear the word of God. Although they did not really want to hear the word of God, they came just out of curiosity, to watch.

II. Receiving Jesus

The fact that the people were pressing on Jesus out of curiosity means that they stopped fishing temporarily. That the fishermen quit fishing means that the sinners quit their sins temporarily. They didn't go to the movies, gamble, or dance. As they paused, the Lord Jesus got on their ship. Some people right when they are striving with ambition in their lives, suddenly hear the preaching of Jesus and they put off their strife—at the time a student is on vacation, or working people are off on sick leave, they hear the gospel of Jesus. Just by this one hearing, Jesus gets into them. They have Jesus in their lives. Oh, friends, when your ship comes to a stop, when you leave the college, when you leave the store, when you leave the ballroom, you hear the word of the Lord Jesus. When your heart quiets down, it makes sense to you to believe in the Lord. This is you receiving Jesus into your ship.

III. Seeing miracles

A. Although Peter received Jesus into his ship, he did not know who Jesus was. He was just letting Jesus use his ship. Only after Jesus performed a miracle on his ship, with the multitude of fish, did Peter realize that Jesus was not only a Nazarene but also the Lord of the universe.

B. Many people did not know who the Lord was at the time

they received Him. They thought that Jesus was One with high morality, an example for men to follow. They did not know that Jesus was the creator of the heavens and the earth. One day after they had received Jesus into their lives, they received a revelation from the Lord. Then they knew that Jesus was the Lord of the heavens and the earth. One may have failed in business. At the time he had no way out, the Lord performed a miracle. In this way that one really got to know the Lord. Another may have been sick, and may have learned who Jesus was through being healed.

Many people still think Jesus is only a great man, although they have received Jesus and have been baptized. Still they do not know who Jesus really is; they will only learn that He is the Lord after He performs a miracle in their home or in their career. Some Christians do not know the Lord for their whole life. When they were about to die, they saw a miracle, and then they were really saved.

IV. Knowing one's self

  A. Once a man knows the Lord, he gets to know himself. When Peter saw that the Lord was the creator, he said, "Lord! Depart from me; for I am a sinful man, O Lord."

  B. Once a man knows that Christ is the Lord and God, he realizes that he is a sinner. If I say that you have sinned, you would deny it. But when you meet Jesus Christ, there will be the feeling of sin in your conscience. Even if you confess you sin, you may not really see that you are a sinner. Only when you meet Jesus do you really see your sin.

V. The Lord's salvation

  A. As soon as Peter confessed that he was a sinner, the Lord said, "From henceforth thou shalt catch men." His living changed as well as his life. Peter changed his job from catching fish to catching men. His livelihood changed because his life had changed. His whole life had changed.

  B. Once we know the Lord and confess our sins, our sins

are forgiven, and we receive the Lord's life. Our whole life is changed. This change of life is salvation.

VI. The result of being saved

A. Forsaking the past. Once Peter was saved, he forsook the lake, the ship, and the net. He forsook the life of self and sin.

B. Following Jesus. Just as Peter forsook all to follow Jesus, we should also forsake all to follow Jesus.

Subject Eighty-three

THE ONE MOST FORGIVEN

Scripture: Luke 7:36-50

I. Receiving Jesus

A. This is a story about a Pharisee named Simon, who invited Jesus to have dinner at his house.

B. Today there are also many who, like Simon, have heard of the fame of Jesus and want to study about Jesus. They even want to have some contact with Christianity. Do not treat Simon's invitation as a sincere one or one coming out of believing; he only cared to investigate a little.

II. Knowing Jesus

A. Although the Pharisee invited Jesus, he really did not know who Jesus was. He had no idea that Jesus was the Lord. He even questioned whether Jesus was a prophet, saying, "This man, if he were a prophet would have perceived..." (Luke 7:39).

B. Today there are many who study Christianity, but they still do not know who Jesus is. Some even consider Jesus inferior to Confucius or some other great philosophers.

C. While the Pharisee was trying to figure out in his heart who Jesus was, Jesus perceived the intent of that Pharisee. The Pharisee was talking to himself in his heart, but Jesus knew. This proves that Jesus is an extraordinary One. The Lord is not only a prophet, but One who knows the intent of man. The fact that Jesus knew the intent of the Pharisee proves that Jesus is God who knows the heart of man.

D. The answer of the Lord was intended to show the Pharisee that the Lord Jesus was not only a prophet but also his Lord, and even the One to whom he was indebted, the One whom he had offended. There is a twofold meaning in the way that the Lord Jesus showed him that He was the Lord: (1) the Lord Jesus is God, and (2) the Lord Jesus is the One to whom he is indebted. The Pharisee considered Jesus only a good rabbi, but what the Lord Jesus did showed him that the One speaking to him was the very Lord who knew the hearts of men, and who was the One to whom all men are indebted.

III. Knowing himself

A. The Pharisee knew only the sinful woman. He did not know the Lord Jesus, and he did not know himself. Many have studied about the Lord Jesus, but never knew who Jesus is. In due time the Lord Jesus let them know that He is God, and that He is the One to whom they are indebted. Today many know only the sins others have committed, but they do not know themselves, much less the Lord Jesus whom they have offended. Many false Christians fit into this category.

B. The words of the Lord Jesus helped the Pharisee to know himself. While the Pharisee was doubting in his heart about the Lord Jesus, the Lord Jesus said right away: "Simon...a certain lender had two debtors: the one owed five hundred shillings, and the other fifty" (Luke 7:40,41). The Lord showed him that although he may not have sinned and owed as much as that woman did, nevertheless at least he owed fifty. The woman was like a robber on a large scale, and he was like a thief on a small scale, the difference being the difference between fifty and five hundred. Not one can say that he does not owe anything. There may be some difference in the size of the debt, large or small, much or little, but all are debtors. The Lord showed him that he owed at least fifty. Furthermore, the Lord showed him that he was unable to pay back even that fifty. However large or small a sin he had committed, he still remained a debtor.

IV. Knowing grace

A. The Lord said that both their debts, the five hundred shillings or the fifty, were equally forgiven.

B. The forgiveness of the Lord is neither casual nor careless, because the Lord is not only gracious but also righteous. The Lord's grace caused Him to forgive, and the Lord's righteousness caused Him to die in our stead. The Lord's forgiveness must be based upon His righteousness. True, the Lord's forgiveness is due to His grace, but it is also based upon His righteousness.

V. The result of forgiveness

A. The Lord forgave men so that men would love Him. The Lord said the reason the sinful woman washed His feet with her tears, wiped them with her hair, and anointed them, was that she received more of the Lord's grace. The reason the Pharisee who invited the Lord Jesus for dinner did not wash His feet—showing that he neglected the Lord—was that he received less grace of the Lord. One to whom much is forgiven loves much, and one to whom little is forgiven loves little.

B. It is not that love produces grace and forgiveness, but that forgiveness produces love. Love is the result of forgiveness. The reason that woman loved the Lord more was that she had received more grace and forgiveness.

VI. The assurance of forgiveness

A. There is a difference between the fact of forgiveness and the assurance of forgiveness. Some received the fact of forgiveness but not the assurance. That woman had received the fact of forgiveness long before the Lord spoke, but she did not have the assurance. Therefore, she did not know whether her sins had been forgiven or not.

B. The assurance of forgiveness is found in the words of the Lord. The Lord said to her, "Thy sins are forgiven" (v. 48). Many have believed in the Lord Jesus and were really saved, but they did not have the assurance because they did not lay hold of the words of the Lord as their assurance of salvation.

VII. After receiving forgiveness

Go in peace. After being saved, you should walk the way of peace and live the life of peace. You should refrain from doing anything that makes you feel uneasy toward God or toward men. Do only what you feel at peace in doing.

Subject Eighty-four

WHO IS MY NEIGHBOR?

Scripture: Luke 10:25-37

I. How the law evaluated eternal life

A. One day a lawyer came to ask Jesus, "Teacher, what shall I do to inherit eternal life?" This means that someone who stood on the position of the law and represented the law was considering the price of eternal life.

B. The Lord Jesus asked him, "What does the law say?"

C. Based on the law, he said that in order to receive eternal life he must pay the price of twofold love. Love toward God includes four *all's,* and love toward men contains only one *as. The four "all's" and one "as" should be emphasized when preaching the gospel.* We know that men can neither love with *all,* nor love *as.* These four *all's* and one *as* defeat everyone. If you are in a store shopping and see that the prices are too high, you will be scared away because you cannot pay the price. All you can do is window shop. The law evaluates eternal life with these four *all's* and the one *as.*

You must pay the price with all of your spirit, soul and body. To love with all your heart (the spirit), your soul, your self (the soul), and your strength (the body) means to love to the uttermost. In addition to these, you must love others as yourself. If you can pay such a high price, then you can inherit eternal life.

D. The Lord replied, "If you do these, you shall receive eternal life." It was as if the Lord were saying, "Do not think the Christians do not care for their behavior; rather, they are the ones who care for their behavior the most. But the question is: Can you do it?"

E. Did the Lord mean for man to do it himself? If He did, He would be asking man to build a heavenly ladder to go to the heavens by himself, which is definitely an impossible task. Although the Lord said, "You do this," it was not that He intended man to do it, for He knew that man could never do it. Therefore this is not a matter of paying the price, but a matter of evaluation. The logic here is very deep. After reading this portion of the Bible, some would kneel down before the Lord and ask the Lord to give them the strength so that they could measure up to the four *all's* and one *as*. They have misunderstood the words of the Lord, because the Lord meant for them to understand that the higher the price, the less man is able to pay. For example, in the figure $1,000,000 there are six zeros. If you have six or even sixteen zeros with the number one in front, how can you pay the price? So this is not a matter of paying the price, but a matter of evaluation.

II. The condition of man

A. The lawyer found out the evaluation of eternal life, and the Lord also confirmed his evaluation was correct. But he wanted to justify himself. All those who try to justify themselves from the standpoint of the law are self-righteous. Therefore he asked, "Who is my neighbor?" The law says that I should love God; on that point I am clear. But in order to love my neighbor as myself, I need to know who then is this neighbor. So the Lord gave an answer.

B. The Lord's answer shows him that what he needs is not a neighbor for him to love, but a neighbor to love him. He did not know himself, thinking that he had the strength to love his neighbor, but the Lord showed him that he was only a desolate sinner, needing a neighbor to love him.

C. Therefore the Lord told him a story: "A certain man went down from Jerusalem to Jericho..." This man was one who left the ground of peace, the dwelling place of God, Jerusalem, and was going down. Anyone who tries to keep the law by his own good behavior is going down. Jericho is a cursed place, so he fell among robbers. The robbers here speak of the law and those who stressed the law. Strictly speaking, the law itself is not the robber. This one who was going from Jerusalem down to Jericho depicts the lawyer. The lawyer beat others with the law, and he stripped them of their clothing, which is to strip them of their good behavior. Before the law, man's good behavior is but filthy clothing and is unable to cover the body. To beat a man until he is half dead is to sentence him to death. Although he (the law and the lawyer) does not send you to Jericho (hell) now, he has already sentenced you and is waiting for you to perish eternally.

D. Can such a one, already beaten until he is half dead, love others and pay the price for eternal life? The Lord Jesus meant to let him see that the evaluation of eternal life is so high and the condition of man so low that it is impossible to obtain eternal life by the law.

III. The uselessness of religion

A. Now there came a priest, a religionist. The priest was also on his way from Jerusalem to Jericho. Even the religionists, pastors, and so-called priests are departing from God and going downhill.

B. The priest was walking on the same road and having the same problem as that man, so he passed by and

went on his way. If the priest is helpless in his own situation, how can he help others? So religion and the
religionists cannot give man eternal life.

C. There are two classes of people in religion:

   1. The priests were those ministering to God.

   2. The Levites were serving people, such as those
      involved in humanitarian efforts. The Levites were
      walking on the same road with the others. Do not
      think that serving humanity is going upward; actu-
      ally it is also going downhill. The Levites are also
      useless to that man who had been beaten.

IV. The deliverance of Christ

A. The Samaritan is the Lord Jesus. He came to the
place where the wounded man was. In Greek, the
word *journey* indicates that the direction He walked
was different from that of the previous three. The
direction of this Samaritan was different from that of
the previous three; He was coming from the opposite
side. Toward the end of John 8, the Jews considered
Jesus as a Samaritan. The Lord Jesus was the
despised Nazarene. Today He is coming to the place
where you are.

B. The Lord Jesus was moved with compassion.

C. The Lord Jesus poured oil and wine upon his wounds.
The oil speaks of the Holy Spirit, and the wine speaks
of life and blood. The Lord Jesus was moved with compassion, and as the Holy Spirit He came to touch,
enlighten, and comfort him. Then He poured wine
upon the wounds. Wine is made of grape juice, which
is the blood of the grape and its life. So here the wine
signifies the Lord's blood and His life. The oil is to
moisten or to anoint, and the wine is to give healing
and strength.

D. He set the wounded man on His own beast. Here the
beast symbolizes the way the Lord Jesus worked on
this earth. To mount His beast is to behave in the way
the Lord Jesus worked, that is, to serve God like the
humble Nazarene.

E. Then the Lord brought him to an inn. Here the inn speaks of the church. The church is an inn on the earth for men to receive the supply.

F. The Lord took out two pieces of silver and gave them to the host for taking care of the wounded man. Here the silver signifies the gift of the Holy Spirit to the responsible ones in the church, so that they may use the gift to take care of the saved ones.

G. Besides the silver, there were the extra expenses. Such extra expenses speak of the care out of love, for which there will be compensation when the Lord comes back. Silver is the gift, and for the care out of this gift there will be no reward when the Lord returns. Only the care out of love will be rewarded at the coming of the Lord. These seven items are the elements of the Lord's salvation.

V. Conclusion

A. The lawyer asked the Lord, "Who is my neighbor?" The Lord replied that he needed a neighbor to love him instead. The lawyer thought that he had the strength to love others, but the Lord said: "You are just a pitiful person. You need someone to love you."

B. "Go and do likewise." The Lord's real intention was not that he would go and do it likewise. Instead the Lord wanted him to realize that by doing it, he was not the Samaritan, but the wounded man. It is impossible to obtain eternal life by our own behavior. Do it, and you will realize that you cannot make it; you need someone else to have mercy on you. Only the everlasting Lord is our neighbor. We need Him to love us.

Subject Eighty-five

CHRIST AND THE JUDGMENT

Scripture: Luke 11:29-32

I. The evilness of this age

A. The Lord Jesus said that this is an evil age.

B. Illustrate how evil this age is. Give concrete examples of the evil in the homes, in the schools, in the offices and in the midst of the crowds of people.

II. Christ as the salvation to the present age

A. The Lord said that there is a sign with Jonah, that is, that Jonah was in the belly of a great fish three days and three nights.

When Jonah came out of the belly of the fish, he became the salvation to the Ninevites. This Jonah typifies the resurrected Christ. Christ, like Jonah, entered into death and stayed in the depth of the earth three days and three nights; therefore, like Jonah, Christ is the salvation to the present evil age. Christ was resurrected because He had died. His death is to bear the sins of the world; His resurrection is to impart life to man. Just as Jonah was a sign to the Ninevites, so is Christ a sign to this present age. This sign is a sign of the taking away of the sins of men and the imparting of life to them. It is a sign of God's salvation.

B. Here Christ also mentioned the queen of the south coming to Solomon to learn from him. Solomon typifies Christ. Solomon spoke to the queen of the south concerning the ultimate issue of life. Today Christ can tell us much more of the ultimate issue of life. To receive wisdom you need to come to Christ. To this age, Christ is not only the One who has died and been resurrected, but He is also the Christ who is the sum of all wisdom. On one hand, like Jonah to the Ninevites, Christ is salvation. On the other hand like Solomon to the queen of the south, He is wisdom. Christ is not only salvation to men, but also wisdom for men.

III. Judgment in the future

A. If today men will not receive Christ as their Lord of resurrection out of the dead, nor receive Him as their Lord of wisdom, one day in the future they shall meet the judgment.

B. Before the throne of judgment, the Ninevites will testify against them, and so will the queen of the south. The Ninevites will condemn you because you would not receive the salvation of the Christ who was resurrected out of the dead, the sin-forgiving and life-imparting salvation. The queen of the south will condemn you because you would not receive the Lord of wisdom, that you might know the ultimate issues of life.

C. There is no escape from the future judgment. If you refuse to receive Christ today, it will be too late for you to repent in that day. If in this age you heard about Christ, and knew that this Christ is the Lord of resurrection out of the dead, and that He is the Lord of wisdom, but you would not receive Him—like the Ninevites who received Jonah or like the queen of the south taught by Solomon—you will be judged in the future, and you will receive eternal punishment.

IV. How to deal with Christ

A. Receive Him like the Ninevites received Jonah, and receive His words like they received the words of Jonah. When a man receives Christ, his sins are forgiven, and he obtains life, for Christ is the Lord of resurrection.

B. Learn from Christ, for He is the Lord of wisdom, who is able to teach you the proper way to live as a man.

Subject Eighty-six

A FOOLISH MAN

Scripture: Luke 12:13-21

I. Man has two possessions

A. Man has the physical, material things (the body and all the things this physical body needs).

B. Man also has a soul and a spirit, which are real although they are intangible.

C. Prove the existence of the soul and the spirit, and explain the nature of each.

(Refer to Subject 65, "The Value of the Soul.")

II. Two directions for man's attention

A. Man can pay his attention to the physical, material things, or may pay his attention to the soul and the spirit.

B. Most people pay attention to the material things, the things of the physical life, and very few pay attention to the soul and the spirit. The lower class of people pay attention to the material things; the higher class of people pay attention to the soul and spirit.

III. A foolish man

A. This passage of the Bible tells about a man who asked the Lord Jesus to divide his inheritance for him. To divide the inheritance is to pay attention to the material things, the possessions of the family.

B. The Lord Jesus let him know right away that He came not that men would pay attention to material things, but that men should pay attention to the soul and the spirit, that is, to pay attention to life. The Lord said that a man's life does not consist in the abundance of the things which he possesses, in other words, not in material things.

C. The Lord spoke a parable, and in that parable the one who came to Him was a foolish rich man.

D. The Lord said that the rich man was foolish, because he cared only for his physical and material needs. That man had such a plentiful harvest that he did not have enough storage space, so he wanted to tear down his barns to build some bigger ones. He intended to rely on these material provisions, so that he might take his ease, eat, drink, and be merry. No one knew that on that very night God would require his soul. This was his foolishness.

IV. The choice of the wise

A. Consider how much more important the soul and spirit are than the body.

B. Treasure the spirit and the soul, and despise the body.

C. Receive Christ as your Savior.

Subject Eighty-seven

THE WARNING TO REPENT

Scripture: Luke 13:1-5

I. The sins of human living

A. Man is born in sins.

B. Man grows up in sins.

C. Man lives in sins (referring to all the normal living).

D. Man wallows in sins (referring to all the abnormal living).

II. The calamity of human living

A. Sin is the source of disaster. Disaster is the result of sin.

B. Because man is born in sins, grows up and lives in sins, and even wallows in sins, man is apt to fall into calamity.

III. God's tolerance

A. According to the condition of man's sins, calamity should strike man down immediately as punishment from God. But God is so tolerant that such calamity is temporarily suspended.

B. The reason God could suspend calamity and tolerate man is that there is a Savior in this universe, and there is redemption. According to man's sins the earth should be turned upside down, and man should perish forever in calamity. But because Christ as man's Savior has accomplished redemption, God can tolerate man and suspend calamity.

C. God tolerates man so that man could repent.

IV. The warning to repent

A. Since calamity is a result of sin, each calamity therefore is a warning, with the intent that men may be delivered from sins.

B. Whenever you see calamity strike, whether it hits you or someone else, either a natural disaster or one caused by man, you should understand that it is God's warning that men should repent.

V. How to repent

A. Believe that sin has its consequence.

B. Confess your own sins.

C. Receive Christ and His redemption.

Subject Eighty-eight

MEN'S EXCUSES FOR REFUSING SALVATION

Scripture: Luke 14:15-24

I. God's preparation of salvation

A. God prepares salvation like a man preparing a feast.

B. God's salvation feast is prepared by the Lord Jesus, and all things are ready.

C. Provided in God's salvation are: firstly, the redemption of the Lord Jesus; secondly, Christ's resurrection life. The redeeming blood and the resurrection life are the food at the salvation feast. Every time we come to the Lord's table, we are coming to God's salvation feast, and what we eat and drink is the Lord's blood and the Lord's life.

II. God's invitation to salvation

A. God not only has prepared the feast of salvation through Christ, but also has extended the invitation for salvation through the Holy Spirit.

B. The invitation of the Holy Spirit is through those who preach the gospel and the gospel messages. Today you are here listening to the gospel. You have been invited to the gospel feast.

III. Men's excuses

A. Men made excuses because of their own riches and their own capability. Give the examples the Lord used: some bought a piece of land, some bought some oxen, and some are getting married. All these excuses illustrate men's riches and capability. *Speak seriously according to these principles.* As long as men are rich and capable, they will excuse themselves from the invitation of the gospel.

B. Riches and capability can be related either to material things or to morality. Land, houses, and buying and selling are the material riches; doing good is the moral riches.

IV. The ones who accepted the invitation

A. All the ones who accepted the invitation were the maimed, the blind, the lame, the poor and the weak ones.

B. To respond to God's invitation to salvation, you must become a poor and weak one. Friends, if you think that you are rich and capable, you cannot respond to God's invitation.

V. God's constraining

A. The ones who are naturally poor and the ones who are willing to be poor are few in number. They cannot fill up the seats of salvation. The naturally poor ones are the ones who were poor originally; the ones willing to be poor are the ones who were rich but are willing to become poor.

B. Therefore God has to constrain people to accept His invitation.

C. God's constraining is to strip men and to wound them. To strip men is to turn their riches to poverty; to wound men is to turn their capability to incapability. Give some examples, such as many who were unwilling to receive God's salvation until the family was broken, or there was a death of someone close to them, or they were critically ill with pneumonia. Such constraining is the great care and mercy of God for you.

VI. How to respond to the invitation

A. Be humble and confess that you are poor and incapable.

B. Repent and turn to God.

C. Receive Christ and His redemption.

Subject Eighty-nine

THE SHEPHERD FINDING THE LOST SHEEP

Scripture: Luke 15:3-7

I. Man is God's sheep

A. Man was made by God, so man belongs to God.

B. Man is not only made by God, but also fed by God and cared for by Him, like a sheep under the care of a shepherd.

C. God is man's shepherd; therefore, God is man's master.

II. Man is lost

A. Man is born lost. On this point you need to prove that it seems that man knows everything; yet he does not know where he came from, where he is going, or to whom he belongs. Who is your master? Everything has an owner. You may be a big man, yet you do not know to whom you belong. If a wife says that her husband is her master, she still would not be able to say to whom she would belong if her husband should die. If you say that your parents are your masters, to whom would you belong if your parents were dead?

B. Man is lost because of sin. Man is born in sins, grows up in sins, and lives in sins; therefore, man is lost.

C. Man is lost because man has lost God. Man is created by God, and he is fed by God. Now because man has lost God, man himself is lost.

III. God comes to seek man

A. Man does not know that he is lost; neither does he have any desire to seek God. But God comes to seek man.

B. The way God seeks man is by coming Himself as man's savior. This is the One incarnated in the flesh, Jesus of Nazareth. So Jesus is not only man's Savior, but also man's shepherd.

C. God seeks man through the Lord Jesus. On the cross the Lord Jesus found man and recovered man. Through

death and resurrection the Lord Jesus imparts life to
man. This is to recover man, because through the resurrection life man is brought back to God.

IV. How to receive God's seeking

A. Confess that you are lost, and that you have lost God.

B. Repent and turn to God.

C. Receive Christ and His redemption.

D. Leave the place where you are lost.

E. Receive life and come back to God.

Subject Ninety

THE WOMAN SEEKING THE LOST COIN

Scripture: Luke 15:8-10

I. Men are God's property

A. Men are created by God; therefore, naturally, men
belong to God.

B. God considers men as His property, as His treasure,
just like the woman who considers the ten pieces of
silver as treasure.

II. Men are lost

A. Men are born lost. To be lost is to be separated from
the original owner. If you do not know to whom you
belong, that is a proof in itself that you are lost.

B. When you are lost, you fall into the dust. Here the
dust represents sins. To fall into the dust is to fall into
sins.

C. So the result of being lost is to fall into the filth of
sins, and to live in a heap of sins.

III. God comes to seek men

A. The first parable in Luke 15 speaks about God as the
shepherd coming to seek the lost sheep. This second
parable speaks about God as the woman seeking the
lost money. The shepherd seeks the lost sheep out in
the field, whereas the woman seeks the money inside

the house. The first parable is objective; the second is subjective.

B. The woman seeking the lost money typifies the Holy Spirit coming into our heart to seek us. Just as the shepherd typifies Christ, so the woman typifies the Holy Spirit. In the first parable the objective seeking is the coming of Christ to this earth nearly 2,000 years ago. In the second parable the Holy Spirit comes into our heart, which is the subjective seeking.

C. The steps the Holy Spirit takes to seek men:

1. The first step is to light the lamp. Because there is darkness, there is the need to light the lamp. The lamp typifies the enlightening of the Holy Spirit. This is related to the fact that within man is darkness. The Holy Spirit comes to enlighten us through the words of the Bible. Friends, the gospel which you are listening to today is the enlightening of the Holy Spirit.

2. The second step is to sweep the house. The house represents man's heart. The sweeping represents the moving of the Holy Spirit. The heart which has not been swept is not only dark and dirty, but also quiet. After the Holy Spirit lights the lamp and sweeps the heart, the heart is tossed about and becomes restless.

3. The third step is to seek diligently. The diligent seeking of the Spirit causes you to have a thorough consideration and a keen feeling. As the Holy Spirit enlightens and moves within you, you will begin to consider the past and the future.

4. The fourth step is the finding. The Holy Spirit will seek until you are brought back to God.

IV. How to receive God's seeking

A. Confess that you are a lost one.

B. Repent and turn to God.

C. Receive the enlightening and the leading of the Holy Spirit.

Subject Ninety-one

THE LOVING FATHER
RECEIVES THE PRODIGAL SON—
The First Contrast in Luke

Scripture: Luke 15:11-24

I. Man being from God

A. This parable likens the relationship between man and God to that of a son and his father. This indicates that as a son is from his father, so man is from God.

B. Man is made by God. Although man did not receive God's life, man's life today comes from God. Thus, from the aspect of creation, man is God's son.

II. Man departing and going far away from God

A. One day the younger of two sons took his portion of his father's substance, left his father, and went to a far country.

B. This is a picture showing that man goes far away from God even after he has received all his natural ability from God.

III. Man living in sin

A. In a country far away from his father, this younger son wasted all his substance with riotous living. As a result he became poor and had to make a living by feeding swine.

B. This shows that when man leaves God, he begins to live a sinful life. Wasting all that he has, he falls into sin. Feeding the swine symbolizes living the sinful life because swine are dirty. Describe how man lives a life of feeding the swine. When you go to the movie theaters or when you go dancing, you are going to the swine pens.

IV. Man waking up

A. While he was in his poverty the son woke up. He came to himself and began to remember the goodness of his father's house.

B. This shows that a man in sin, who is living in sins, remembers God and His blessing when he comes to

his end. Describe how poverty helps man to wake up.
It is hard for some to wake up until they have sinned
to the uttermost. When they have reached the end of
dancing or gambling, then they wake up.

V. Man turning to God

A. When the younger son came to himself and remembered his father, he decided to return to him.

B. This shows that when a man wakes up from sin, it is
natural for him to remember God and turn to Him.

VI. Man wanting to work for God

A. When the son was about to return, he remembered his
sins and felt that he was no more worthy to be his
father's son. He was willing to be a servant instead,
and was going to ask his father to hire him. So he prepared four sentences for meeting his father: first, "I
have sinned against heaven"; second, "I have sinned...
in thy sight"; third, "I am no more worthy to be called
thy son"; and fourth, "Make me as one of thy hired
servants."

B. This shows that when a sinner wakes up and turns to
God, it is natural for him to feel that he has sinned
against God and is unworthy of God's blessing. In
other words, he feels unworthy of receiving anything
from God freely. Because of this, he depends upon
trading his work and good behavior for God's goodness. He thus hopes to improve himself before God.
This is the wrong concept of every repenting sinner, to
think he should be a servant instead of a son. Because
of this concept, man always tries to establish his own
merit in order to exchange it for God's goodness.

VII. Man not realizing the heart of God

A. Although the younger son had a humble heart in feeling unworthy to be a son and in wanting to be a
servant, he did not realize the heart of his father. In
his father's heart was the longing for his son.

B. Many sinners may have such a humble heart, but they
do not realize the heart of God. God's heart is not that

repenting sinners would work for Him, but that they would be His sons. While a hired servant must earn what he gets and must work for what he receives, a son receives everything from his father freely.

VIII. God receiving man

A. As the younger son was returning to his father, it was far from his realization that his father would be waiting to receive him. He was expecting that he would have to knock many times, and that his father would eventually send someone else to open the door. Yet even while the son was returning and was still afar off, his father saw him coming and ran out to meet him. While the son thought it was a matter of his returning to his father, even the more it was a matter of his father's waiting to receive him.

B. This tells us that many think that they must pray to God for a long period before He will answer them. They have no realization that God has been there waiting to receive repenting sinners. But actually, even while such a one is repenting and turning to God, God is waiting to receive him.

C. When he saw the son, the father was moved with compassion. Because his heart was moved, it caused him to run and fall on his son's neck, and to kiss him. This running shortened the time and the distance between them. Running involves the feet; falling on the son's neck involves the hands; kissing involves the mouth, which is able to express emotion. So we can see that the father's whole being was moved for his son.

D. This signifies that when God in heaven sees a sinner repenting, He is moved with compassion, and runs to meet him. With His whole heart He embraces the repenting sinner. Before repenting, many think that God is terrible and fearful, but after repenting they discover that God is so dear and so near.

IX. God justifying man

A. After the father kissed him, the son immediately began his prepared speech. But when he had just finished his first three sentences, the father interrupted him. The son had just said, "I am no more worthy to be called thy son," but the father said to the servants, "Bring forth quickly the best robe, and put it on him." The heart of the father could not stand the son saying that he was unworthy to be called his son. So he commanded his servants to bring forth the best robe. The word *the* is an important word. *The* best robe was the robe that had been prepared a long time ago. When the father spoke, the servants knew which one it was. The father only had to say "the best robe," and the servants understood right away. The father also put a ring on the son's hand and shoes on his feet and killed the fatted calf. All of these were beyond the son's expectation.

B. Just as the son did, we prepare a speech, *but* God brings forth the best robe. *The word BUT should be stressed. It is a big word in the New Testament.* This *but* makes us saved. A brother once had a big sign, "BUT," hanging on his living room wall. It is quite meaningful. We should be condemned, *but* God justified us; we should be going to hell, *but* we go to the heavens instead. God prepared the best robe and put it on us, so that we could match Him. Putting on the robe signifies Christ as our righteousness. When a sinner puts on Christ, he matches God and is justified.

The father also put shoes on the son. Shoes separate man from the earth. When a man returns to God and is justified and sealed by the Holy Spirit, he is able to be separated from the earth. After putting the shoes on his feet, the father killed the fatted calf. Killing the fatted calf signifies Christ prepared for us as our life and enjoyment. Only when Christ comes into us can we be filled and happy.

X. God and man making merry together

A. It was at this time that the father and the son ate and drank and were happy together. Before the son came back, the father had no joy. While the son was away from home, wandering and suffering, the father was also suffering at home.

B. This shows that when sinners are away from God, wandering and suffering, God is unhappy. Only when sinners are at home with God, eating and making merry, is God joyful.

XI. Result

A. The younger son who had been lost was found; he had been dead, and was alive again.

B. This means that a sinner away from God is both lost and dead; but when he returns to God, he is received and justified by Him. In other words, he is found and he is alive.

Subject Ninety-two

THE RICH MAN AND LAZARUS—
The Second Contrast in Luke

Scripture: Luke 16:19-31

The stories in Luke 15 through Luke 23 are all in contrast.

I. Two different persons

One is rich; the other is poor.

II. The difference while alive

A. The rich man was clothed in purple and fine linen and was living in mirth and splendor every day. To be clothed in purple indicates that he was honorable and wealthy. To be clothed in fine linen indicates that he was living in abundance. Describe how the rich man enjoyed his life.

B. The poor man was full of sores, and was laid at the gate of the rich man.

III. The difference after death

A. Describe the condition of the beggar after he died. In this portion of the Bible, it mentions the rich man first and then the beggar, because it was the rich man's world while they were alive. On the street, you see that the rich man walks in front and the beggar follows after. But after their death, the order was reversed. It mentions the poor man first and then the rich man, because it was the poor man's world after death. Dogs came and licked the poor man's sores while he was alive. When he died, he was carried away by the angels. How lonesome he was when he was laid at the gate of the rich man. Yet after he died, he was in Abraham's bosom. How comfortable and how sweet it was then!

B. The rich man also died. Not only the poor ones will die, but the rich ones too! Money cannot buy life. As the poor people will die, so also will the millionaires die. *Emphasize the word "also."* No one can escape death. Poor or rich, lowly or honorable, man or woman, young or old makes no difference. They all will die someday. And one day you *also* will die. Use the word *also* to cover all classes of people, such as the laborers, college students, taxi drivers, university professors, guards, school superintendents, etc. The sick ones shall die, so also shall the doctors die.

C. The rich man was buried. The rich man had quite a funeral, but there were no angels coming to carry him, nor was he put into the bosom of Abraham; rather, he was in torment in Hades. And he lifted up his eyes, and saw Abraham afar off and Lazarus in his bosom. He used to drink soda, coke, beer, and wine, but now he could not even get a drop of water. Formerly his tongue enjoyed blessings—his speech was so powerful and influential, and with his tongue he scorned so many people. But now it is in torment in the flame. This is only the flame of Hades, not the flame of the lake of fire yet. Abraham said, "Son, remember that thou in thy lifetime receivedst thy good things, and Lazarus in like manner evil things: but now here he is comforted, and thou art in anguish. And besides all this, between us and you there is a great gulf fixed, that they that would pass from hence to you may not be able, and that none may cross over from thence to us." If you do not ask God in your lifetime, it will be too late to ask God after you die.

IV. The reasons for the difference

A. Their difference was not a matter of being rich or poor, nor was it a matter of enjoying or suffering in their lifetime.

B. Their difference was a matter of whether they believed in God's words. For the Lord said clearly that they should believe in Moses' words. To believe in God's words is to believe in Christ, because God's words are centered on Christ. Here "the one from the dead" refers to Christ. The rich man would not believe in the Bible or Christ in his lifetime so he was in torment in the flame after he died.

C. Because the rich man did not believe in God's words, so in his lifetime he indulged himself in all kinds of luxurious pleasure and never cared about his future problem. The poor Lazarus believed in God's words, so he could be careless about his suffering in his lifetime.

D. Friends, if you do not believe in God's gospel, if you only care for the present life and never take thought about after your death, how pitiful it is! Please quickly believe in God's words and believe in Jesus.

Subject Ninety-three

THE CONDEMNATION OF THE SELF-RIGHTEOUS AND THE JUSTIFICATION OF THE SELF-ABASED— The Third Contrast in Luke

Scripture: Luke 18:9-14

I. Two men praying

A. In terms of action, this passage of the Scripture is not talking about two different people doing two things, such as a good person committing a sin or a bad person not committing a sin. No, the two were praying and were drawing close to God.

B. Their actions were the same, but the persons were different, and their positions were also different. One was a Pharisee, and the other a publican, a tax collector. The Pharisee represented a high-ranking person, and the tax collector, a despised person.

II. A self-righteous man

A. The self-righteous man was the Pharisee. He was self-righteous not before his audience, but before God. He prayed, "God, I thank thee, that I am not as the rest of men, extortioners, unjust, adulterers, or even as this publican. I fast twice in the week; I give tithes of all that I get." In essence, in his prayer he was asking God to thank him. Because of self-righteousness, he was saying, "I am not like other people. I am not like my colleague who is sitting in front of me. I am not like my classmate who is sitting beside me. I am not like the professor living next door."

B. Nearly all the religious people are self-righteous; so are moral people. The Pharisee represents both of these two groups of people, the religious people and the moral people. He fasted twice a week, and gave tithes. These are religious matters. He was neither an adulterer nor an extortioner. These are moral matters.

C. The Pharisees are false religionists and false moralists.

III. A humble man

A. Describe the way the tax collector prayed. He stood afar off and dared not lift up his eyes toward heaven but smote his chest saying, "God, be Thou merciful to me a sinner."

B. Nearly all the immoral, sinful people have a humble feeling.

IV. The results of self-righteousness and self-abasing

A. The one who humbled himself was justified. Humbling oneself is not a virtue but a confession which affords God a chance to grant His mercy.

B. The self-righteous one was condemned, because self-righteousness shuts off God's mercy.

C. Christ has accomplished redemption. A man who humbles himself and believes in Christ shall be justified. A man who is self-righteous and unbelieving shall be condemned.

Subject Ninety-four

IMPOSSIBLE WITH MEN
BUT POSSIBLE WITH GOD—
The Fourth Contrast in Luke

Scripture: Luke 18:18-27; 19:1-10

I. Two rich men

A. In Luke 18 a ruler is mentioned who was a rich man. In Luke 19 a chief publican is mentioned. He was also a rich man.

B. The rich man mentioned in Luke 18 was a young, moral official, respected by men. The rich man in Luke 19 was an old, despised official, rejected by the Jews of that time.

C. Both of them loved their wealth dearly.

II. The honorable rich man

A. The young ruler in Luke 18 was one who was wealthy, moral, and seemingly benevolent. So the question he asked the Lord Jesus was concerning what to do in order to inherit eternal life. Because he was wealthy and charitable, he paid attention to the matter of good work.

B. The Lord Jesus showed him that to call the Lord "good" is to acknowledge that the Lord is God, because only God is good. This means that the Lord was also showing this rich man that he was not such a good man, but a sinner.

C. Then the Lord brought him to the realization of his lack. He felt that he had kept all the commandments, but the Lord said that he lacked one thing; that is, to sell all that he had and distribute it to the poor and

then come and follow the Lord. What he lacked was to
dissolve his wealth and care for the poor on the one
hand, and to follow the Lord on the other. Many
thought that they were good. The Lord often brought
them to realize what they lacked. You might have
done ten good things, but the Lord would say that you
still lack one. Maybe you love your parents, but you
lack loving your brothers. Or maybe you are humble,
but you lack patience.

D. When that rich man heard what he lacked, he went
away sorrowful. He went away because: (1) toward men,
he was wealthy but really not charitable, because he
could not distribute his wealth to the poor; and (2)
toward God, he had an idol in his heart. The first of the
ten commandments is not to have any idol before God,
and next is to love thy neighbor. Outwardly he had
obeyed the ten commandments, but in reality he did not
obey them at all. The Lord was showing him that he had
transgressed against the law.

E. According to the written letters you may have obeyed
the ten commandments, but according to the reality, no
one can obey the ten commandments. Between you and
God, are there absolutely no idols in your heart? Toward
men, is your heart full of love? Since no man can attain
to that level, it is impossible with men. It is impossible
with men because men are rich. When a man is rich, he
has an idol toward God, and he has no love toward men.
Your knowledge, wealth, and good family life are your
riches. When you did not know so much, you had love
toward men. But now that you know so much, you have
no love toward men. So the ones who feel rich can never
be saved. This is impossible with men.

III. The despised rich man

A. The rich man mentioned in Luke 19 lived in Jericho.
Jericho was a sinful and cursed place. But Jesus passed
through there. Jesus would not pass through the place
where the honorable rich man lived, but today He is
coming to the fallen, sinful place.

B. Here the rich man was rich but not good. He specialized in scandal and deceit.

C. He was there not to ask Jesus questions but to see Jesus. To ask Jesus questions is like the study of Jesus as religion. This cannot save you. Look at Jesus, and you will be saved.

D. Because all were crowding Jesus, Jesus was concealed. Today Jesus is also concealed by so many false Christians and Catholics.

E. You must overcome the concealing. There are two reasons for this concealing: (1) there were too many people, and (2) he was short in stature. To be short in stature is something natural; to be too crowded is environmental and speaks of a man-made situation. To overcome these overshadowings you need to run ahead of the crowd. Do not be running blindly in their midst, lest you run into hell with them. You need to pass them, leaving behind those false Catholics and false Christians. Also, you need to climb up the tree in order to overcome your natural problem. Though short in stature, once he climbed up a sycamore tree he could see what others could not. He really knew how to do business. Some people may have heard the gospel over a hundred times and still not be saved, but he only heard the message for a few minutes, and he was saved. If you don't know how to read the Bible, and you ask someone else to read it for you, that someone is like your sycamore tree. If you don't know how to pray, and you ask someone else to help you to pray, that person is like your sycamore tree. Or like today with so many people around, you hesitate to get saved; but you would wait until most are gone and would stay around to have some talk and prayer, this will be like climbing up the sycamore tree. If you stay in the midst of the crowd, you may be listening to the gospel all your life and still not be saved. But if you would run ahead and climb up the sycamore tree, you will be saved.

F. He wanted to see Jesus, but actually Jesus saw him first. When Jesus came to that place, He looked up and saw him. He called him by name and said to him, "Zaccheus, make haste, and come down." When you believe in the Lord, right away you will sense that the Lord is calling your name. He calls your name because He knows you. You are saved when the Lord calls you. The Lord knows your living situation. He also knows what sins you have committed. Because He knows you, He calls your name. Among so many people, Jesus only called Zaccheus, because Zaccheus had a heart for Him.

G. When he heard Jesus, he received Him joyfully. Have you ever received Jesus? Have you let Him live in you? The first rich man only studied the truth, but this rich man received Jesus into him. *Emphasize the words* receive *and* live.

H. After he received Jesus into him, something happened. Immediately he said, "Lord,"—Jesus became his Lord— "the half of my goods I give to the poor; and if I have wrongfully exacted aught of any man, I restore fourfold." Now he is rich and charitable. He has forsaken the idol. This power did not come from himself but came as a result of his receiving Jesus.

I. The Lord said, "Today is salvation come to this house." Where Jesus is, there is salvation. Mere letters are something dead; the more you study them the more you are dead. But, as soon as Jesus comes in, man is saved.

J. It is possible with God.

Subject Ninety-five

SALVATION OF A THIEF—
The Fifth Contrast in Luke

Scripture: Luke 23:39-43

I. Two thieves

A. The two thieves who were crucified with Jesus committed the same sin and received the same punishment.

B. Of the two, one believed and the other did not. Formerly they were both thieves. The only difference was that later on one believed and one did not.

II. One railed on Jesus

A. The first thief, being very sinful, railed on the sinless Jesus.

B. Today many are really deep in sins, yet they rail on Jesus.

III. The other one asked Jesus

A. The other thief railed on Jesus as the first (cf. Matt 27:44).

B. But when he thought about God, a godly fear came up within him, and he said, "Dost thou not even fear God?" The reason men repent and call on Jesus is that men think about the matter of God. As he thought about God, he thought about the matter of eternity. He knew that his sins would be resolved before the law by his execution but would still be unresolved before God. So he was afraid when he thought about God; he was afraid of entering into eternal perdition.

C. He knew himself. Because he was afraid of God, his conscience caused him to confess before the Lord, acknowledging that he deserved the punishment of death.

D. He knew the Lord. He also acknowledged that the Lord Jesus had done nothing amiss to deserve such punishment, and that the Lord Jesus was bearing his sins and dying for his sake.

E. He asked. So he asked the Lord Jesus to save him, to remember him when the Lord would come in His kingdom.

F. He was saved. As soon as he asked the Lord, the Lord's salvation came to him. He was asking for the future, but the Lord promised him, saying, "Today shall thou be with me in Paradise." Just ask, and you will receive. To ask is to show your faith. Your asking is a proof that you have believed. So, just ask and you will be saved.

G. He received assurance of his salvation. The assurance of his salvation was in the Lord's words, "Today shall thou be with me in Paradise." The Lord has given us many words, and these words are the assurance of our salvation. For example: "He who believes in the Son has eternal life" (John 3:36); "He that hath the Son hath the life" (I John 5:12). Just lay hold on one verse, and you will be saved.

Subject Ninety-six

THE WORD BECAME FLESH

Scripture: John 1:1, 14, 16-18

I. The Word is God

A. The Word is the spoken word. The spoken word expresses and defines.

B. The Word in this universe is God. God is the meaning and the definition of the universe.

II. The Word became flesh

A. In the beginning there was the Word, because the Word was God. In the beginning, that is, in eternity past, before the beginning of time, was the Word. The Word was there in eternity past.

B. "The Word became flesh" means that the Word came into time.

C. The flesh is man; for the Word to become flesh, God became man.

D. This man, who was the Word becoming flesh, was Jesus, the Nazarene. Here, the emphasis is on the fact that Jesus has both the divine nature and the human nature. He was a man in His outward form, but God was embodied in Him. This Jesus was God becoming man, with the divine nature lived out in the human nature.

III. The purpose of the Word becoming flesh

A. The Word became flesh in order to express God. No

man has ever seen God; only Jesus, as the Word incarnated to become flesh, has declared Him.

B. By becoming flesh the Word brought grace and reality to man. Grace is God enjoyed or gained by man; reality is God realized by man. All the things in this universe are as light as air and as contemptible as dung; only God is weighty and precious. Therefore, nothing really counts; only when God is enjoyed by man, that is the real grace. All the things in this universe are temporary, changeable, and subject to vanity. God never changes, so only God is reality. Reality is just truth. Everything that can be seen by man is vanity. Only God is reality. Therefore, to see God is to see the truth.

C. The Word became flesh to enable man to receive grace and to see the truth; this means to enjoy God and to know God.

IV. How to treat this Word

A. Confess that He is God incarnated to become man.

B. Receive Him.

C. Believe in His word. He Himself is the Word. As the Word, He has spoken many words. If we receive Him, we must also believe in His word.

D. When we receive His word, we receive His life. This means we receive Himself. The result is the Word becomes flesh in us and mingles with us.

Subject Ninety-seven

THE RESULT OF RECEIVING THE LORD

Scripture: John 1:11-13

I. The Lord came into mankind

A. The Lord is God. He became man and dwelt among men.

B. Today, the Lord is still coming to mankind by His Spirit and His Gospel.

II. Man receiving the Lord

A. The Lord came into mankind for men to receive Him, that is, that He would be enjoyed by men.

B. To receive the Lord does not require either the seeing with our physical eyes or the touching with our physical hands. It only requires the believing in the heart.

C. To believe in the heart means to believe by hearing, and to believe by hearing is all that is necessary. Verse 12 says, "But as many as received Him...to those who believe in His name." Thus, to believe by hearing is just to receive Him.

D. It is very difficult for man to see the Lord, or to meet Him. Yet, to hear His name is the easiest thing. To receive the Lord is to believe in His name with the heart. Therefore, it is possible for anyone to receive the Lord at any time and at any place. This point is important. One can receive the Lord when he is washing his face, on the bus, or even when hearing this word.

III. The result of receiving the Lord

A. To be born of God. The Lord is God become flesh. When we received Him, He came into our being, that is, God came into us to become our life. Since we have the life of God in us, therefore we were born of God.

B. To have the life of God. Because we were born of God, naturally we have received His life. This life is our right to enjoy all the portions of God. A child who was born in the royal family has the life of the royal family, and this life is his right to enjoy all the portions of the royal family.

C. To be the children of God. We were originally just the creatures of God, having our origin from God, yet we did not have God's life and God's nature. Our relationship with God was just a relationship between a creator and the creatures, without the relationship of the Father and the children. Once we received the Lord, our relationship to Him advanced from that of the creatures to that of the children. Once we have the life of God, we can enjoy all the portions in the Father's house.

Subject Ninety-eight

THE LAMB OF GOD

Scripture: John 1:29, 36

I. The meaning of the lamb

A. We have to see this from the type revealed in the Old Testament. We see in the Old Testament that when Adam sinned, he should have died. But God killed a lamb for him and clothed him with garments from the skin of the lamb to cover up his nakedness. This shows us that when man sinned, he should have died, but God used the lamb to be the substitute for man, to shed its blood for the sins of man; thus the lamb became the clothing for man to cover himself before God. From that time on, throughout all the generations man could only come before God through the lamb. It is only through the shedding of a lamb's blood for our sins that we can be accepted by God. The offering of the sacrifices by the Israelites can also be mentioned here.

B. The great significance of the lamb is in its death and the subsequent shedding of blood for the remission of our sins. Because God is righteous, He cannot forgive the sins of man. Therefore, the provision for the forgiveness of sins is the shedding of the blood of a lamb.

II. The Lamb of God

A. The Bible tells us that God prepared a Lamb for man even before the foundation of the world. Therefore this Lamb is called the Lamb of God. All the many lambs in the Old Testament were prepared by man, so they are called the lambs of man. Only this Lamb is prepared by God for man, so it is called the Lamb of God.

B. The Lamb of God is the Son of God, Jesus Christ.

C. When the Son of God, Jesus Christ, came to this earth, His forerunner John the Baptist testified of

Him saying, "Behold the Lamb of God Who takes away the sin of the world." When John preached these words to the Jews, it was very easy for the Jews to understand what he was preaching. From the days of their forefathers up till that time, the Jews were offering sacrifices every day. Therefore, on that day when John said, "Behold, the Lamb of God Who takes away the sin of the world," they immediately knew what this referred to.

III. To bear the sins

A. The reason God prepared a Lamb for man was that man had sinned. God needed man, therefore He created man. He loved man, so He saved man. Since man had fallen, sinned, and had created a problem between himself and God, God had to use some means to take away the sins of man. The saving way for our sins is to have a Lamb to bear and take away the sins.

B. The place where the Lamb of God, Jesus Christ, bore the sins of man was on the cross. When He was dying, He cried out, "My God, My God, why have You forsaken Me?" God forsook Him not because He was sinful, but because God had put the sins of all mankind upon Him.

C. Because He bore and took away the sins of man in such a way, today, the blood He shed can wash away the sins of man and solve the problem between man and God.

IV. How should one treat the Lamb of God?

A. Confess that He died for your sins.

B. Repent.

C. Receive the Lamb of God as your Savior.

Subject Ninety-nine

THE FIRST SIGN—WATER CHANGED INTO WINE

Scripture: John 2:1-11

I. The Lord came to Cana

A. The Lord came to Cana. Cana means a land of reeds,

signifying weak and fragile people. Isaiah 42:3 says, "A bruised reed He will not break." So the reeds refer to those who are weak, fragile, and bruised. The Lord coming to Cana meant He came to the place of fragile people. Cana is in Galilee, a place despised by people.

This message uses the weak and fragile people as a base, so it talks about man's weaknesses. Man is weak and bruises easily. Once pressed, he is bruised; once touched, he falls.

B. The Lord came to Cana on the third day, the day of resurrection. This means the Lord came to the fragile people in resurrection, or the resurrected Lord came to the fragile people. The foregoing chapter talks about the Lamb of God who takes away the sins of the world. When the Lamb of God took away the sins of the world, He entered into resurrection; that is, He came the third day to bring enjoyment to man's life.

II. The Lord was invited to the wedding

A. Marriage is the most important event to man, and wedding signifies the enjoyment of life. Human life depends firstly on the creation of God and secondly on marriage. Without marriage, there would be no continuation and therefore no existence of man. Thus marriage is human life, and wedding is the enjoyment of the human life. The Lord coming to the wedding meant He had come into human life and into the enjoyment of the human life.

B. The center of the wedding feast was wine. Wine is the life-juice of the grape. Though it is a liquid, it is different from water. Water does not grow out from something, but wine does. The center of the wedding is the wine, signifying that the enjoyment of human living depends on life. Without life, there is no enjoyment.

C. The wine is limited; it runs out. This signifies our human life will die. Not only the old couples die, but also the young couples die. If, in a couple, one dies, the enjoyment is also gone. This is the running out of wine in the wedding. When life ends, the human living and the enjoyment of human life also ends. A newlywed couple might get tuberculosis while they are enjoying the pleasures of human life; then there would be the running out of the wine. An old couple married for fifty years is also running out of wine. If they drink a little more, it would still run out.

III. The Lord changed water to wine

A. He did not follow man's will. Mary first told Him that there was no wine, but the Lord did not do anything then. This is to say that the Lord does things not according to man's will. You might be very anxious in hoping your husband, wife or children will be saved, but the Lord purposely slows down His work.

B. The Lord does everything according to His own will. When all the opinions of man have ceased, then He starts doing something.

C. Before the Lord changed water into wine, there were six stone waterpots. Six is the number of man, for man was created on the sixth day. Stone is natural, thus six stone waterpots signify the created human beings and those that do not have God.

D. There was only water in the stone waterpots. Water signifies death, and wine signifies life. The Lord used His life with His creating power to change water into wine, that is, to change death into life.

E. This wine is not a natural wine, but a miraculous wine. The wine in the wedding feast was natural wine, which meant the center of the enjoyment of life depended on the natural life, and this life will run out. Since the Lord had come in, the life which man received was God's eternal life. The enjoyment of this new life is endless, and causes the wedding to last until eternity.

IV. This is the beginning of signs

A. All the signs which the Lord did had this sign as a beginning. All the work which the Lord has done upon us is that of signs, to change the death in us into life. Giving us life is the beginning of all His works.

B. The Lord changing death into life was a miracle among miracles and was the biggest miracle in all His miracles. Moody once said that the biggest miracle which the Lord ever did was to give life to those who were dead in sins.

V. Results

A. To satisfy the enjoyment of human life.

B. To express God's glory and God Himself. God's glory can only be manifested when man receives the resurrection life.

Subject One Hundred

THE NEED OF THE HIGH CLASS PEOPLE

Scripture: John 3:1-15

I. A moral man

Nicodemus was an upper class man. He was a moralist, a teacher, and a "master of Israel." He also feared God, so he was qualified to represent the moral people.

II. The matter of human behavior

A. This man came to Jesus and discussed with Him the matter of human behavior.

B. Nicodemus focused on the matter of human life as a matter of behavior. He called Jesus "Rabbi," and he also said that Jesus was a teacher come from God. A teacher is one who teaches people how to keep the law and how to behave themselves before God.

C. The Lord's answer revealed to him that man's real need before God is not to improve himself, but rather it is a matter of life. The Lord answered him, "Unless a man is born anew, he cannot see the kingdom of God." The Lord's answer was to change Nicodemus' concept. What Nicodemus asked was a matter of behavior, but what the Lord answered was a matter of life.

D. The Lord uses this answer to show that the real need of the moral people is not to improve their behavior but to be regenerated with the divine life.

III. The need to be reborn

A. The human life received by natural birth is corrupted and cannot be improved any more.

B. For man to reform himself is vain.

C. Man's real need is to have the divine life remake him; that is, to be born again.

IV. The meaning of regeneration

A. The definition of regeneration is to be born anew. But Nicodemus thought regeneration was to enter the second time into his mother's womb and be reborn.

B. Although the definition of regeneration is to be born again, yet the meaning of regeneration is not to enter the second time into your mother's womb and be reborn, but rather to be born of God.

C. To be born of God is to be born of the Spirit. It is when the Holy Spirit comes into us that we receive the life of God.

D. To be born again is to receive God's life in addition to our own life.

V. How to be regenerated

A. On the objective side—through the death and resurrection of Christ. The death of Christ eliminated the sins of man; the resurrection of Christ released His life. His death has erased the problem of sins; His resurrection has dispensed His life into man.

B. On the subjective side—firstly, we need to confess that our human life is corrupted and cannot be improved. Secondly, we have to confess that the Lord has died and was raised for us. Thirdly, we have to receive this resurrected Christ as our Savior. We must look upon Jesus on the cross as the Israelites looked upon the brass serpent. By looking upon that brass serpent, they lived.

Subject One Hundred One

THE NEED OF THE LOWER CLASS

Scripture: John 4:3-32

I. Jesus went to Samaria

A. Samaria was a place no one cared for—it was an unde-
sirable and disliked region. In that place different
nationalities and races were interbred and mixed.
Thus, they were confused.

B. The Lord went to Samaria to the well. Water comes out
from the well, so it represents something to quench
man's thirst. The Lord went to Samaria, which was a
low (vile, base) and thirsty place. The important point
seen about Samaria is the well. This shows us that the
problem with the lower class is thirst.

II. The Savior—Jesus—related to the lower class

A. The Lord sat on the well and was waiting.

B. This lower class woman was confronted by the Lord.
Their confrontation was because of the Lord's waiting;
it was not an accident or a coincidence.

C. Why did the Savior, Jesus, go to this well and wait for
the Samaritan woman?

1. The Savior needs the sinner.

2. The sinner needs the Savior.

The Savior went to the well because of His thirst, as
did the woman. The place where they met was the
well. The subject of their conversation was the water,
the cure for their thirst.

D. The position of the lower class as seen in the woman.

1. She is one who has no morality. No one has any
respect for this kind of person. She has had five
husbands and now is living with another man who
is not her husband.

2. She is the "scum of the earth."

3. She is probably not educated.

4. She is probably not too old.

5. She does not fear God.

E. The higher class person, Nicodemus, went to find the Lord at night, while the lower class person came to the Lord in the daytime, at noon. The higher class person talked about proper behavior while the lower class person talked about the quenching of her thirst.

III. The realization of her need and knowledge of the Savior

A. Jesus asked the woman for some water to drink. Why? He did this to make her aware of her own need that she might then realize the Savior, Jesus, and His salvation. When the Lord first asked for water, she only knew that He was Jewish. She was offended that He, a Jew, asked for water from a Samaritan. Then Jesus said, "If you knew the gift of God, and Who it is that says to you, Give Me a drink, you would have asked Him, and He would have given you living water." When Jesus spoke this, He wanted her to realize her need and then also to see who He was. The woman said, "Sir, give me this water..." Jesus told her first to call her husband. With this, she realized that He was a prophet, and finally that He was the Messiah, the Christ.

B. The Lord caused her to realize how to know the Savior and how to quench her thirst.

IV. How to meet the need

A. The Lord caused her to know her sinfulness. When she saw her need for the living water and also realized that Jesus was the giver of this water, only then did she ask for the water. Then Jesus asked her concerning her husband. "Husband" represented the history of her sinful life.

B. She talked to the Lord Jesus about worshipping God. The Lord showed her that to really touch God one needs to be in the spirit.

V. The outcome of their conversation—she received the living water

A. When the Samaritan woman got the living water, she

immediately left her waterpot and departed from the
well.

B. From that time on, she never could depend upon her
own way to satisfy her thirst. Because of her past life,
the fact that she had become fully satisfied was now a
wonderful testimony to Jesus Christ.

Subject One Hundred Two

THE NEED OF THE WEAK

Scripture: John 5:1-14, 21, 24-26, 39-40, 43, 46-47

I. The Lord went to Jerusalem

A. Jerusalem is the foundation of peace, the dwelling
place of God, and the capital city of the King—a place
full of peace, joy, and honor.

B. The Lord went to Jerusalem in the time of a festival. A
festival is for man's happiness and rejoicing.

C. When the Lord came, it was the Sabbath day. The
Sabbath is for man to rest. So this particular day was
a time for peace, joy, and rest.

II. Jesus met the weak person

A. In Jerusalem on that day, men should have been
rejoicing, but everyone whom the Lord Jesus met
was suffering; they were all lying in sickness and in
pain.

B. Pain and weakness are due to sickness. The weakness
caused by sickness in this man signifies the weakness
of death caused by man's sin. Sin brings in death.
Death is the ultimate weakness; death is weakness to
the uttermost.

C. We find that the weak man's suffering is not only
because he is sick, but because he knows how to do what
is needed and what is right but cannot do it because he
lacks the strength. Man's suffering today is not only due
to his weakness caused by sin; but rather due to knowing that he should do good but being unable to do so.
This is the agonizing weakness of people today. People

know how to do what is good and what is right, but they
cannot do it.

D. In front of this weak man is a way for him to be healed,
the water from the pool. When the water is moving, those
who get to it first get healed instantly. Although the way
to heal him is here, because of man's weakness he has no
energy to do it. This signifies that although there is a
way to be good, because of weakness, man cannot do it.
Brother Austin Sparks says this man's suffering on his
back for thirty-eight years represents the people of
Israel, who, after they received the law of God, just laid
down in the wilderness for thirty-eight years.

III. The Lord's salvation

A. The salvation of the Lord was completely unexpected
by this weak man. All his attention was fixed on the
water of the pool. So he never expected the Lord's salvation.

B. The Lord in His salvation was seeking out the man,
rather than the man seeking out the Lord. The Lord
asked him, "Do you want to get well?" The man did
not ask the Lord for help, yet the Lord healed him and
became his salvation.

C. The reason the Lord's word can save people is that
there is life in His word. The reason weak people are
so weak is that there is death in their weakness. The
healing of the death depends on the life. There is life
in the Lord's word. Once man receives His word, the
weakness is changed to strength.

D. The Lord's saving is by His life. From a human view,
this man is in weakness, but from the Lord's view, this
man is in death. So the Lord said, "An hour is coming
and now is, when the dead shall hear the voice of the
Son of God, and those who hear shall live." The Lord's
way to save man is to give him life and make him a
"living" creature.

IV. The Lord's saving power

A. The Lord's salvation was not only able to cause him to

rise up and walk, it also caused him to pick up his bed and walk. Formerly, he depended on his bed, so he was being controlled by his bed. But now he controls the bed. He governs the bed, rather than vice versa. For some people, their bed is movies, wine, cigarettes, gambling, etc.

B. He not only made the weak man become strong, but He made him strong to the point where he could overcome all kinds of habits and obstacles.

V. **The result of the Lord's salvation**

A. Peace. Although it was a Sabbath day, this man was lying down without peace and without rest. After he rose and walked, he had peace and rest.

B. Joy. When you have God's life, you have a real joy and a real feasting. Once you are saved, you have the feast of salvation. Then you can enjoy your salvation. You have God's presence. God becomes your companion, and you are in Jerusalem.

Subject One Hundred Three

THE NEED OF THE HUNGRY

Scripture: John 6:22-37, 47-58, 63

I. **The dissatisfied human living**

A. In this passage John recorded that there was a great multitude surrounding the seashore seeking the Lord. The sea is where demons live. It signifies the world corrupted by Satan. The seashore represents the place where fallen mankind lives. The place where fallen mankind lives and the dwelling place of demons are adjacent to each other. Men's sinful way of living on the seashore is very close to the demons' life, if not exactly equal to it. In such a sinful living, nothing can satisfy men, and nothing can supply and sustain them.

B. They were seeking the Lord on the one hand and living a sinful life on the other. They lived in sins, expressing the dissatisfaction of human life. *Emphasize that men live in sin and do not feel sinful; they only feel dissatisfied.* Give real examples to prove how unsatisfying human living is. Tell them that each and every one of them is not satisfied.

C. These people who came to seek the Lord felt a need inside, but they did not know what their need was. They thought what they needed was the physical bread. They did not realize that what they needed was the eternal bread. So the Lord spoke to them with many words and showed them that their real need was not the physical bread, but eternal life. Friends, you may feel that you need something, but you don't know what that something is. Maybe some of you feel that you need a degree, a family, or something else. But even if you get all of these, someday you will still feel empty, because what you need is not these things, but the bread of life.

II. The Lord is the bread of life

A. That day the Lord's words were to lead them to realize that only the Lord could supply their need, because their real need was not the physical bread, but the bread of life.

B. The Lord told them that He was the bread of life which came down from heaven to give life to the world. The real need of man is the Lord Jesus Himself.

C. The bread of life is the life of the Lord Himself. It is also the Lord Himself coming as the life of man. Explain clearly that man's real need is life. For example, without life all of the human affairs will be terminated, because all of man's desires and endeavors depend upon life. Because man lacks life, human living is fraught with shortages. Man's life is a life of shortage and vanity; it cannot meet the need of man. The life of the Lord Jesus is abundant, eternal, and fulfilling. That is why His life can meet all the needs of human living. Only the Lord's life can supply man in such a way, so He said, "He who comes to Me shall by no means hunger." Not to be hungry means not to be lacking or empty.

III. How the Lord gave Himself to man

A. The Lord is the "bread of life," which implies that He is for man to enjoy.

B. Anything to be taken in by man must pass through death. Things such as rice, wheat, and all kinds of vegetables and fruit must first go through death and be broken before they can be enjoyed by man.

C. For the Lord to become the bread of life, He must also pass through death. So He said, "My flesh is true food, and My blood is true drink." Flesh and blood being separated signifies death. When the Jews heard that the Lord could be eaten as the bread of life, they were puzzled. But the way the Lord gave Himself to man is by passing through the separation of death. When He died, His blood was separated from His flesh, so that He could be enjoyed by man. *Stress the Lord's death.* The Lord's flesh and blood were separated on the cross so that He could be enjoyed by man on the one hand, and so that His life could be received by man on the other.

IV. How to receive the Lord as life

A. In principle, the way to receive the Lord as life is by eating and drinking. For man to receive any food for nourishment, he must take the food by eating and drinking. For man to receive the Lord as life, he must likewise take the Lord in. The Lord's flesh and blood were separated so that we may take Him in.

B. As we believe that the Lord gave His body and died on the cross for us, we are eating His flesh. As we believe that the Lord bore our sins and shed His blood on the cross for us, we are drinking His blood. When we thus believe, we fully receive Him into us.

C. This kind of believing by eating and drinking is the believing of receiving the Lord as Savior and as life.

So in John chapter six the Lord said that, on one
hand, he who eats His flesh and drinks His blood has
eternal life, and, on the other, he who believes in Him
shall have life. This points out that to eat His flesh
and drink His blood is to believe.

Subject One Hundred Four

THE NEED OF THE THIRSTY

Scripture: John 7:37-39

I. The thirst of human living

A. It was the feast of tabernacles in Jerusalem. A feast is
a day of joy.

B. On the last day of the feast Jesus stood and cried out,
saying, "If anyone thirst...." The last day of the feast
is absolutely related to the thirst. Man is thirsty
because the feast has its last day. A feast is a period of
joy in the human living. But the last day of the feast is
the termination of the joy. When the joy of human
living reaches its end, man immediately begins to feel
the thirst. There is an end to everything: a ball game,
a movie, a birthday party, a wedding, etc. When the
end comes, the crowd breaks up and each person goes
back, exhausted. In any feast there is a last day, and
when the last day comes, man begins to feel thirsty.
All the joyous occasions only produce the thirst. The
more you pursue the fashion of this age, the more
fashion you have to pursue; the more you desire
beauty, the more beauty there is for you to go after.
But the end only makes you more thirsty and dissatisfied.

II. The Lord has the living water

A. The Lord cried out and said, "If anyone thirst," because
He wanted man to realize what man's real need is. His
crying was not only to make man realize he is thirsty,
but also to show that He has the living water to
quench man's thirst. So He said, "If anyone thirst, let

him come to Me and drink." The feast cannot quench the thirst; only the Lord's living water which is flowing forever can quench man's thirst.

B. The living water of the Lord is the Lord's life and the Lord's Spirit.

III. How the living water flows out from the Lord

A. The Lord's life-giving water came out of His broken body through the death on the cross, just like the living water which came out of the smitten rock. As soon as the Lord was glorified after His death and resurrection, His life-giving water flowed out, that is, He descended as the Spirit.

B. The Lord's life-giving water is in the Holy Spirit. It flowed out through the Holy Spirit. Today if you are moved by the Holy Spirit, the living water has flowed unto you. If you receive it, this water will then be flowing inside of you.

IV. How to receive the Lord's life-giving water

A. The only way to receive this water is to drink. This is why the Lord said here, "If anyone thirst, let him come to Me and drink."

B. To drink is to believe. After saying, "Come to Me and drink," the Lord continued, "He who believes in Me." So to believe is to drink. Believe in what? The Lord said, "Believe in Me." To believe is to receive the Lord into you, that is, to believe that the Lord died for you on the cross and released His life. When you thus believe in Him, you are receiving Him in, and His Spirit and His life will flow into you.

C. Such a believing not only results in the living water flowing into you, but also causes the living water to become rivers of living water flowing out of you. Give examples to illustrate how a person is satisfied and happy when he drinks of the living water, the life-giving water. As a result of drinking, rivers of living water just flow out of him to meet others' needs and to quench others' thirst.

Subject One Hundred Five

THE NEED OF THE SINNER

Scripture: John 8:1-11, 24, 34, 36

I. A sinful woman

A. When the Lord was in the temple, those supposedly moral people brought an immoral woman to the Lord Jesus to question Him.

B. Woman represents man's position before God. Man's position before God is that of a woman.

C. The greatest sin of a woman is adultery. Adulterous means impure. Man's greatest sin before God is that man is impure before God. Man lusts for many things other than God. So, spiritually speaking, all men (women) have committed adultery. This immoral woman represents all of us who have sinned.

II. All have sinned

A. Those supposedly moral people only saw that the woman sinned, but they did not see that they were just like her. Because they did not know themselves, they brought the woman to Him and questioned Him. They did not realize that their condition was exactly the same as the woman's, and therefore, that they were actually bringing themselves before the Lord for judgment.

B. They said that according to the law such a woman must die. But they asked the Lord, "What then do you say?" They were trying to put the Lord on the spot. But the Lord's answer shut their mouths: "He who is without sin among you, let him be the first to throw a stone at her." The Lord's words were a judgment upon them. In essence He was saying, "You saw this woman committing adultery. But have you seen that before God you are committing the same sin?" Those who heard the Lord's words were judged by the Lord.

C. The Lord's words touched their conscience. Each one of them acknowledged that he was a sinner by walking away, beginning with the older ones until the last. This indicates that both the condemned one (the woman) and those who were condemning were all sinners. Not only those who commit outward sins are sinners, but also those who do not. Not only those immoral ones are sinners, but also those who are moral. Not only the ones being judged in a court are sinners, but also the judge. Not only the lawbreakers are sinners, but also the lawmakers and the law enforcers. Not only the troublemakers are sinners, but also those who keep the law and order. Not only the defenders are sinners, but also the prosecutors. Not only those who steal are sinners, but also those from whom things are stolen.

III. There is only One who never sinned

A. After the Lord said, "He who is without sin...," everybody went away. There was only one left—the Lord Jesus.

B. The Lord did not walk away because He never sinned and He could not sin.

C. So only the Lord is qualified to condemn others.

IV. The Lord would not condemn man for his sins

A. Those who tried to condemn others were exposed by the Lord. They were sinners themselves. How could they, then, condemn others?

B. Although the Lord never sinned and was qualified to condemn others, He did not condemn man for his sin because He came to this world in order to save man from sin.

C. The Lord did not condemn man for his sin because He bore man's sins on the cross. He is the righteous God. According to His righteousness, He should have condemned man for his sin.

D. Because He bore man's sins on the cross, He does not condemn man for his sins; rather, He saves man from sin.

V. The Lord can deliver man out of sin

A. That day the Lord not only told the woman, "Neither

do I condemn you," but also said, "From now on sin no more." He wanted her to be delivered out of sin.

B. In the following passage the Lord said, "Everyone who commits sin is a slave of sin." If a man does not believe in Him, he shall die in his sins.

C. The Lord also said that only He can set people free. That is the real freedom. So the Lord can deliver man from sin.

VI. How to obtain forgiveness and deliverance from sin

A. Confess that you are a sinner.

B. Believe that the Lord is the great "I Am." "I Am" means God.

C. Believe that the Lord is God coming as our Savior. By the Lord's shed blood we obtain forgiveness; by God's coming into us as our life, we are delivered from sin.

Subject One Hundred Six
THE NEED OF THE BLIND

Scripture: John 9:1-11, 35-41

I. Man is born blind

A. The Lord met a person who was born blind.

B. Blindness is the absence of sight. A blind person cannot see anything. Although man's outward eyes can see, his inward eyes are blind. Man does not know from where he came, nor where he is going. Man does not know what life is all about, nor what is his relationship with God.

II. The Lord is the light of the world

A. Blindness is synonymous with darkness. As darkness prevents man from being able to see, so also does blindness.

B. The Lord is the light of the world. Only the Lord can dispel man's darkness; that is, only the Lord can resolve man's problem of blindness and cause man to regain his sight. Only the Lord can dispel man's darkness and restore his sight.

III. How the Lord causes man to see

A. That day the Lord spat on the ground and made clay of the spittle and anointed the eyes of the blind. The spittle signifies the words which proceeded out of the mouth of the Lord, and clay signifies man who was made out of the dust of the ground. The words entering into man and mingling with man through the moving and anointing of the Holy Spirit enable man to see clearly.

B. That blind person went to wash in the pool of Siloam. Siloam means "sent." To be sent, one must first believe and obey. Whatever the Lord says to you, you must believe and obey. So here the washing includes both believing and obeying. Washing also signifies baptism. If you believe now, you should also be baptized now. The baptismal is the pool of Siloam. To wash in the pool of Siloam means that you believe and are baptized. At the time the Lord asked him to go and wash in the pool of Siloam, it did not seem very meaningful. There were many places with water in Judea. Why must it be the pool of Siloam? This commandment is to test and see if you are willing to obey. If you obey, your eyes will be opened.

C. The Lord not only healed the blind person so that he could see, but also led him to realize that the Lord was the Son of God. So the real eye opening is to realize that Jesus Christ is the Son of God.

The words at the end of chapter 9 can be included in this subject. You may mention briefly that although the Pharisees had eyes to see, they were blind.

Subject One Hundred Seven
THE NEED OF THE DEAD

Scripture: John 11

I. A man had died

A. First mention that a man was sick, and his sisters came to ask the Lord for healing.

B. When he was sick, the Lord would not come to heal him. This is to say that if a man only admits that he has some problems but will not admit that he is dead, the Lord will not come to save him, because the Lord's salvation is not to heal but to cause the dead to resurrect. The Lord's salvation is not to cause man to be healed, but to cause man to be enlivened. Healing is a matter of correction, whereas enlivening is a matter of life. The Lord's salvation is not to correct man's problem, but to enliven man that man may receive His life. *This point needs to be emphasized.*

II. The Lord is life

A. The need of the dead is to receive life. The only way for a dead person to be healed is to receive life. Only life can vanquish death.

B. Give examples to prove that man is dead.

1. A dead person is weak and impotent in doing good.

2. A dead person has no consciousness in doing evil. The fact that man is weak and impotent in doing good and yet has no consciousness in doing evil is a proof that man is dead.

3. A dead person is in bondage. The dead Lazarus was bound with burial cloths and confined in a tomb. Many today are bound in a theater, and the theater is their tomb.

C. The Lord said that He is life. Only the Lord can meet the need of the dead.

III. How the Lord causes man to receive life

A. The Lord's life is in His words. The basic principle in gospel preaching is to cause man to receive the Lord's life. So you must cause man to believe in the Lord's words. The Lord's words are the Lord's voice, which is the Lord's gospel. Today the gospel is being preached to you so that you may believe in His words, for in His words there is the Lord's life.

B. What caused Lazarus to be resurrected from death

that day was the Lord's words, saying, "Lazarus, come forth!" The dead Lazarus heard the Lord's words and was quickened. John 5:25 says, "An hour is coming and now is, when the dead shall hear the voice of the Son of God, and those who hear shall live."

C. Today the words of the gospel are the voice of the Lord. Friends, if you will listen to this voice, you will live. Those who believe are the ones who have really heard His voice. Some of you here may have heard these words superficially, but you still do not believe. The reason you do not believe is that you have not heard. Those who have really heard the words are the ones who believe. Quote to them the verses in the Bible regarding how to obtain the eternal life.

IV. The result of obtaining the Lord's life

A. Lazarus lived when he heard the words of the Lord, and he came out of the tomb. Today as you hear the gospel, you have also heard the words of the Lord, and you live. Because you are living, you will surely come out of the movie theaters and other sinful pits.

B. Freed from the bondage. Eating, drinking, whoring, and gambling are all bondages. They cause you to be unable to move an inch. When you receive life, you will be freed from the bondage.

V. Remarks

The story about the resurrection of Lazarus in chapter eleven and the miracle of changing water into wine in chapter two are similar in figure. In Cana there was a wedding feast, signifying the joy of human living; the center of the feast was wine, signifying life. This means, likewise, that there was joy in the house of Bethany, and the center of the joy was dependent upon life. But the life of those three was as weak as the reed. When life was terminated, the joy of human living was gone, just as when the wine ran out. John chapter two is a picture, whereas John chapter eleven is a description of that picture. The following is a comparison between these two chapters.

Chapter Eleven

1. There was joy in the house of Bethany.
2. Lazarus was dying.
3. Martha, Lazarus' sister, came and told the Lord that Lazarus was sick.
4. The Lord did not act according to Martha's words.
5. The Lord acted in Bethany according to His own will.
6. Lazarus was absolutely dead and buried in the tomb.
7. The Lord caused Lazarus to resurrect from death and to receive life.

Chapter Two

1. There was a wedding feast in Cana.
2. The wine was running out.
3. Mary, Jesus' mother, told the Lord that the wine was running out.
4. The Lord also did not act according to Mary's words.
5. The Lord also acted in Cana according to His own will.
6. The wine ran out. Only six stone water pots remained. Water typifies death.
7. The Lord changed water into wine, and caused men to obtain the joy of life.

Subject One Hundred Eight

GOD LOVES THE WORLD

Scripture: John 3:16

I. God

In this section we should prove the existence of God.

A. Prove it from the existence of the universe.

B. Prove it from the existence of men, that is, from the physiological and psychological aspects of men.

    1. Physiologically illustrate the wonderful structure of the human body.

    2. Psychologically explain that in men there is a hunger for God and there is condemnation in the conscience.

C. Prove it from the heavenly principle.

    1. The universe is ruled by God. If men disobey His rule, they defy the heavenly principle. Men will then be peaceless or even die.

2. If men walk according to the heavenly principle, they will have peace and blessing. This shows that there is a ruler in the universe. The Chinese concept of the heavenly principle emphasizes the ethics and the recompense of good or evil.

II. God loves

A. God is love.

B. God's heart is love. His love centers on men and has men as its object. His creation of air, sun, and food for men proves that God loves men.

III. Men

A. Men are lost.

B. Men are sinners.

C. Men are dead.

IV. God so loved the world that He gave His only begotten Son

A. Starting from Genesis explain how that after man's fall He came to seek and save man.

B. God loved men to such an extent that He even gave them His only begotten Son.

V. That every one who believes in Him should not perish, but have eternal life

A. God loves men, and in return He wants men to believe in Him. His love is His giving, and our believing is our receiving. Love is the issue of God's heart, and believing is the issue of our heart. Giving is the expression of God's hand, and receiving is the expression of our hand. Love causes God to extend His hand to give to us, while believing causes us to extend our hand to receive from God. Love compelled God to give His Son to us, and believing causes us to receive God's Son. There are two hearts in the universe—love and believing. There are also two hands in the universe—giving and receiving. Love is God's heart and believing is our heart. Giving is God's hand and receiving is our hand.

B. Originally men were all sinful and were destined to die and to perish. But since the Lord bore our sins and died for us, if we believe in Him, we shall not perish.

C. Eternal life is the life of God. Once we believe in the Lord, we have the life of God.

Subject One Hundred Nine

HE THAT BELIEVETH IS NOT CONDEMNED

Scripture: John 3:18

I. Men all have sinned

To prove that men have all sinned, pick up two or three important sins, such as telling lies, stealing, and so forth.

II. Men are all under the condemnation

A. Since all men have sinned, they are all condemned before God. Because God is righteous, He cannot reckon those that have sinned as without sin.

B. Men are also condemned in their own conscience. Friend, today do you have peace in your conscience? Many people have tried to suppress their conscience. Though they could be at peace for a short while, nevertheless, when alone at night the sense of unrest rises up again.

C. Condemnation of the conscience is the evidence of the condemnation of God. For example, when a man is condemned by a police station, he is also condemned by the country.

III. The Lord Jesus bore the sins of men

Speak on the redemption of the cross.

A. God should condemn our sins, but since He loves men, He has accomplished a saving way for us. His saving way is to lay all of our sins on His Son.

B. The Lord Jesus did not die on the cross as a martyr, but rather, to be our substitute to be judged by God. Therefore, the blood that the Lord Jesus shed on the cross is able to cleanse us from our sins.

IV. He that believeth is not condemned

A. What to believe? Firstly, believe that the Lord Jesus is the Son of God and came to be our Savior. Secondly, believe that the Lord Jesus bore our sins on the cross, shed His precious blood, and then rose up from the dead to be our Savior.

B. As soon as a man believes in the Lord Jesus, that is, receives Him, all his sins before God are forgiven. God's judgment has passed over him. Therefore his conscience will not condemn him any more.

C. So men are saved from the eternal judgment and perdition. (The word 'condemned' here in the original text also means 'judged.')

V. He that believeth not is condemned already

A. Since all men are sinful, they are condemned before God.

B. Since God had the Lord Jesus bear our sins, if we do not believe in Him, we would naturally remain under God's condemnation.

C. Therefore all those who do not believe are condemned already. They can only wait for the eternal judgment and perdition.

Subject One Hundred Ten

HE WHO BELIEVES HAS ETERNAL LIFE

Scripture: John 3:36

I. Eternal life

A. The eternal life is not just a blessing, but even more, it is another life.

B. The eternal life is a life that is eternal. It is God's life. Only God's life is an unlimited life, a powerful, holy, bright, loving, and righteous life.

II. Man's life

A. Man's original life is a fragile life. Being hit by a car or taking a little too much tranquilizer will immediately terminate it. It is also a limited life. Men live fifty, sixty, eighty, or even one hundred years and die. The life span is limited and life soon vanishes away.

B. Man's life is also evil and is destined to die. Speak on sin and death.

Items I and II are the comparisons of God's life with man's life.

III. How to obtain eternal life

A. The eternal life is in God's Son. It is the life of God.

B. In order to have the eternal life men must have the Son of God.

C. The Son of God is God and is also the Spirit. In order to have Him men must receive Him with their spirit, that is, believe in Him.

D. After receiving Him with their spirit, after believing in Him, men will have the eternal life. As the Scripture says, he who believes in the Son has eternal life.

IV. The consequence of not believing

A. Men who do not believe will not have eternal life because the eternal life is in God's Son. If you do not believe, you will not have eternal life.

B. If you do not believe, the wrath of God is upon you. The eternal life is in the Son of God, while the wrath is according to God's righteousness. If you believe in the Son of God, you will have eternal life. If you do not believe in the Son of God, you will remain under the wrath of God. God's wrath is like the thunder ready to roll. When it rolls, men will perish.

Subject One Hundred Eleven

PASSED OUT OF DEATH INTO LIFE

Scripture: John 5:24, 25

I. Men were born in sin

A. Describe how men were born in sin.

B. Use examples to illustrate the condition of men born in sin, such as telling lies, hating others, and so forth. There is no need to learn how to sin. Men were born in sin.

II. Men are living in death

A. Sin brings in death. Wherever sin is, there is death. Because men are in sin, men are also in death.

B. Use examples to show that although apparently men are living, actually they are dead. Prove the following three points:

1. Men are incompetent to do good.

2. Men commit sins without any feeling.

3. Men are bound and have no freedom.

How do you know that men are in death? Because men are incompetent in doing good and in pleasing God. In addition, men commit sins without feeling. The living have feeling, but the dead have no feeling. So they that are without feeling are dead. The dead are also under much bondage. Much bondage paralyzes them. Death is a tremendous bondage.

III. The Lord is life

A. The Lord came to be the Savior, to give life to the dead. Because the salvation that the dead need is life, any kind of improvement is useless. Washing and beautifying the dead is the work of the mortuary. Confucianism, Buddhism, and moral practices are but the work of the mortuary. All the practices of self-denial are equivalent to the beautifying of the dead. The Lord Jesus did not come to improve men. He came to be life to men.

B. The life that the Lord gives to men is God's life. God's life is powerful, unlimited, holy, merciful, bright, mighty, and righteous.

IV. Passed out of death into life

A. After men have heard the name of the Lord and the gospel, that is, the word of the Lord, and have believed in the Lord, they immediately receive the forgiveness of sins and obtain God's life.

B. Therefore the Scripture says that he who believes is not condemned and is passed out of death into life.

C. Use examples to illustrate that as soon as men believe, they are made alive.

D. Use verse 25, "An hour is coming and now is, when the dead shall hear the voice of the Son of God, and those who hear shall live." You should repeat these words again and again. If you can drive these words strongly and solidly into them, they will be saved.

Subject One Hundred Twelve

HE THAT COMETH SHALL NOT BE CAST OUT

Scripture: John 6:37

I. One great big word—COME

A. When the Lord Jesus was on the earth, He often uttered this word: come. Come and find rest. Come and have life. The Lord is always calling us to come.

B. To come is to draw nigh to the Lord, to call on Him, and to believe in the Lord.

II. The need of coming

A. Because of sin there is a need of coming. The sinners need to come to have their sins forgiven.

B. Because of burden there is a need of coming. You should point out the many burdens of this life.

C. Because of perdition there is a need of coming.

III. How to come

A. Come with your sins. Do not wait until you improve yourself. Do not wait until you get rid of all your sins. Do not wait until your conscience does not bother you anymore.

B. Come with your burden.

C. Come as you are. Do not wait until you improve yourself. It would be good to sing the hymn "Just As I Am."

D. Come according to the word of the Lord. The Lord is calling us to come. So when we come, we do not have to be afraid that we are coming without an invitation. The Lord says, "Come." You reply, "Amen, I come."

IV. The Lord's promise

Emphasize this strongly.

A. In this universe there is at least one promise made by the Lord for us, as sinners: "Him that comes to Me I will by no means cast out." This is not only a definite word, but also a promise. It is neither guessing, nor postulating. It is firm and cannot be changed. Whatever can be changed is not a promise.

B. Even a gentleman will fulfill what he has promised. How much more shall this faithful Lord fulfill His own promise.

C. In this sentence there are three words: "by no means." These words mean that it does not matter what your condition is. When someone is coming to the Lord, he often hesitates because of his poor condition. The Lord said, "Him that comes to me I will by no means cast out." He did not say, "Him that comes to me must be in good condition so that I will not forsake him." Once when Dr. Torrey was preaching the gospel, one among the audience asked him, "Will the Lord not even forsake one like me?" Dr. Torrey used this verse to help him get saved. *You should emphasize the words "by no means."* Men must believe "by no means" firmly and never doubt, then they will be saved.

Subject One Hundred Thirteen

THE LIGHT OF LIFE

Scripture: John 8:12; 1:4

I. The darkness of human life

A. Men were born into darkness.

B. Men do not know human life, cannot distinguish right from wrong, and do not understand themselves. Furthermore, they do not know God. These few points prove that men are in darkness. John 8:1-11 illustrates how the Pharisees did not understand themselves. They themselves were the sinners, yet they brought a female sinner to the Lord Jesus. Eventually the Lord exposed their hidden condition. They were fully put to shame. They were going to judge others, but eventually they were judged. Then the Lord continued to say, "I am the light of the world; He who follows Me shall by no means walk in darkness, but shall have the light of life." Those Pharisees did not know the Lord. They did not follow the Lord. So they were in darkness. They only saw others committing sins, but failed to see that they themselves were sinners.

C. The reason that men are in darkness is that men have sins and sins bring in death. They who are in death are in darkness.

II. The Lord is the light of men

A. Darkness needs light. Nothing else can dispel darkness. When light comes, darkness disappears.

B. Men's darkness issues from men's death. Those in death are in darkness.

C. The Lord can deliver men from sins and cause them to obtain His life. This life dispels men's darkness as well as their death. Therefore this life is the light of life. Chapter 8 of John reveals to us how the Lord can forgive sins and give both light and life to men. Only they that have life have feeling. To have feeling is to be in the light. Some committed sins without any feeling. One day they received the life and were brought into the light. Therefore this life is the light of men.

III. Follow the Lord

A. The Lord is the light of life. If we want to have the real shining, we have to follow Him.

B. The first step in following the Lord is to receive the Lord as Savior, as life, and as the light of life.

C. The second step in following the Lord is to obey Him. As soon as you receive Him, He comes right into you. Then you will start to have feeling. From this time on you must walk by obeying this inner feeling. "He who follows Me shall by no means walk in darkness, but shall have the light of life."

Subject One Hundred Fourteen

REAL FREEDOM

Scripture: John 8:32, 34, 36

Today everybody talks about freedom. Now we will see what real freedom is.

I. All they that sin are the slaves of sin

A. The slave is under bondage, having no freedom. Everyone who commits sin is the slave of sin, under the bondage of sin.

B. Today those who talk about freedom are, in fact, the slaves of sin. The high class educationalist and the intellectuals all are the slaves of sin. Playing chess, smoking, dancing, and being under the bondage of various habits are the symptoms of being the slaves of sin.

II. Real Freedom

A. The inability to escape from sin reveals the lack of freedom. The ability to escape from sin shows the real freedom.

B. Today many do not have the real freedom because of the bondage and oppression of sin. Many are aware of the bondage of sin and seek for deliverance, but are unable to achieve it. Therefore there is no freedom.

C. The real freedom means the absence of the condemnation of the conscience and deliverance from the bondage of sin.

III. The real freedom is dependent on the Lord

A. The Lord is truth. Only He can cause men to know the reality of human life. Only He can cause men to know the mystery of human life. Only He can cause men to know God, and God is the source of freedom.

B. To bear the sins of men, the Lord died and rose again from the dead. So He is able to forgive men's sins. He also can deliver men from their sins. His blood brings in the forgiveness of sin and sets men free from the condemnation of the conscience. The Lord's life enables men to escape from the bondage of sin, so there is the real freedom.

IV. How to be free

A. Whoever wants to be free has to confess that he is the slave of sin.

B. He must also receive the Lord and His salvation. In His salvation are blood and life. His blood provides for the forgiveness of men's sins, and His life enables men to be delivered from the bondage of sin.

Subject One Hundred Fifteen

THE GOOD SHEPHERD

Scripture: John 10:10-11

I. Men are the sheep of the Lord

A. Men are created by the Lord and are the Lord's.

B. Men are also watched over and shepherded by the Lord.

II. The Lord is the good shepherd

A. The Lord looks after us and shepherds us. This shows that He is a good shepherd.

B. His shepherding us not only provides us with the ordinary supply, but also with His life. Ordinary shepherds give something outside of themselves to supply the sheep. The Lord, as a shepherd, not only supplies us with something outside of Himself, but also with His life. His life is His own self, so He supplies us with His own self.

C. Since the Lord wanted us to have His life, He had to give up His life for us. He is the good shepherd who gives His life for the sheep.

III. How do we receive the Lord's shepherding?

A. We must confess that we are out from Him and of Him.

B. We must confess that we have not obtained the Lord's life, and have not had any life relationship with Him.

C. We must receive the Lord as our life.

D. We must follow the inner sense of life that the Lord gives us.

Subject One Hundred Sixteen

THE LORD IS THE DOOR OF THE SHEEP

Scripture: John 10:9

I. God's sphere

A. Everything has its own sphere. God and the blessing He bestows also have a sphere. Heaven, eternal life, and God Himself also have a sphere.

B. A sphere is for separating the outside from the inside. Whatever is inside has the portion of the sphere; whatever is outside has no part of that portion. God and whatever belongs to Him also have a sphere; this sphere separates what is outside of God from what is inside.

II. God's door

A. To enter any sphere one has to go through an entrance door. It is the same in God's sphere.

B. The entrance door of God's sphere is the Lord Jesus. In order to enter into God's sphere, men have to go through the Lord Jesus.

C. If there were no Lord Jesus in this universe, men would have no entrance to God's sphere. But thank God, He has established a door which is the Lord Jesus.

D. The Lord Jesus on one hand bore men's sins and took away the barrier of sin between God and man. On the other hand, He released His life and took away the barrier of creation between God the Creator and man the creature. The Lord's bearing of sins and shedding His blood is an entrance. The Lord's death and releasing life is another entrance. Today if men want to enter into God's sphere, they must enter through the Lord's blood and the Lord's life. The blood takes away the barrier of sin between God and man, and the life takes away the barrier of creation between God and man. When men receive the Lord, they immediately enter into all that God is.

III. The Lord is the door of the sheep

A. We belong to God. God wants us to unite with Him.

B. The Lord is the door through whom we can enter into whatever God is. So through the Lord we can enter into God's forgiveness, life, blessing, and habitation.

IV. How do we enter through the door?

A. We must confess the existence of the barriers. There is the barrier of sin, and there is the barrier between the Creator and the creature.

B. We must confess that the Lord shed His blood for us that He might be our Savior.

C. We must receive the Lord Jesus in order to have His life.

Subject One Hundred Seventeen

ETERNAL SALVATION

Scripture: John 10:28-29

I. Salvation is eternal life

A. The salvation that the Lord gives us is His eternal life. The characteristic of His life is eternal. Therefore the characteristic of His salvation is eternal and will never change.

B. To obtain salvation is to obtain something eternal. So it is eternal salvation.

II. To be saved is to be in the Lord's hand

A. The saved ones not only have the Lord's life, but also are in the Lord's hand.

B. The Lord will never change. The Lord's hand is a mighty hand which will never lose its power. So because of His power, they that are in the Lord's hand will never perish.

III. To be saved is to be in God's hand

A. To be saved is to have eternal life in us; it also means that we enter into two hands, that of the Lord and that of the Father.

B. While the Lord's hand is a mighty hand, the Father's hand is a hand of love. Because of the Lord's power and because of the Father's love, we shall never perish.

IV. The proof of not perishing

A. The fact of not perishing is based on the Lord's life as well as on both the Lord's hand and the Father's hand. One life and two hands are the fact of our not perishing.

B. The basis of our not perishing is the word of the Lord. The Lord said, "They shall by no means perish forever." This word is the basis of our not perishing. Furthermore the Lord said, "I give to them eternal life." This word is the basis of our obtaining eternal life.

Subject One Hundred Eighteen

THE LORD IS THE WAY

Scripture: John 14:6

I. The way is the method

A. To do anything we need a way. In other words, we need a method.

B. To be saved, to be forgiven, to have eternal life, and to have God, all need the way, the method.

II. The Lord is the way

A. The Lord said that He is the way; that is, He is the method.

B. Man needs a way to be saved, to be forgiven, to have eternal life and to have God. The way is a living person, the Lord Jesus Himself. Develop this in detail.

III. How can we have the Lord as the way?

A. We must confess that we ourselves have no way, no

method. Concerning the matters of sins being forgiven or of being saved or of having eternal life or of having God, men have no way, no method. They can only sigh for having no way, no entrance.

B. We must confess that the Lord is the Son of God to be our Savior, our way, our method.

C. We must receive Him as our Savior, that is, receive Him as our way and as our means.

Subject One Hundred Nineteen

THE HOLY SPIRIT CONVICTS THE WORLD

Scripture: John 16:7-11

I. The Holy Spirit came

A. God not only sent His Son to accomplish redemption for us, but also sent the Holy Spirit so that we may understand the redemption.

B. After God's Son had accomplished redemption and ascended to the heavens, God's Spirit was poured out so that men may understand God's redemption.

II. The Holy Spirit convicts the world

A. The Holy Spirit causes man to know God's redemption by means of convicting him. Speak thoroughly on this point. Describe that the Holy Spirit's working in men and causing men to know God's redemption is the work of convicting the world.

B. The Holy Spirit's convicting work is to cause man to know himself, Christ, and Satan.

III. The Holy Spirit convicts the world concerning sin

A. The first aspect of the working of the Holy Spirit is to cause man to be convicted concerning sin. This is to cause man to know that he is a sinner.

B. The Holy Spirit causes man to see that he is born in sin, brought up in sin, and living in sin; that he is a sinner in every respect, and that he is under condemnation. *Expound on these five points.*

C. The Holy Spirit causes man to see that he is a sinner in Adam and is under condemnation; He reveals that the only way to depart from sin and to obtain forgiveness is to believe in Christ. If a man does not believe in Christ, he can only remain in sin and under condemnation. The Scripture says that the Holy Spirit convicts the world in respect of sin because man does not believe in Christ.

IV. The Holy Spirit convicts the world concerning righteousness

A. The Holy Spirit's convicting man concerning righteousness is to cause man to know Christ.

B. The working of the Holy Spirit in man firstly causes man to see that he is a sinner in Adam under condemnation, and secondly causes man to see how he can be justified in Christ and become righteous. The Holy Spirit causes man to see that Christ has died for men according to God's righteousness, that Christ's death has fulfilled all of God's righteous requirements, and that God has resurrected Him so that He can be the righteousness to those who believe in Him. Whosoever believes in Christ is justified and made righteous.

V. The Holy Spirit convicts the world concerning judgment

The Holy Spirit's convicting man concerning sin is to cause man to know his condition in Adam. Man is sinful and condemned. The Holy Spirit's convicting man concerning righteousness is to cause man to know Christ. The Holy Spirit's convicting man concerning judgment is to cause man to know Satan. The Holy Spirit shows that Adam is sinful, Christ is the Redeemer, and Satan is the one judged. Man in Adam is condemned because of sin. Man in Christ obtains forgiveness of sins and is justified. However, if man follows Satan, he shall receive the judgment of sin. Since Satan is the originator of sin, he must also receive the judgment of sin. Although man in Adam followed Satan and committed sins, becoming a sinner, he can be redeemed in Christ, and be freed from the judgment of sin. But if man would not believe in Christ and would continue to remain in Adam and to follow Satan, then he can only be the companion of Satan, sharing the judgment with Satan. So the Scripture says that the Holy Spirit convicts the world concerning judgment because the ruler of this world, Satan, has been judged.

VI. The result of the Holy Spirit's convicting the world

A. Causes man to confess that he is sinful and condemned.

B. Causes man to receive Christ as the resurrected Savior, that he may be justified.

C. Causes man to reject Satan and be freed from the pending judgment.

VII. Summary

The three main points of this message are sin, righteousness, and judgment. These three things make up the history of the universe. Also in this universe there are three persons who are related to our salvation or perdition. The result of following the first person, the sinful Adam, is that man is condemned. The result of following the second person, the redeeming Christ, is that man is justified. The result of following the last person, the judged Satan, is that man is judged.

Subject One Hundred Twenty

THE BLOOD AND WATER OF THE CROSS

Scripture: John 19:34-37

I. Men's twofold need

A. Men have sins. Because of this they need the forgiveness of sins.

B. Men also are destined to die. For this reason they need the eternal life, the life of God. *Elaborate more on this point.*

II. The Lord's twofold salvation

A. Since men have sins, the first aspect of the Lord's salvation is redemption.

B. Since men are destined to die, the second aspect of the

Lord's salvation is to give men a life that will never die, an eternal life.

III. The twofold meaning of the cross

A. The Lord's salvation is by means of the cross. Without the cross there is no salvation.

B. The first aspect of the salvation of the cross is redemption, the forgiveness of men's sins. This is why the Lord shed His blood on the cross. The blood is for redemption. The blood is the price for redemption to redeem men from under the condemnation of the law. The blood speaks to men that the crucified Christ has already borne their sins before God. The shedding of the blood declares that men's sins may be forgiven.

C. The second aspect of the salvation of the cross is the releasing of the Lord's life. This is why on the cross not only blood, but also water came out from the Lord. Originally the Lord's life was in the Lord Himself; it could not enter men to be men's life. The death on the cross caused the Lord's body to be broken and through this, the life within Him flowed out. Now, men only have to receive Him to obtain His life.

IV. How to receive the twofold salvation of the blood and water

A. Confess that you are sinful as well as in death.

B. Believe that the Lord Jesus died and resurrected for you. Confess that His blood has redeemed you from your sins. Also realize that His resurrection life causes you to have God's life.

C. Receive Christ as your personal Savior.

Subject One Hundred Twenty-one

CHRIST'S RESURRECTION

Scripture: Acts 2:23-24, 32-33; 3:15; 5:30-31

I. The Lord is the Lord of life

A. Christ is God incarnated. Since the life in God is the eternal life, the life in Christ is also the eternal life.

B. Because the eternal life is in Christ, the Bible refers to Him as the Lord of life; and He is not only the Lord of life, but also the life itself.

C. Because He is the Lord of life, He cannot be held by death. Death is a tremendous power; when it comes, no one can resist it. But the power of life overcomes the power of death. Since the Lord Jesus is the Lord of life, death has no power over Him. Though He entered into death, yet He came out of death and was resurrected.

II. The Lord has fulfilled the requirement of death

A. Since men have sins, death has a requirement upon men. Sins bring in the requirement of death upon men.

B. Christ died to bear men's sins; He died to taste death for all.

C. Men's sins cause the law of God to sentence men to death. God's law says that he who commits sin must die.

D. Christ's death satisfies the requirement of the law of God. It takes away the death that was the result of the requirement of the law.

E. Since Christ has both fully tasted and taken away the death required by the law, death not only has no power over Him but also has no power over those who are redeemed. This is why He died and rose again. *In giving this message, more development is needed. Only a few main points have been presented here.*

III. The meaning of the Lord's resurrection

A. The resurrection of the Lord is the proof that His death has satisfied the requirements of the law of God. It frees men from sin and death.

B. The resurrection of the Lord causes men to have His life and causes men to be united with Him.

C. The resurrection of the Lord makes men righteous, justified, and accepted by God.

IV. Believe the resurrection of the Lord

A. To believe in the Lord is to believe that the Lord has been resurrected. To believe the resurrection of the

Lord includes the confession that the Lord died for you.

B. When one believes the Lord's resurrection, he is united with Him. By this he is justified and has life.

C. When one believes the Lord's resurrection, he receives the peace of mind and the power of life. He is reconciled to God and can live a life that is acceptable to God.

Subject One Hundred Twenty-two

WHAT SHALL WE DO?

Scripture: Acts 2:36-39

I. We should repent

A. We are those who have turned our backs toward God and who live in sins.

B. God wants us to turn to Him and be freed from sins.

C. Repentance starts with the turning of the mind until the whole being is turned to God. Repentance in Greek means a change of mind. Originally your mind is toward sins and toward the world. Now God wants you to turn to Him, to turn your mind toward Him and then to turn your whole being to Him.

D. We must confess that we have our back toward Him and must reject all our sins.

II. We should believe in Jesus Christ

A. The word "in" in the phrase "in the name of Jesus Christ" means believing.

B. To believe in Jesus Christ does not mean to agree, or to recognize, but to receive. To receive Him is to unite with Him. This word "in" has also the meaning of uniting.

C. Jesus Christ is God as the Savior. God is Spirit. As the Spirit, He is omnipresent and available to us. Because we have a spirit within, we can use our spirit to receive the Spirit of God. When we confess that we are sinners, repent and turn away from sins, our spirit is opened to receive Jesus Christ to be our Savior. His Spirit then comes into ours to unite us with Him.

III. We should be baptized

A. Believing in Christ is the inner reality, while baptism is the outward expression. With the inner reality the outward expression is still necessary. This means that in addition to the believing in Christ with the heart there is the need of the baptism.

B. What baptism shows is firstly the severing of the relationship with sins and that we are being put into God. Secondly, it shows that we are being freed from ourselves and being immersed into God.

C. Baptism is the declaration with a physical action that the former conduct and former person have altogether been concluded, have died, and have been buried. From now on there is no more former person and no more former conduct; but a uniting with Christ, a living out of Christ.

IV. The result of such doing

A. Having our sins forgiven. This includes being freed from the punishment and dominion of sins.

B. Receiving the Holy Spirit. The Holy Spirit is another form of Christ Who is the embodiment of God. Therefore, to receive the Holy Spirit is to receive Christ and to receive God. It is also to have the eternal life of God.

Subject One Hundred Twenty-three

REPENT AND BE CONVERTED

Scripture: Acts 3:19, 26

I. Men are in sin

A. Describe men living in sins.

B. Use examples to illustrate the picture of men living in sins.

II. Men have no rest

A. Sins cause men to have problems with God. Men's consciences also condemn them constantly because of sin. They often encounter God's judgment. Therefore, they often lose their peace. There is no peace either in their conscience or in their environment.

B. Sins also often cause men to have problems with one another. The discord between husband and wife, manager and clerk, classmates and colleagues are examples of men's problems with one another.

C. Sins also cause men to have problems with themselves. Sinners destroy themselves. They live a contradictory life. Their mind urges them to do good, but the lust within them compels them to do the opposite. Their mind urges them to take care of their family, fame, position, and health; but sins cause them to destroy all of these. The agony within such men is beyond description.

D. Since men have problems with God, with one another, and with themselves, they have no peace. Both in the outward environment and in the inward sensation in their conscience, they lose the normalcy, the peace; therefore, they have no rest. *When describing the absence of rest within men, elaborate on it thoroughly.*

Subject One Hundred Twenty-four

NO OTHER NAME WHEREBY WE MUST BE SAVED

Scripture: Acts 4:12

I. Only Jesus is both God and man

A. Men commit sins, and the forgiveness of sins is the exclusive authority of God.

B. In order to save men, God had to become a man. Because it was men who committed sins, God had to become a man to bear sins for men. Although as God He had the authority to forgive sins, yet He would have made Himself unrighteous had He forgiven men their sins without first becoming a man to bear those sins.

C. The Savior not only has to be a man, but He also has to be God. As a man He can bear sins for men. As God He can forgive men's sins. If the Savior were only God and not man, then He could not bear sins for men. If He were only man and not God, He could not forgive men's sins. In order that He could both bear sins for men and forgive sins, He must be both God and man.

D. Only the Lord Jesus is both God and man. Only He can bear sins for men, and at the same time forgive men's sins. Only He can be man's Savior. Therefore, besides Him, there is no other salvation.

II. Only Jesus died and rose again

A. Since men have committed sins, men have to die according to the requirements of God's righteous law. Because there is death, men cannot escape the punishment of sins.

B. Men cannot stop sinning because of the sinful nature of man. They cannot stop trespassing God's righteous law.

C. Thus the Savior had to die. Only death could take away the punishment for sins. There also had to be a life for men to receive, so that men could overcome the sinful nature.

D. Only the Lord Jesus died for men's sins to take away the punishment for sins. He rose from the dead, giving life to those who believe in Him, freeing them from their sinful nature. Therefore, only the Lord Jesus can be men's Savior. Besides Him there is no salvation.

III. There is no salvation apart from Jesus

A. All the founders of religion are merely men and not God. Regardless of how perfect, good, and kind they are, they cannot bear sins for men, much less can they deliver men from sin. (I and II are the base and III and IV are the main emphasis of the message.)

B. All founders of religion can only teach. They can only teach methods of self-denial. None of them could die for man. None of them could give life to the dead. They cannot save men from the punishment of sin, much less free men from their sinful nature.

C. Only Jesus is both God and man to be the Savior, the resurrected One from the dead. Only He could die to bear men's sins and to give life to men. He can take away the punishment of sin and free men from their sinful nature. Only He can be the Savior. Therefore, besides Him, there is no salvation. *This must be said emphatically.*

IV. How to be saved

A. Repent and confess your sins.

B. Believe in Jesus' name. The Scripture says, "For neither is there any other name under heaven, that is given among men, wherein we must be saved."

Subject One Hundred Twenty-five

REPENTANT HEART AND REDEEMING GRACE

Scripture: Acts 5:30-32

I. Men are sinners

A. Men are born in sin, raised up in sin, and living in sin.

B. Use examples to prove the sinful condition of men.

II. Jesus is the Savior

A. His crucifixion on the cross has borne the sins of men.

B. Having been raised from the dead, He has become the living Savior of men.

III. Repentant heart and redeeming grace

A. Since men have sins and the Lord Jesus has accomplished redemption, God sends the Holy Spirit to move men to repentance. This repentant heart does not come from one's self but is given by God through the Holy Spirit.

B. The repentant heart firstly includes a turning of the mind toward God. Secondly, it includes regret and sorrow for sins. Thirdly, it includes confession before God. Fourthly, it includes a forsaking of sinful deeds.

C. Redeeming grace comes by the redemption of Christ and is given to us through the Holy Spirit. When we repent, the Holy Spirit brings the peace of forgiveness of sins into our heart. This peace proves that we have received redeeming grace.

IV. **How to have a repentant heart and the redeeming grace**

A. Do not harden your heart against the moving of the Holy Spirit. Now the Holy Spirit is moving in your heart. Do not harden your heart. You should soften your heart.

B. Repent and confess your sins.

C. Receive Christ and His redemption.

Subject One Hundred Twenty-six

THE SALVATION OF THE EUNUCH

Scripture: Acts 8:26-39

I. **The eunuch was one that sought after God**

A. He was an official.

B. He was a Gentile from a great distance.

C. Though he was a high official and lived a great distance away, he was a man who sought after God. There are two proofs: (1) He came from a remote region in Africa to the temple in Jerusalem to worship God. (2) He read the Bible and was seeking for God in the Bible.

D. He came to Jerusalem to seek for God. He sought after God in the temple, but he did not meet Him. Neither did he meet God by reading the letter of the Bible. This shows that the outward effort is in vain.

II. **God allows men to find Him**

A. All man's effort in seeking after God is in vain. It is

only when God allows men to find Him that their seeking is not in vain.

B. Though man's seeking after God is in vain, man's seeking heart is precious. God does not value man's effort, but he treasures man's heart. He will fulfill every heart that is seeking for Him.

C. Although his effort of seeking after God was in vain, this official's seeking heart was fulfilled by God. When he was returning home in disappointment, having gained nothing, God allowed him to find Him. He thought that he could find God in the temple, but he never thought that he could find God in the wilderness. He thought that he could meet God in the letters of the Bible, but instead he met God through the mouth of a man without the Bible. Today many come to the chapel to seek for God and leave in disappointment. Yet on the way home they may meet a believer, and after talking with him, meet God. Many come to the letter of the Bible to find God, but cannot find Him. One day, through one of His own people, God speaks one or two words and their eyes are immediately opened to see Him.

III. The revelation of the gospel

A. The eunuch read the Bible. When he was reading in Isaiah concerning Christ, he could not understand anything because he had no revelation.

B. The revelation of the gospel is to unveil Jesus Christ to men. That day the eunuch happened to read that particular passage of the Bible unknowingly. His reading was of the Holy Spirit, because the passage touched his relationship with Christ. The Holy Spirit on the one hand moved him to read that passage while he was unoccupied, and on the other hand moved in Philip to explain it to him. After Philip had explained, his eyes were opened and he understood.

C. The revelation of the gospel is the revelation of Christ. The gospel tells men that Jesus Christ is God who came to be a man, was crucified, and shed His blood for men.

IV. How to receive the gospel

A. Believe the word of the gospel. When this official heard what Philip told him about Isaiah 53, he believed.

B. Believe in the Son of God. To believe in the Son of God is to receive a living Savior.

C. Be baptized into the Lord.

V. The result of receiving the gospel

A. Our sins are forgiven. When the eunuch believed that the Lord was the Lamb of God bearing the sins of the world, his sins were then forgiven.

B. We obtain the life of God. Since he received the Son of God, he obtained the life of God.

C. We walk on the path of rejoicing and live a happy life. He who has not met God has an unhappy life. After being saved, the eunuch's life was changed and he went on his way rejoicing.

Subject One Hundred Twenty-seven

THE SALVATION OF ONE WHO OPPOSED THE LORD

Scripture: Acts 9:1-19

I. One who served God zealously also opposed the Lord

A. Saul, a young man serving God with zeal, was an orthodox religionist. He was not only an orthodox Jew, but also an orthodox Jewish religionist. He received the orthodox teaching of Judaism. Not only was he not a Gentile, he was even a Jew who feared God.

B. Though he served God with zeal, he, in his zeal, became one who opposed God.

C. He then obtained letters authorizing him to bind those who called on the name of Jesus. On the one hand he zealously served God, on the other hand he opposed Christ.

D. The fact that he could oppose Christ at the same time he was serving God with zeal shows that there is a difference between believing in Christ and being zealous for religion. Do not think that serving God is believing in Christ. Many serve God and are zealous for religion, but they offend the Lord more than those that love the world and live in sin. You may be very zealous for religion, but your zealous activities are opposing Christ. *Elaborate fully on this point. It is important to let people see that believing in Christ is entirely different from being zealous for religion.*

II. Christ met him

A. When Saul was zealously serving God, that is, opposing Christ with zeal, unexpectedly, Christ met him.

B. He knew that there was such a man as Jesus, but he did not know that Jesus was the Christ. According to him all the preaching about Christ was false. Today there are also many who have some concept of Jesus but fail to realize that Jesus is God, Christ, and the Savior. Today these people consider as false the preaching that Jesus Christ is God.

C. During the time he thought that the preaching about Christ was false and unbelievable, he met Christ. It was obvious that he had met Christ, yet he still asked, "Who art Thou, Lord?" The Lord answered, "I am Jesus whom thou persecutest." God's salvation is not a doctrine, not mere hearsay, but a living Lord whose name is Jesus. He is God and He is Christ. Every man can turn from opposing and not believing in Christ to believing in Christ as soon as he meets Christ. Many have listened to preaching for years and yet have not met Christ. Today men can oppose many doctrines, but they cannot oppose the living Lord. One day the Lord will meet you.

III. The result of being met by the Lord

A. You will see the light. Before, this man served God with zeal, but he had no light. Once Christ meets you, then you have the light. Some have been pastors for twenty years, or have been elders for eighteen years, but they are still in darkness, without any light. Not only pastors and elders may be in this kind of condition, but also many other religionists.

B. You will fall down. You cannot get up again. You cannot go on the same way you went before. The way you acted as a pastor or an elder cannot continue. You cannot go to the movies any more. All your activities have been terminated.

C. You will become blind. The light is indeed bright, but you do not see. This is a paradox. Before, when you were a pastor or an elder, you had a way to handle everything. Now everything is unclear. Whenever your concept about things becomes unclear, you know that Christ has met you.

D. You will go into the city to wait for someone to teach you.

IV. What should be done after meeting Christ

A. Repent.

B. Believe.

C. Be baptized.

D. Serve Christ.

The above four points must be expounded according to the record of the Bible.

V. The result of this change

A. You will preach Christ and testify Christ.

B. For Christ's sake you will suffer persecution. Just as Saul persecuted others formerly, after he believed, he was then persecuted by others.

Subject One Hundred Twenty-eight

A GOOD MAN STILL NEEDS SALVATION

Scripture: Acts 10:1-5; 11:4-18; 10:34-43

I. A good man

A. Cornelius was a godly, that is, a good man.

B. Both he and his household feared God.

C. He often gave alms to the poor.

D. He prayed to God.

E. The Lord heard his prayer.

F. All the above five points prove that Cornelius was a good man. However, he was not a saved man. *Emphasize strongly that he was a godly man, but he was not saved.* Yes, he feared God, but he was not saved. He always gave alms, but he was not saved. He prayed to God, and God heard his prayer, but he was not saved.

II. Why he was not saved

A. He was a good man, but he was still a sinner. *Emphasize strongly that a good man is still a sinner.* He was a good man; he had all the preceding five good points, but it cannot be said that he had no sin. A man is not without sin just because he honors his parents, is honest, meek, merciful, and compassionate. He was a good man, but he was not yet saved.

B. He was a good man but would still die. No matter how many good points a man possesses, eventually he has to face death. A man who goes to the Sunday service, contributes regularly, and fears God will still have to die someday.

C. All his goodness, fear of the Lord, and giving of alms were of his own effort. Since he did not have the life of God, he needed to be saved.

III. The gospel of salvation

A. The gospel of salvation is not man's invention. Cornelius thought that as long as he had good behavior and was a godly man, he would be saved. This is absolutely wrong.

B. The gospel of salvation is a revelation from God. While Cornelius tried his own way to touch God, God appeared to him in a vision saying, go get Peter, he will show you the revelation of salvation. Only that kind of revelation can save you.

C. The revelation of the gospel is to show that Jesus is the Lord of all, and that He is God come as man to be our Savior.

    D. The gospel is to show people that Christ died and res-
urrected to be the Savior of mankind, to forgive sins,
and to be life for man.

IV. How can a good man be saved?

    A. A good man as well as a bad man needs to be saved.

    B. A bad man has to repent. A good man also has to
repent. A bad man may have a hundred sins to confess, and a good man may have at least ten sins to
confess. Therefore, a good man also needs to repent.

    C. Just as a bad man needs Jesus to be his Savior, so also
a good man needs Jesus to be his Savior.

Subject One Hundred Twenty-nine

EVERYONE WHO BELIEVES IN HIM
SHALL RECEIVE FORGIVENESS OF SINS

Scripture: Acts 10:43

I. All are sinners

    A. Man has sinful deeds.

    B. Man is under condemnation.

II. Jesus is the Savior

    A. Jesus is God incarnated to be the Savior of man. He
died on the cross for our sins.

    B. He resurrected from the dead and His resurrection
became the basis of our faith.

III. Believe in Jesus

    A. To believe in Jesus is to believe that He is the Son of
God.

    B. Believe that He resurrected from the dead.

    C. Believe all the words of the Scripture.

    D. In spirit receive Him as your Savior.

IV. The result of believing in the Lord

    A. Your sins are forgiven.

    B. The assurance of the forgiveness of sins is found in this
verse: "Everyone who believes in Him shall receive forgiveness of sins."

Subject One Hundred Thirty

A SAVIOR WHO FORGIVES AND JUSTIFIES

Scripture: Acts 13:38-39

I. The futility of depending upon works

A. The human disposition is corrupted. Although man would do good, his goodness has a limit. Sometimes he might be able to do a little bit of good, but even that he can never do perfectly.

B. Human works are imperfect and defiled. In fact, man has no power to do good. Even in honoring our parents, our motive within is impure.

C. Therefore, no man is justified in the presence of God by his own works.

II. The trustworthiness of Christ's forgiveness

A. The death of Christ resolves the problem of man's sins.

B. The resurrection of Christ enables man to obtain the position and life of justification.

C. Christ, by His death, has paid the ransom for man's sins, therefore He is able to forgive sins. Because of Christ's position and life in resurrection, He is able to justify man. Therefore, the Scripture says, "that through this man is proclaimed unto you remission of sins: and by Him everyone that believeth is justified from all things."

III. How to obtain Christ's forgiveness and justification

A. Confess that you are sinful, and that you have no strength to do good.

B. Confess that Christ has died and resurrected for you.

C. Receive Christ as your Savior.

Subject One Hundred Thirty-one

THE PROOF OF GOD'S EXISTENCE

Scripture: Acts 14:15-17; Psa. 19; Rom. 1:20

I. The existence of God

A. God exists in the universe.

B. God exists in human living.

C. God exists in the thoughts of man.

D. God exists in human conversation. The fact that people talk about God's existence or non-existence is a proof that God exists.

E. God exists in the dictionary. The fact that every dictionary has the word "God" is a proof that God exists.

II. The proof of God's existence

A. The creation of the universe proves that God exists.

B. The very operation of nature proves that God exists. Consider the showers from heaven, the growth of produce from the earth, and the distance between the sun and the earth that keeps a suitable climate for human living.

C. Human psychological faculties prove that God exists. For instance, within man there is the capacity for joy. Psalm 16:11 says "...in Thy presence is fullness of joy..." This verse shows that man's capacity to be filled with joy is related to God. Whatever God does in this universe is to make man full of joy. Friends, today is your joy full? If not, your lack of joy shows that you do not have God. If you are full of joy, that shows that you have received Him and proves that God exists.

III. What should you do with God?

A. Confess that you are far from Him, that you are sinful, and that you come short of His glory.

B. Repent and turn back to Him.

C. Receive the Son of God, Jesus Christ, as your Savior.

D. Through Christ enjoy and serve God in spirit.

Subject One Hundred Thirty-two

THE SALVATION OF THE JAILER

Scripture: Acts 16:19-34

I. A hard man

A. The one who was saved was a keeper of the prison, a jailer. All jailers are hard men, otherwise they would not be able to keep the prison.

B. Some jailers may be a little soft-hearted, but this one thrust Paul and Silas into the inner prison, even making their feet fast in the stocks, above that which was commanded by the officer.

C. A hard man is a hard-hearted man.

II. God's way of dealing with the hard-hearted man

A. God makes him hear the gospel. The prayers and praises offered to God by the two apostles became the gospel when they reached the ears of the jailer. He never knew anything about God; but when he heard the two apostles praying and singing, he got some realization of God. Dear friend, can you say that you have never heard the gospel before? When you heard people joyfully praying and singing to God, you heard the gospel.

B. By means of an earthquake. This hard-hearted man heard the gospel, but his heart was not touched at all. So God had to cause the earth to shake. The foundations of the prison were shaken, all the doors were opened, and every prisoner's bands were loosed. After you hear the gospel, your heart is still very hard. Eventually God has to cause your wife to get sick, your business to go bankrupt, the loss of your job, or your contracting of tuberculosis. When God shakes you in this way, you will get saved. Sometimes you will encounter a real earthquake or hurricane. When the hurricane blasts and the earth quakes then you will truly believe in God.

III. The result of God's dealing

After the shaking, the hardened heart was softened. Many are saved through this kind of shaking. The gospel of God is the Word of God and the shaking of God is the action of God; after He speaks, His action follows.

IV. How to be saved

A. After being shaken by God, the hard-hearted jailer was softened and said immediately, "Sirs, what must I do to be saved?"

B. And they said, "Believe in the Lord Jesus, and thou shalt be saved, thou and thy house."

C. Then the jailer and his whole house were baptized.

V. **The result of being saved**

A. The jailer received forgiveness of sins and obtained life.

B. Having received the Lord, the jailer and his house were filled with joy.

Subject One Hundred Thirty-three

BELIEVE IN THE LORD JESUS

Scripture: Acts 16:30-31

I. **Who is the Lord Jesus?**

A. He is the Lord who created the universe. He is also the God who is our Savior.

B. He is Jesus who is God become a man. He is the One who is God and also is a man.

C. He became man to bear our sins. And because He is God, He is also able to forgive our sins.

II. **What did the Lord Jesus do?**

A. He died and shed His blood on the cross for our sins.

B. He resurrected from the dead in order that we might have life.

C. Because of His death and resurrection He became the Savior of our whole being.

III. **What should we do with the Lord Jesus?**

A. Acknowledge that He is the Savior of all mankind.

B. Acknowledge that He is our Savior, that He died and resurrected for us.

C. Receive Him as our Savior.

IV. **The unit of the Lord's salvation**

Even though the salvation of the Lord comes to an individual, God's intention is that the entire household unit receive salvation. The salvation of the Lord comes not only to an individual, but also to the whole household.

Therefore the Word says, "Believe on the Lord Jesus, and thou shalt be saved, thou and thy house."

V. The result of salvation

A. Sins are forgiven.

B. Eternal life is obtained.

Subject One Hundred Thirty-four

AN UNKNOWN GOD

Scripture: Acts 17:22-29

I. The God who created the universe

A. The universe came into being by the creation of God.

B. This God, unknown to man, is the God who created the universe.

II. The Lord of heaven and earth

A. The universe was created by God and hence belongs to God. Therefore it says that He is the Lord of heaven and earth. The Lord means the ruler.

B. He is the Lord of the universe, and the administrator as well. We need to know God both through the creation and through the administration of the universe.

III. The source of mankind

A. This God is the creator not only of the universe, but also of mankind. The Scripture says, "...He Himself giveth to all life, and breath, and all things; and He made of one every nation of men..." This word tells us that He is the creator of mankind and also is the source of mankind.

B. Man is not only from Him, but is also taken care of and fed by Him. The human life is given by Him, and human existence is sustained by Him. Man came out of Him and depends upon Him. He is the source of all mankind. Without Him man could never have come into being, neither could there be any human living. Verse 28 says, "For in Him we live, and move and have our being...'For we are also His offspring.'"

IV. The Lord's ruling of man

A. This passage of the Scripture says that man came out of God and depends upon God. Man is ruled and controlled by God. After He created him, God put man on the earth and appointed the times and bounds of his habitation. Every man is ruled and appointed by God in time and space. Even the time and place of your birth are not decided by you; they are appointed by God. When someone decides to get married, he may choose the date. But may I ask you a question? Did you choose the time and place of your birth? Whether you are born in China or in the United States, in a wealthy family or in a poor family, none of this is up to you.

B. Since God rules over our time and space, not one thing related to us is outside of His ruling.

V. God can be found

A. Man always thinks that God is too mysterious, too far away from us, and that He cannot be found or apprehended. On the contrary, God can be found. We are able to realize something of God by the creation of this universe, the existence of all the things, and even by the existence of human life itself. Therefore the Scripture says, "For the invisible things of Him from the creation of the world, being apprehended by the things made, are clearly seen..."

B. Since we can apprehend God, then knowing God is not only a matter of outward perceiving, but also of inward reasoning. To apprehend is to think and to reason within ourselves. It involves psychological functioning. Therefore, we know God through creation outwardly and through our psychological apprehension within. When we look at nature without, we cannot help but admit the existence of God. When we turn to our heart within, we know clearly that God exists. Therefore, God can be found!

VI. What should you do with God?

A. When we think of God, naturally we would want to worship Him. This desire to worship God is in our blood. In every human race, there is such a concept. Human beings try to worship God—even though many worship the wrong god—for worshipping God is a natural instinct in man.

B. Do not worship idols as if they were God; neither worship God as if God were an idol. We are made by God, therefore we should not make God an idol. All the idols of gold, silver, wood, or stone are made by man, so how can we worship these idols?

C. Confess that you are far away from God. Repent and turn back to God.

D. Receive Jesus as your Savior.

E. Worship God in spirit after receiving the Lord.

Subject One Hundred Thirty-five

THE THREE DISPENSATIONS OF GOD'S DEALING WITH MAN

Scripture: Acts 17:30-31

I. The first period—God was overlooking

A. In the first period, God allowed man to do whatever he wanted. It seems that God did not concern Himself too much with what man did. This was God's overlooking.

B. This period was also the time of man's ignorance. Because the gospel had not yet been preached, and because man was without the light of God's revelation, he was in ignorance. Prior to the gospel age God overlooked much and let man go his own way.

II. The second period—God commands men to repent

A. During the second period, God concerns Himself with what man does. This is the period when God visits men, seeks men, and saves men. He commands all men to repent and be saved.

B. Since the beginning of the human race, the things concerning God were never preached in such a clear way until the gospel age. In this period, God gives special revelation to man. Through the gospel He gives light to men that they may know God. So there can be no excuse for men not knowing God.

C. This period is called the gospel period. During this time God's purpose is to save men, and God's work is to have the gospel preached that they may be saved. Therefore, in this period man should repent, believe, and receive God's salvation.

III. The third period—God will judge men

A. When the gospel period has passed, God will judge the whole world in the day which He has appointed.

B. The future judgment will be according to God's righteousness as well as man's deeds or works. But because by works no one is perfect, all will be condemned and the result will be eternal perdition.

C. While today God saves man through Jesus Christ, in the future God will judge man through Jesus Christ. As He is the Savior today, so shall He be the Lord of Judgment in that day.

D. If a man receives Christ today, to him Christ is a Savior. If a man does not receive Christ today, he will still have to meet Him in the future. At that time Christ will be the Lord of Judgment to him. Sooner or later all men will face the Lord. No man will be able to escape His presence. If today, under grace, you do not get involved with Him as your Savior, you will still have to get involved with Him that day. Today, He is your Savior; if not, in that day He will be your Judge. Whether He is your Savior or your Judge is not up to Him; it is up to you. You cannot avoid this decision; please make your decision now.

IV. God's saving way

A. God raised Jesus from the dead; this is God's saving way. By Jesus' death, man's sins are taken away, and by His resurrection, man may obtain eternal life. This eternal life is the very life of God.

B. Today, as we are in the gospel period, those who do not believe in Jesus' death and resurrection nor accept

His salvation will come under His judgment in that day.

C. Jesus died and was resurrected. This is a faithful saying. When you receive the Lord Jesus you are not receiving a historical figure, but a living and real Savior. How do you know that Jesus died for sinners? Because Jesus was resurrected! Jesus is not a dead historical figure, but a living and real Savior. He works miracles, brings men from darkness into light, makes the weak strong, turns the hearts of men, and hearkens to the prayers of men. All these prove that Jesus is a living Savior.

D. Men receive God's salvation by believing. Believe that the Lord Jesus has died and resurrected to save you from sin and from judgment.

E. To believe you must first repent. In the gospel period, God specifically wants men to repent. Repent and believe, and you will be saved, and will not be judged in that day.

Subject One Hundred Thirty-six

THE BLESSINGS OF THE GOSPEL

Scripture: Acts 26:18

I. Eyes are opened

A. Man is born blind. He does not know God, life, or even himself.

B. When man hears the gospel and believes in Jesus, his eyes are opened by the Holy Spirit. He then is able to know God, life, himself, and the Savior.

II. Men are turned from darkness to light

A. Man is born in darkness. This is evidenced by two facts.

1. Man cannot see God; he can neither know nor understand the things of God.

2. Man has no joy; this is because there is misery in darkness.

B. Though we are born in darkness, when we believe the gospel and receive the life of Christ, we are turned to light. The gospel of God is light, because God is light and the life of Christ is also light. When we have the light within, we are able to see clearly and we have joy.

III. Men are turned from the power of Satan unto God

A. Man is born under the power of Satan and is controlled and enslaved by Satan. For example:

1. A man commits sins not merely by himself. Many people do not want to do evil, but they cannot help themselves. Some even commit crimes. This is because man is under the control of Satan. Please tell me, who wants to do evil? Man does evil which he does not want to do. This proves that man is under Satan's control.

2. Because man is under the power of Satan, he cannot refuse death. He cannot be free from sin, neither can he be free from death.

B. When a man hears the gospel and receives Christ, he is freed from the power of Satan. Through His death on the cross Christ destroyed the one who had the power of death, the Devil. When one turns to Christ, he is delivered from the power of Satan unto God and is freed from sin and death.

IV. Forgiveness of sins is received through faith

A. Man is of the world from his birth; he is common and unholy. He has nothing to do with God and is unable to partake of the riches of God's inheritance.

B. When he receives Christ, he is separated from the world and is sanctified unto God. Now he is the partaker of God's divine nature as well as God's inheritance.

C. The inheritance of God includes present and eternal blessings. In order that we may actually obtain this inheritance, God has granted us both the life and the foretaste of this inheritance. The life is the life of God, and the foretaste is the Holy Spirit. These qualify us to enjoy and obtain this inheritance.

V. How to obtain the blessings of the gospel

A. Repent and believe.

B. Receive Jesus as your Savior.

Subject One Hundred Thirty-seven

THE POWER OF THE GOSPEL

Scripture: Rom. 1:16-17

I. The gospel is the power of God

A. The gospel is not only a blessed message, but it is also the power of God.

B. Since the source of the gospel is God, therefore it is the power of God. The power of the gospel is equal to the power of God.

C. Give practical examples to prove that the gospel is powerful in saving all kinds of people. The entire life and living of a great sinner is changed after he believes in the gospel. There has never been any teaching as powerful as the power of the gospel.

II. The power of the gospel is based on God's righteousness

A. This portion of the Scripture shows us that the gospel is powerful because God's righteousness is in the gospel. Any religious method demands that man cultivates a moral conduct, that is, establish his own righteousness. There is no need to explain what righteousness is. Do not say that righteousness means lawfulness; people understand that it refers to man's works. Only the gospel of God is based on God's righteousness. Man's righteousness is imperfect and weak, but God's righteousness is perfect and powerful. Man's righteousness is changeable, but God's righteousness never changes. The religious method is based on man's righteousness, and teaches that a man can be saved only if he can do good. But the fact is that no one can do good. God's saving way is that through His righteousness God has accomplished the work of salvation for us.

B. We are all sinners before God. According to God's right-eousness, we all should be sentenced to death. But God sent the Lord Jesus to die for our sins. Thus the death of the Lord Jesus fulfilled the righteous requirement of God.

C. Because the death of the Lord Jesus has fulfilled God's righteous requirement, today God's righteous-ness demands that He must forgive and justify those who believe in Jesus. Thus God's righteousness, through the death of Christ, saves all those who receive the Lord Jesus. Because it is unchanging and powerful, God's righteousness makes the gospel pow-erful.

III. The power of the gospel is based on God's life

A. The gospel of God not only contains God's righteous-ness but also God's life. Romans 1:17 says that the gospel gives life to those who believe, and this life is the life of God.

B. God's saving way is that man may be forgiven of his sins and delivered from perdition on the negative side, and that man may be one with God on the positive side. The negative side is accomplished by God's right-eousness; the positive side is accomplished by God's life.

C. The gospel of God causes man to obtain righteousness as well as God's life. To obtain God's righteousness is to be justified; to obtain God's life is to be regenerated.

IV. How to receive the power of this gospel

A. Confess that you have no righteousness, only sin; that you have no life, only death.

B. Believe that the Lord Jesus died and was resurrected. The death of Jesus takes away our sins, fulfills God's righteousness, and gives us His righteousness. The resurrection of the Lord abolished death and gives us the life of God.

C. This gospel is out of faith unto faith. The Scripture says that the just shall have life and live by faith.

Thus you must believe in Christ and in the word of the gospel. By believing, you will receive the power of the gospel of God, the righteousness of God, and the life of God.

Subject One Hundred Thirty-eight

GOD MAY BE KNOWN

Scripture: Rom. 1:19-20

I. God has manifested Himself among men and in everything related to man

A. The fact that there are parents proves that there is a God. Everyone was born with a certain set of parents. You should ask the question, "Where did my parents come from?" Continue with this question and you will have to trace it to God.

B. The structure of your body is wonderful and complete, both physically and psychologically. You should ask how this came about.

C. Many things which you encounter make you feel that they cannot be mere coincidences. You cannot help but believe that there must be the arrangement of God in it. These coincidences are the manifestation of God.

D. Just study the universe a little, and you cannot help but acknowledge that God exists. Consider the laws of nature, the revolution of the planets, and the changing of the seasons. Who is the One that arranges and rules all of these? You cannot help but confess that there is a God.

II. Creation manifests the existence of God

A. The Scripture says, "For the invisible things of Him from the creation of the world, being apprehended by the things made, are clearly seen, both His eternal power and divine nature." It shows that the existence of the universe is the manifestation of God.

B. Here the Scripture says that the creation and existence of the universe especially manifest God's eternal power and His divine nature. *Emphasize that God's power and nature manifest God Himself.*

1. God's eternal power makes Him known. The earth is rotating in space, and man living on this earth is pulled by gravity. Both are a matter of power. Where does the power come from? This wonderful power is the manifestation of God.

2. God's divine nature makes Him known. Many good things in this universe such as light, kindness, and mercy, all symbolize God's divine nature.

III. God is clearly seen

A. All the foregoing examples show that God is clearly seen. Facts speak louder than arguments. All of creation is a strong proof of God's existence. How can a sensible person deny the existence of God if he is fair and honest within?

B. If you still insist on saying that there is no God, then you are the fool mentioned in Psalm 14, which says, "The fool hath said in his heart, there is no God." Only a fool would say that there is no God, because God is so clearly seen.

IV. What should you do with God?

A. Appreciate that God's existence may be realized through His creation.

B. Repent and turn to God.

C. Believe that the Son of God is your Savior.

D. Worship God in spirit.

Subject One Hundred Thirty-nine

THE UNGODLINESS AND UNRIGHTEOUSNESS OF MEN

Scripture: Rom. 1:18-32

I. The ungodliness of men

A. Man's first relationship is the relationship between man and God. Chinese people talk about five ethical principles. Actually, on top of these five there should be one more principle, namely, the principle of the relationship between man and God. The first of these five principles is the principle for the relationship between man and his parents. In fact, the relationship between man and God is much higher than that between man and his parents. No doubt man is born of his parents, but he was born because God firstly created mankind. God is the source of our being; therefore man should worship and serve God. If man's relationship with God is normal, man will have the virtue of godliness. The word godliness is not used here to describe the relationship among men, but rather the relationship between man and God.

B. Man should keep a normal relationship with God, but such was never established. Instead, men turn away from God and worship idols; consequently men become ungodly. There are some who do not worship idols, yet they deny the existence of God. They, too, are ungodly.

II. The unrighteousness of men

A. Human beings not only have a relationship with God, but also a relationship with men. The five ethical principles are concerning the relationship between men. The abnormal relationship among men is called unrighteousness. A man is unrighteous if he does not honor his parents, and if he is without respectfulness, loyalty, faithfulness, courtesy, righteousness, purity, or a sense of shame.

B. Mention all the unrighteousness in Romans item by item; there are altogether twenty-nine items. Some of these refer to the sinful deeds, and others refer to the sinful people. Read these items beginning with verse 18. Sometimes the working of the Holy Spirit can really touch people's feeling. Do not read through all at once. Pause and ask the audience how they feel after reading each paragraph.

III. The relationship between ungodliness and unrighteousness

A. Ungodliness is toward God; unrighteousness is toward men. Man is ungodly toward God first and then

unrighteous toward men. All unrighteousness comes
from ungodliness.

B. Therefore, if man does not worship God, he definitely
will be a source of trouble to his fellow man. Luke
chapter 18 describes a man who does not fear God nor
respect men. If man's relationship with God is not
right, his relationship with men is definitely wrong.
Atheists definitely are immoral. Homes without God
are definitely dark homes. If man is improper toward
men, it is because he is improper toward God.

IV. The result of ungodliness and unrighteousness

A. Ungodliness and unrighteousness cause man to damage himself. If a man worships lower animals, he is
destroying himself. There is no unrighteous man who
does not destroy himself. The result of unrighteousness is destroying one's reputation, family, status, and
position.

B. Ungodliness and unrighteousness not only bring self-
destruction, they also bring the wrath of God. Sometimes man meets the small anger of God, such as car
accidents, sickness, or bankruptcy, etc. In the future
he will meet the great wrath of God which is eternal
perdition.

V. How to depart from ungodliness and unrighteous-ness

A. Repent and confess that you are ungodly and unrighteous.

B. Change your mind and turn to God.

C. Receive Christ as your Savior.

D. Be one who serves God.

Subject One Hundred Forty

THERE IS NONE RIGHTEOUS

Scripture: Rom. 3:9-20

I. All are under sin

A. Man is born in sin.

    B. Man grows up in sin.

    C. Man lives in sin.

    D. Man wallows in sin.

    E. All men are under sin.

II. There is none righteous

    A. A righteous man is just and faultless before God.

    B. Using "just and faultless" as a yardstick to measure a man, we find that there is none righteous, because man is not normal toward God and is not just toward man.

III. There is none that does good

    A. "Righteousness" is up to the standard of justice, but "good" is exceeding the standard of justice. Whenever you do something more than what you ought to do, you are doing something that is good. For example, you hired a servant and promised to pay him $600 monthly. If you pay him only $580, you have done something unrighteous. If you give him $650, you have done something good.

    B. But even if you do something good, there is none that can do good out of a pure heart. Most good works contain side effects which expose that the heart is not pure. Consequently, there is none that does good, not even one.

IV. The conditions of man

    A. There is none that understands. All are confused and foolish, not knowing how to behave themselves before God and before men.

    B. There is none that seeks God who is the source of righteousness, the origin of all good. There is none that seeks Him; therefore there is none righteous and none that does good.

    C. All have turned aside.

    D. All have together become useless.

    E. Their throat is an open grave. Everything that comes out of men is stinking and dead.

F. Their tongues work deceit.

G. The poison of asps is under their lips.

H. Their mouths are full of cursing and bitterness.

I. Their feet are swift to shed blood.

J. Ruin and misery are in their ways.

K. They know not the way of peace.

L. There is no fear of God before their eyes.

After talking about these twelve points of man's condition, all will have to bow down their heads and confess that there is none righteous, none that does good, not even one.

V. The world is under the condemnation of God

A. Man has sins, and God has the law. The sins of man conflict with the law of God.

B. According to His law, God has to condemn man.

C. Since all have sinned, all are under God's condemnation.

VI. How can a man become righteous?

A. Confess that you are not righteous, neither can you become righteous. In other words, admit that you have no righteousness, and that you can do nothing that is righteous.

B. Believe in the Lord Jesus, and receive Him as your righteousness.

C. Receive the Lord Jesus as your living Savior. He makes you righteous and causes you to live out His righteousness.

Subject One Hundred Forty-one

ALL HAVE SINNED

Scripture: Rom. 3:23

I. The source of man's sin

A. Sin came from Satan.

B. Sin came into the world through Adam.

C. Man is born in sin. Because man is the seed of Adam, man is sinful since his very birth.

II. Man's sinful life

A. Man is born in sin, therefore man lives in sin.

B. If man lives in sin, all his living is sinful, whether consciously or unconsciously, intentionally or unintentionally.

C. Give practical examples of how man commits sins.

III. Man comes short of the glory of God

A. The glory of God is the standard of human morality. The glory of God is the manifestation of the character and the disposition of God. This glory should be the standard for man's living and man's morality. Whether a man is sinful or not should not be judged according to man's moral standards, but according to God's glory. Some deeds are not sinful according to human moral standards, but they are quite short according to God's glory. For example, God's divine disposition is manifested when He forgives man's sins. But man thinks to himself, "As long as I do not offend others, it is not a sin for me not to forgive them when they offend me." How short is this lack of forgiveness when compared to the glory of God.

B. According to this divine standard, we realize that there is no comparison between man's moral standard and God's divine disposition and character. Not only to hate people is sin, but also not to love people is sin.

C. Man is made according to God's image. Man is the picture of God to express God. But now, because sin came in through Adam, man is full of sins and filthiness; so certainly man comes short of the glory of God.

IV. The way to salvation

A. Confess that you are short of the glory of God.

B. Christ is the effulgence of the glory of God. Receive Christ as your Savior, and He will enable you to live out the glory of God.

C. Live in the presence of God by the life of Christ.

Subject One Hundred Forty-two

GRACE, REDEMPTION, AND JUSTIFICATION

Scripture: Rom. 3:24

I. Grace

A. Grace is the expression and manifestation of God's love.

B. Grace is something freely given of God or done by God.

C. God freely saves and justifies us; He did something for us and gave us something freely.

II. Redemption

A. Redemption is necessitated by God's righteousness. God's righteousness requires that He accomplish redemption for us.

B. God's redemption is accomplished by the crucifixion of Jesus Christ.

C. The death of Christ on the cross satisfies the requirement of God's righteousness so that God's grace can come to us freely.

III. Justification

A. Justification is the grace of God to save us according to the righteousness of God. Therefore, justification is both grace bestowed upon us and God's righteousness accomplished for us.

B. It is God's love that causes Him to have grace upon us, and God's righteousness which causes Him to accomplish redemption for us.

C. Therefore, because of justification, God can reckon us righteous and is able to save us.

Subject One Hundred Forty-three

THE PROPITIATION-COVER OF GOD

Scripture: Rom. 3:25-26

The propitiatory sacrifice is the propitiation-cover in the original language.

I. God set forth a propitiation-cover through Jesus

A. In the Old Testament the Holy of Holies in the tabernacle is the meeting place for God and man. In the Holy of Holies there is an ark which contains the tablets of the ten commandments. The ten commandments express the righteous requirement of God. This means that if a man wants to be in the presence of God, he has to fulfill all these ten commandments. But the real condition of man is that rather than keeping the ten commandments, he breaks them. Therefore, according to the ten commandments, God has to condemn man.

B. However, God is also full of compassion. His love causes Him to be gracious to man. Here we see that God's love is conflicting with God's righteousness. In order to fulfill both His righteousness and His love, God sent Jesus to be our propitiation-cover.

C. Jesus Christ was given to us by God's love and grace, but the shedding of Jesus' blood for the forgiveness of our sins is according to God's righteousness. Because His blood satisfies the righteous requirement of God, enabling God's love to come upon us, Jesus becomes the propitiation-cover of God.

D. In the Old Testament, the propitiation-cover is on the top of the ark, completely covering the law inside the ark. This signifies that Jesus Christ and His redemption completely satisfy the righteous requirement of God. Thus, God can no longer put the demands of the law upon man.

II. By the blood of Jesus

A. In the Old Testament, the blood was sprinkled upon the propitiation-cover for the people of Israel. Every year on the Day of Atonement the high priest had to bring the blood of atonement into the holiest of all and sprinkle it upon the propitiation-cover. Then, upon the propitiation-cover, God manifested Himself to meet with man. There man also was able to meet God and obtain grace from God. Under the propitiation-cover there was the righteous law of God, while upon the

cover there was the blood of atonement. The righteous
law was putting demands upon man, but because of
the blood on the propitiation-cover the demand of the
law was satisfied.

B. Likewise, in the New Testament, the blood of Jesus
Christ satisfies the righteous requirement of the law
of God. With the blood of Jesus Christ, God's righteous
law can no longer put any claim upon us. Thus, the
blood of Jesus Christ opens a way for God to grant us
His grace without causing God to be unrighteous.
Therefore it was through this blood that God established the Lord Jesus as the propitiation-cover.

III. By the faith of man

A. The righteousness of God has already accomplished
everything for us so that we might obtain God's salvation. However, we must receive this salvation by faith.
To receive is to open our heart to believe in Christ and
His redemption.

B. To believe is not only to agree or to confess, but also to
receive in the spirit.

IV. To manifest the righteousness of God

A. By our faith, and through Christ, God not only gave us
grace, but also manifested His righteousness. Every
believer who obtains redemption through faith in Christ
has both the grace and the righteousness of God. Because Christ has accomplished redemption, His blood
has satisfied the righteous requirement of God. Thus
today if we believe in Christ and His redemption, God
has to forgive us and justify us for His righteousness'
sake. If God would not forgive or justify us, He would be
ungracious and unrighteous. So today God's forgiving us
and justifying us by faith manifests not only His grace
but also His righteousness.

Subject One Hundred Forty-four
JUSTIFIED BY FAITH

Scripture: Rom. 3:22a, 28, 30; 5:1

I. The works of man fail

A. The requirement of God's law is perfect.

B. In contrast, the works of man are imperfect and defiled.

C. Therefore no one can be justified according to his own works.

II. The redemption of Christ is sure

A. The redemption of Christ is entirely according to the requirement of the law.

B. Christ's redemption also satisfies the requirement of the law.

C. Thus the redemption of Christ enables man to be justified by God.

III. Justified through faith

A. Since the works of law are not dependable, but the redemption of Christ is so dependable and sure, justification must not depend upon man's works, but upon the redemption of Christ.

B. In order for man to depend on the redemption of Christ he must believe in Christ and His redemption; in other words, he must receive Christ and His redemption.

Subject One Hundred Forty-five

REWARD AND GRACE

Scripture: Rom. 4:4-5; 6:23a

I. Wages are justly received

A. Wages are earned through working.

B. Wages are a payment according to righteousness, according to the work a person renders.

II. Grace is freely received

A. Grace does not require working.

B. Grace is freely bestowed, and not earned.

III. Man's sin earns him the wages of condemnation and death

A. In the eyes of God, all of man's behavior is sin, and

this behavior is man's work. Man does no other work but to sin. Therefore, before God we have done only the work of sin.

B. Man's work of sin earns the wages of death. Thus, the Bible says, "The wages of sin is death."

IV. **God's grace is freely bestowed through the righteousness of Christ**

A. Through the righteousness of Christ, grace came to us. The redemption of Christ has already fulfilled the righteous requirement of God, thus enabling God to bestow grace upon us.

B. Grace is bestowed upon us through the redemption of Christ. This is possible because His redemption reckons us righteous.

Subject One Hundred Forty-six

THE BLESSEDNESS OF FORGIVENESS AND JUSTIFICATION

Scripture: Rom. 4:7-8

I. **The blessing of having sins forgiven**

A. Unforgiven sin issues in condemnation which leads to perishing; thus this condemnation is a suffering.

B. With the forgiveness of sin man avoids destruction; thus this forgiveness is a great blessing.

II. **The blessing of being reckoned righteous**

A. On the negative side, the blessing of forgiveness of sin is the saving of man from destruction. On the positive side, the blessing of being reckoned righteous is the acceptance of man by God.

B. Forgiveness of sin is to be forgiven after you have sinned. To be reckoned righteous is to have God see you without sin as though you have never sinned. So Romans 4:8 says, "Blessed is the man to whom the Lord shall by no means reckon sin."

III. **How to obtain the blessing of being forgiven of sin and being reckoned righteous**

Develop this point.

Subject One Hundred Forty-seven

THE CRUCIFIXION AND
RESURRECTION OF CHRIST

Scripture: Rom. 4:25

I. Crucifixion

A. The crucifixion of Jesus is not a sacrifice or a martyrdom, although it is commonly considered to be so.

B. The crucifixion of Jesus was to redeem sinners and
bear the sins of men. In this passage, it says that
Jesus was delivered for our offenses and raised for our
justification. His being delivered refers to His going to
the cross.

II. Resurrection

A. On the negative side, the crucifixion of Jesus took
away our sins; on the positive side, the resurrection of
Jesus justified us.

B. Through this resurrection we not only receive a righteous position, but also a righteous life—the life of God
in Jesus Christ. This life enables us to live out a kind
of righteous life that exactly matches our righteous
position.

III. How to partake of the crucifixion and resurrection of Jesus

Develop this point.

Subject One Hundred Forty-eight

FOR WHOM DID CHRIST DIE?

Scripture: Rom. 5:6-8

I. Christ did not die for the righteous man

A. The righteous man is one who is just and faultless
toward God and man; he is one who has completely
fulfilled his duty.

B. There are very few people, if any, who would die for this kind of man.

C. But Christ did not die for the righteous, because actually there are not any righteous men in the entire universe.

II. Christ did not die for the good man

A. The good man is a moral person, even surpassing the righteous man. What the good man does goes beyond his human duty; he is not only just and faultless, but kind as well.

B. There might be a few who would be willing to die for the good man.

C. But neither did Christ die for the good man, because strictly speaking, there are not any good men on the earth.

III. Christ died for the sinner

A. A sinner is not a good man or a righteous person.

B. Christ died for such sinners who are neither good nor righteous persons.

C. Whoever considers himself a good and righteous man is not one who is saved by Jesus' death; thus he cannot obtain the salvation of the Lord Jesus.

D. Jesus died for the sinners, thus manifesting God's love.

IV. How to participate in the death of Jesus

Develop this point.

Subject One Hundred Forty-nine

RECONCILED TO GOD

Scripture: Rom. 5:1, 9-11

I. Man's conflict with God

A. Since the time Adam sinned, man has had conflict and discord with God.

B. We have had conflict with God from the time of our birth.

C. We are in conflict with God in all our daily living and walk.

II. Man as God's enemy

A. We have not only received from Adam a life that has conflict with God, but also in this life we have Satan's nature and are enemies to God.

B. From the time of our birth, we are against God and are God's enemies.

C. Our human living is against God.

III. Reconciled to God

A. God sent the Lord Jesus to take away our sins through the redemptive work of the cross, thus resolving the conflict between God and us.

B. God sent the Holy Spirit to move us and to cause us to repent and turn to Him.

C. Once we believe in the Lord Jesus, our sins are forgiven and we are justified, accepted, and reconciled to God.

IV. How to be reconciled to God

Develop this point.

Subject One Hundred Fifty

THE ENTRANCE OF SIN

Scripture: Rom. 5:12

I. The origin of sin

A. The originator of sin is Satan.

B. Satan originated sin when he rebelled against God.

II. The entrance of sin

A. Sin entered into the human race through Adam. We can use hereditary disease to illustrate the entrance of sin. For example, the germs of venereal disease are passed down from parents to children. Likewise, sin was passed down from one man, Adam, and entered into the descendants of Adam.

B. All humanity inherited sin; therefore, not one man is without sin.

III. The result of the entrance of sin

A. The fruit of sin is death.

B. Death passed to all men because all have sinned.

IV. How to escape sin

Point out the ways of escaping the punishment of sin and the power of sin.

Subject One Hundred Fifty-one

CONDEMNATION AND DEATH BY ONE MAN, JUSTIFICATION AND LIFE BY ONE MAN

Scripture: Rom. 5:15-19

I. There are only two men in the universe

A. According to God, there are only two men in the universe: Adam and Christ. All men are in one of these two persons; either they are in Adam or in Christ.

B. Whoever is born of Adam is considered by God to be in Adam and to be Adam, because he is born of Adam. For example, if a watermelon is cut into twenty slices, every slice is watermelon. And if a bottle of wine is poured into twenty cups, every cup is a cup of wine.

II. Adam was condemned to die because he sinned

A. Adam sinned, and so all his descendants sinned. Because he sinned, we in Adam have also sinned. For example, if the forefathers are captives, when the grandsons are born, they are automatically captives.

B. The condemnation of Adam is the condemnation of his descendants.

C. Because Adam should die, his descendants also should die.

D. Because of the one man Adam, we all became sinners condemned to die.

III. Through Christ's righteous act we are justified to receive life

A. When Christ died on the cross we also died with Him;

because of this righteous act we were delivered from God's condemnation.

B. The death of Christ not only delivered us from God's condemnation, but also, on the positive side, justified us before God. This is proven by the resurrection of Christ. The resurrection of Christ proves that God accepted Him and His works. God's acceptance of Him is His acceptance of us, because we are all in Christ.

C. Through the resurrection of Christ we receive His life. Through His resurrection from the dead He was accepted by God; we, in the same manner, are accepted by God and justified to receive the life of God.

IV. **How to be transferred from being in Adam to being in Christ**

A. Confess that you are born in Adam.

B. Confess that you deserve death and are condemned to die.

C. Receive Christ as the life-giving Savior.

D. Believe the fact that you are in Christ the moment you receive Him.

Subject One Hundred Fifty-two

WHERE SIN ABOUNDED GRACE HAS MORE ABOUNDED

Scripture: Rom. 5:20

I. **Sin abounded**

A. Man is sinful and commits sins.

B. Man's sin is abounding.

C. Give a real example to prove how man's sin has abounded. The older a man is, the easier it is for him to sin.

II. **Grace abounded**

A. God not only has grace, but He has abundant grace.

B. The more our sin abounds, the more God's grace abounds.

C. All of man's abundant sin needs to be resolved by God's abundant grace.

III. How to receive grace and escape sin

A. Although sin caused grace to abound, we should not continue to be in sin that grace may abound.

B. We have to confess that we have sinned and should be punished for our sin, and that we need grace to save us. We should confess that we are bound by the power of sin and need grace to deliver us.

C. We need to receive Jesus Christ and His salvation.

Subject One Hundred Fifty-three
SIN REIGNED

Scripture: Rom. 5:21

I. The meaning of sin

A. Sin is not only a behavior but also a life. Sin is not a dead thing but a living being with a personality.

B. Sin itself is the life of the Devil, Satan. The behavior of sin is the multitude of wicked things.

II. The power of sin

A. The behavior of sin causes man to suffer punishment of sin, and sin itself is a kind of power dwelling in man.

B. The power of sin dominates man and puts man under the slavery of sin; thus sin can reign in man.

III. The result of the reigning of sin

A. It causes man to sin and do evil against his will.

B. It causes man to die. Once man sins and does evil, he has to die.

IV. How to escape sin

Develop this point.

Subject One Hundred Fifty-four
GRACE REIGNS THROUGH RIGHTEOUSNESS

Scripture: Rom. 5:17, 21

I. The meaning of grace

A. Grace is not only the way God treats man or something God gives man, but grace is a living person with a personality.

B. Apparently, grace is God's doing and something given by God; in reality, grace is just God Himself and God's life.

II. The power of grace

A. Grace not only causes man to receive God's forgiveness, justification, and acceptance, but grace is also a source of power in man.

B. Because grace is God and the life of God, the power of grace is the power of God.

III. Grace reigns through righteousness

A. Although God wants to give grace to man, because there is sin in man, the righteousness of God has to come and judge man's sins. Consequently, the grace of God cannot be bestowed upon him. God—on the other hand—according to His righteousness, sent the Lord Jesus to accomplish redemption for man, and so fulfilled the requirements of His righteousness. Hence, God is able to bestow His grace upon man because of His righteousness, according to His righteousness, and through His righteousness.

B. Today God gives grace to men. In doing so, not only is God not involved in unrighteousness, but even the more, in this is His righteousness manifested. So today, through this righteousness of God, His grace can exert its power upon man. This is grace reigning through righteousness.

IV. The result of the reigning of grace

A. Grace not only enables man to be forgiven and delivered from sin, but also gives man eternal life.

B. Grace not only gives life to man, but also causes man to reign in life. Here there are two reignings. On the one hand, grace reigns that we might receive life; on the other hand, having received life, we can reign in this life.

V. How to get grace

Develop this point.

Subject One Hundred Fifty-five

THE WAGES OF SIN AND THE GIFT OF GOD

Scripture: Rom. 6:23

I. The wages of sin

A. To sin is an occupation; man's entire life is given to the occupation of sin.

B. All occupations demand wages; not a single job is done without earnings. Since wages are rightfully due, a man who works sin should also receive the wages of sin.

C. The wages of sin is death.

D. Illustrate how man sins and thus obtains death. For example, some people gamble daily; consequently, this daily toll of sin causes them to die earlier. There are even those who have died on the gambling table.

E. This kind of death which is the wages of sin means not only the death of this life, the physical body, but even more an eternal death, the death of the soul.

II. The gift of God

A. A gift is a present; God's gift is God's present.

B. A present is freely given and freely received. Since the gift of God is a present, it requires no work in return; it is not wages but a present.

C. The free gift of God is His very life. So, in Romans 6:23 it says, the "gift of God is eternal life in Christ Jesus our Lord."

D. This gift of eternal life from God was given to us in Christ Jesus. God put His life in Christ Jesus to be given to us. So, our receiving the Lord Jesus is to receive the gift that is in Him.

E. Not only does this gift of life enable us today to live before God and to please Him, it also enables us in the future to be in God's presence, enjoying the eternal and heavenly blessings.

III. How to be delivered from the wages of sin and obtain the gift of God

A. Confess that you are sinful and therefore destined to receive sin's wages, death.

B. Believe into Jesus Christ to be your living Savior. God's life is within Him; if you want to receive the life of God, you must receive Him. To illustrate, just as tea is contained within a tea cup, if you want to receive the tea, you must receive the tea cup.

Subject One Hundred Fifty-six

INSEPARABLE LOVE

Scripture: Rom. 8:35-39

I. Love is essential to human living

A. Man as an emotional being needs love, and depends upon love.

B. Without love, human living is desolate; with love, life is wonderful.

II. Love meets man's need for warmth

A. Human emotion needs warmth; only love has this warmth.

B. With love, life is warm; without love, life is forlorn.

C. Love generates the warmest feelings in man.

III. The love of man

A. Man's love is limited and lacking; therefore, it cannot satisfy the need of his emotion. Give some practical illustrations.

B. Man's love will change and cease; therefore, it is not dependable. Illustrate this point also.

IV. The love of God

A. Because God's love is unlimited and complete, it can satisfy man's emotions.

B. God's love is unchanging, unceasing, and dependable. Describe this through illustrations.

C. Since God's love is unchanging and unceasing, it is an inseparable love. No tribulation will cause His love to change or cease.

V. How to partake of God's love

A. God's love is given to us in Christ Jesus.

B. God's love is manifested through the death of Christ.

C. We must believe in Christ and His redemption in order to partake of God's love.

Subject One Hundred Fifty-seven

BELIEVE IN THE HEART AND CONFESS WITH THE MOUTH

Scripture: Rom. 10:6-10

I. Christ has died and resurrected

A. Christ is the very Savior God prepared for man.

B. Since He has descended from heaven, there is no need for us to ascend to bring Him down. Here it says, "Who will ascend into heaven? That is, to bring Christ down."

C. Since Christ has already died and resurrected, there is no need for man to cause Him to die again.

D. Thus, because Christ has already come to accomplish redemption for us, there is no need for us to ask Him to work redemption again.

II. The Holy Spirit has come and is inspiring you now

A. Christ died and resurrected, accomplished redemption and ascended into heaven. Now the Holy Spirit is sent to inspire man so that he can believe in Christ and His resurrection.

B. The Holy Spirit is inspiring you right now; He is putting the word of Christ's redemption into you.

C. This word of salvation is near you, even in your mouth

and in your heart. Once you open your mouth and exercise your heart, you will receive it.

III. Believe in your heart and confess with your mouth

A. Christ's redemption has been accomplished, and the Holy Spirit has sent this redemption into your heart and your mouth.

B. Now, if you open your heart and your mouth just a little, you will be saved.

C. The heart is for believing and the mouth is for confessing. Believe that Christ died and was resurrected, and confess with your mouth the Lord Jesus.

D. Once you believe, you are justified; once you confess, you are saved. Justification means to be accepted before God and salvation means to be separated before man. Before God we are accepted by God, and before man we have separation.

Subject One Hundred Fifty-eight

WHOSOEVER CALLS UPON THE NAME OF THE LORD SHALL BE SAVED

Scripture: Rom. 10:13-14

I. The Lord is the Savior

A. The Lord is Jesus, the very Son of God who came as a man to redeem us.

B. By His death and resurrection, He accomplished this redemption and became our Savior.

II. Call upon the name of the Lord

A. According to our thought, because we have neither seen Him nor touched Him it is difficult to call on the Lord's name.

B. In reality it is easy. We do not need to see or touch Him; once we have heard of His name, we can just call.

C. To call on the name of the Lord is just to call on the Lord Himself.

D. To call on the name of the Lord is also to believe in the

Lord. Romans 10:14 says, "How then shall they call upon Him in Whom they have not believed?" Therefore, calling includes believing.

    E. Believing includes repentance. "Repentance" means to turn our minds to God, confessing our sins.

III. Whosoever calls shall be saved

    A. To call is to believe; therefore, calling results in immediate salvation.

    B. When we call upon the Lord, the Holy Spirit brings God and His salvation to us. This proves that once we call, we are saved.

    C. The fact of our receiving this salvation is not based upon our feeling. If it seems that you have not received after calling, this is simply your feeling. In reality you have received because the Word says, "Whosoever calls upon the name of the Lord shall be saved."

IV. The meaning of being saved

    A. To be saved means to receive forgiveness of sins.

    B. To be saved also means to receive the life of God.

Subject One Hundred Fifty-nine

THE WORD OF THE CROSS

Scripture: 1 Cor. 1:18-21

I. The meaning of the cross

    A. The cross is both the instrument by which the Lord Jesus died and the place where He died.

    B. By His death on the cross the Lord Jesus bore the sins of mankind and saved man from destruction.

    C. Therefore, the cross is able to deliver man from sin and destruction.

II. The word of the cross

    A. The word of the cross includes the meaning of the cross and the teaching of the cross.

    B. Those who regard the meaning and the teaching of the cross as foolishness will perish. Those who receive the word of the cross, recognizing that it is the power of God, will be saved.

C. The reason that the meaning and the teaching of the cross can cause man to be saved is that the cross is God's wisdom and power. Wisdom is God's means; power is God's ability. God's means and ability to save man depend upon the cross.

III. **How to apply the word of the cross**

A. Confess that we have sinned and deserve to perish.

B. Acknowledge that the cross is God's way of salvation.

C. Accept Jesus Christ as the Savior who died on the cross to bear our sins.

Subject One Hundred Sixty

CHRIST CRUCIFIED

Scripture: 1 Cor. 1:23

I. **Who is Christ?**

A. He is the Son of God and also God Himself.

B. He came to be a man whose name is Jesus.

C. He came as a man in order to be our Savior.

II. **Why was Christ crucified?**

A. He was crucified in order to accomplish God's way of salvation.

B. He was crucified to remove the sins of man.

C. He was crucified in order to release His life.

III. **Christ crucified**

A. Christ is the Savior; the cross is the means of salvation. Therefore, Christ crucified is the Savior who accomplished the way of salvation.

B. Although He was Christ crucified, today He is Christ resurrected! He is no longer on the cross. He is not only the Savior who accomplished the way of salvation, but He is living to impart His saving life into man.

IV. **How to receive Christ**

Develop this point.

Subject One Hundred Sixty-one

JESUS IS LORD

Scripture: 1 Cor. 12:3

I. There is a lord of all things

A. Everything has its lord.

B. Who is the Lord of this great universe and the things therein?

C. Who is your lord? Neither your parents, your husband, nor your wife is your lord. If you think they are, who will you belong to once they die? You will be a man without a lord.

II. The creator of all things

A. The universe and all creation has its creator.

B. Man also has a creator.

C. The one who created all is the Lord of all. Since all things were created by Him, all things belong to Him. He is the Lord of all.

III. The ruler of all things

A. There is a ruler in creation.

B. There is a ruler over man and within man's heart.

C. This ruler is the Lord.

IV. The redeemer of all things

A. Man needs redemption because he has sinned.

B. The whole creation also needs redemption because it was corrupted through man's sin. This is clearly seen in the Bible.

C. The redeemer of all is the Lord of all.

V. Jesus is Lord

A. Jesus is the creator and the Lord of all.

B. Jesus is the ruler of creation; as ruler, He is the Lord of all.

C. Jesus is the redeemer of all creation; as the redeemer, He is the Lord of all.

VI. How to receive Jesus as Lord

A. Confess that you are created, ruled, and redeemed by Him.

B. Repent, confess your sins, and receive Him as your Savior.

C. Acknowledge that all that you are and have belong to Him, and that He is your Lord.

Subject One Hundred Sixty-two

FOR WHAT DID CHRIST DIE?

Scripture: 1 Cor. 15:3-4

I. Presumptions of the people regarding Christ's death

A. The Jews said that He died because He was sentenced to death by the Roman officials.

B. The Gentiles throughout the ages said that He sacrificed Himself for a cause.

II. Christ's own explanation

A. He willingly gave His own life, to die (John 10:11, 18).

B. He died to redeem men from their sins (Matt. 26:28).

III. The Bible's explanation

A. God predestined Him to die.

B. He was destined to die for the sins of man.

IV. The witness of the saints

A. They confessed that Christ died for their sins, thus receiving the peace of being forgiven.

B. This confession resulted in a change in that they no longer lived a life of sin.

V. How to deal with Christ's death

Develop this point.

Subject One Hundred Sixty-three

THE STING OF DEATH

Scripture: 1 Cor. 15:55-56

I. The fearfulness of death

A. The most fearsome word in the dictionary is "death."

B. The most frightening sound is the sound of the word "death."

C. Death is the most frightful thing in a man's life. Who is not afraid of death?

II. The power of death

A. There is no power among men that is greater than the power of death.

B. No one can reject the visitation of death.

C. The fact that no one is spared from death speaks of the powerfulness of death.

III. The sting of death

A. Death possesses man not directly, but in an indirect way.

B. Death possesses man through sin. Sin is the sting of death. Everyone who fishes knows that one fishes with a hook. Once the fish is hooked, it is caught. Just as man fishes by using a hook, so death possesses man by sin.

C. Sin is the sting because it is poisonous. Once sin poisons man, it possesses him. The result of sin is death. Because sin is poisonous, it deadens.

IV. How to be spared from death

A. One needs to be freed from sin in order to be spared from death.

B. To be freed from sin one must first believe in the Lord. On one hand the Lord died and shed His blood that we might be spared from the punishment of sin. On the other hand, He resurrected that we might be delivered from the power of sin.

Subject One Hundred Sixty-four

"ONE DIED FOR ALL"

Scripture: 2 Cor. 5:14

I. The One is Jesus

A. Jesus is God coming to be the Savior of mankind.

B. Since He is God incarnated, He is an unlimited person.

C. In God's eyes, all who believe in Jesus are included in Jesus. So Jesus is not only an unlimited person, but One that includes all.

II. All are sinners

A. All the people in the world are sinners.

B. Every sinner that believes in the Lord Jesus is included in this "all."

III. One died for all

A. Apparently Jesus died as one individual, yet actually He died for all. That is, He died for those He redeemed, for all those who believe in Him.

B. The reason that the Lord's death could become effective for all who believe in Him is that He is one with them and they are joined unto Him.

IV. All died

A. "All" refers to all those who are joined unto Christ Jesus. Since He died, all have died in God's sight. It is best to use the example of a nation destroyed.

B. Since all died because of His death, "all" do not need to die again.

V. How to share in Jesus' death

Develop this point.

Subject One Hundred Sixty-five

THE SINLESS ONE MADE SIN

Scripture: 2 Cor. 5:21

I. The sinless One is Jesus

A. Jesus as God incarnated, does not have a sinful nature.

B. Jesus never sinned, even when He was judged. All the examinations of men could not find any sins in Jesus. Even He Himself said, "Which one of you convicts me of sin?" (John 8:46).

II. We are sin

A. We were born in sin.

B. We grew up in sin.

C. We are living in sin.

D. We live out sin.

E. We both possess a sinful nature and commit sinful acts, so we are sin.

III. The sinless One became sin

A. God caused Jesus to be our substitute. He caused the sinless Lord Jesus to replace us, who are sin, by becoming sin for us.

B. God caused the Lord Jesus to become sin in order that He might receive God's righteous judgment on the cross for us.

C. When God judged the Lord Jesus, He actually judged us. By terminating the body of Jesus, He terminated us.

D. Jesus could become sin for us because He became a man in order to be united with man.

IV. The result of His becoming sin

A. He became sin for us that we might become righteousness.

B. We are sin and Jesus is righteousness. When He caused us to be righteousness, He caused us to become Him.

C. He caused us to become Him means that we may be joined to Him. Here "in Him" refers to this joining.

D. This righteousness of His is not only before man but also before God. Not only does it fulfill the requirement and standard of man, but also that of God. Therefore, His righteousness is God's righteousness. So when He became sin for us, He caused us to be joined with Him and in Him to become righteousness before God.

Subject One Hundred Sixty-six
THE SACRIFICE OF LOVE

Scripture: Gal. 2:20

I. The love of Christ

A. Christ loved us, so He left heaven and the throne to be born in this world as a lowly person.

B. Christ loved us, so He passed through thirty-three years of human sufferings.

C. Christ loved us, so He gave Himself up at the cross; that is, He gave up His life through death.

D. Very few lay down their lives for others, although some might die for a good man, or friends. Yet Christ laid down His life for us, even though we were His enemies. This love is a surpassing love (Rom. 5:7-8, 10).

II. The intention of Christ's sacrifice

A. Not only to suffer and die for us, but to take away our sins and redeem us.

B. Not only to satisfy our need, but to fulfill God's requirement.

C. Not only to make us complete, but to accomplish God's means of salvation.

D. His sacrifice was that we might partake of God and all He has.

III. How to receive the love of Christ

Develop this point.

Subject One Hundred Sixty-seven

CHRIST BECAME A CURSE FOR US

Scripture: Gal. 3:13

I. The origin of the curse

A. The curse came from sin.

B. God brought in the curse after Adam sinned. God said, "Cursed is the ground for thy sake" (Gen. 3:17).

II. The sign of the curse

A. The sign of the curse is thorns. After Adam sinned, the earth brought forth thorns because of the curse. So thorns are the sign of being cursed.

B. The outstanding feature of thorns is that they prick, causing pain.

III. The execution of the curse

A. The curse is carried out through the law. The law administers the curse. Once man sinned, God's law then administered the curse upon man.

B. Therefore, the curse is related to the law of God, and is the demand of the righteousness of God upon sinners.

IV. The nullification of the curse

A. When Christ bore our sins, He also took our curse. Since the problem of sin is resolved, so is the problem of the curse.

B. When Christ bore our sins on the cross, He wore a crown of thorns. Since the thorns are a sign of the curse, this shows that He took our curse on the cross.

C. Since Christ was cursed in our stead on the cross, the demand of the law was fulfilled and He could redeem us from the curse of the law.

V. How to have the curse removed

Develop this point.

Subject One Hundred Sixty-eight

CHRIST HAS SET US FREE

Scripture: Gal. 5:1

I. Our bondage

A. We are under the bondage of sin.

B. We are under the bondage of the law.

C. We are under the bondage of Satan.

D. We are under the bondage of death.

II. Christ's setting free

A. Christ dealt with sin for us.

B. Christ satisfied the law for us.

C. Christ destroyed Satan for us.

D. Christ eliminated death for us.

III. The purpose of salvation

A. To forgive our sins and deliver us from sin.

B. To deliver us from the law.

C. To deliver us from Satan's dominion.

D. To deliver us from the power of death.

IV. How to be released

Develop this point.

Subject One Hundred Sixty-nine

REDEMPTION BY THE BLOOD

Scripture: Eph. 1:7

I. The result of sin

A. Sin causes us to be under God's condemnation.

B. Condemnation creates a distance and a barrier between us and God.

II. The demand of the law

A. The law represents God's righteousness, making absolute demands on man.

B. The demand of the law confines the sinner under condemnation.

III. The redemption by the blood

A. Christ bore our sins to fulfill the demand of the law. Therefore, the blood of Christ is able to redeem us from under the law that the law could no longer confine us under condemnation.

B. Since the blood of Christ redeems us from the condemnation of the law, it also abolishes the distance between us and God; thus, we are brought back to God. As sin and the law cause us to depart from God and become distant from Him, so the blood of Christ redeems us from under the law that we may return to God without anything between us and Him.

IV. The result of redemption

A. Our sins are forgiven.

B. We are brought back to God.

V. The accomplishment of redemption is through God's grace

VI. How to obtain redemption

Develop this point.

Subject One Hundred Seventy
DEAD IN SINS

Scripture: Eph. 2:1

I. The meaning of death

A. Death means the loss of function; spiritually, this is the inability to do good.

B. Death also means the loss of feeling; spiritually, this is the unconsciousness of sin.

II. The fact of death

A. The condition of man today is altogether one of death. He is unable to do good and is without the consciousness of sin. Having lost his function and feeling, he is ungodly toward God and unrighteous toward man; he is without the strength to be godly or righteous.

B. Illustrate the facts of death. Show the inability to do good and the lack of consciousness of sin.

III. The source of death

A. Death comes from sin.

B. All who sin abide in death.

IV. The result of death

A. The death of the spirit occurs first.

B. The death of the spirit results in the death of the body.

C. It also causes the soul to suffer in Hades.

D. In the end it will cause the whole being to be cast with its body, soul, and spirit into the lake of fire to suffer the second death, that is, eternal suffering.

V. How to be free from death

Develop this point.

Subject One Hundred Seventy-one
THE SURPASSING SALVATION

Scripture: Eph. 2:4-8

I. The source of salvation

A. The source of salvation is God.

B. The source of salvation is God's mercy.

C. The source of salvation is God's great love.

II. The accomplishment of salvation

A. Salvation is accomplished through the death and resurrection of Christ.

B. Salvation is also accomplished through the ascension of Christ.

III. The surpassing salvation

A. When we were dead in sin, God's surpassing salvation caused us to become alive together with Christ.

B. He also caused us to be raised together with Christ. There is a difference between being made alive and being raised. To be made alive means to have life; to be raised means not only to have life but to be able to move. Not only was Lazarus enlivened in the tomb, but his coming out of the tomb shows that he was resurrected, that he was raised up.

C. Thirdly, He caused us to sit together with Him in heavenly places. This is surpassing! This is God's surpassing salvation.

IV. The manifestation of salvation

A. This salvation manifests the rich and abundant grace of God.

B. This grace is given to us in God's kindness.

1. *Emphasize that grace is God's action in freely saving us.*

2. *Emphasize that kindness issues out of God's mercy and love, out of the intent of His heart.*

V. How to receive this salvation

Stress the matter of faith.

Subject One Hundred Seventy-two

SAVED BY GRACE

Scripture: Eph. 2:8-9

I. The meaning of salvation

A. Salvation means to be forgiven and delivered from sin.

B. Furthermore, salvation means to receive life and be resurrected.

C. Salvation also includes being ascended and transcended.

II. The source of salvation

A. The grace of God is the source of salvation.

B. Grace comes from love. Grace is an active issue, and love is an intention of the heart. So the act of grace is an issue coming from the loving intention of the heart.

C. Because grace is free, salvation is not by works.

D. Since it is by grace and not by works, salvation is out of God and not out of ourselves.

III. The means of salvation

A. Salvation is not by works, but by faith.

B. Grace is the dispensing; faith is the receiving. The dispensing grace and the receiving faith make salvation complete.

IV. The result of salvation

A. That man may not boast in himself. Since salvation is not by the works of man, nor out of man, there is no room for man to boast.

B. That God may be man's boast and glory.

Subject One Hundred Seventy-three

THE HUMAN LIFE HAS NO HOPE

Scripture: Eph. 2:12

I. The situation of man

A. Describe how man is born, raised up, encounters sicknesses, and dies. The human life can never depart from these four things: birth, aging, sickness, and death.

B. Conclude that everything is vanity.

II. The hopelessness of the human life

A. Use further examples to illustrate that once a man dies, that is the end of everything for him.

B. Conclude that the human life is hopeless.

III. The reason for hopelessness

A. The reason why the human life is hopeless is that man has lost God. Without God there is no hope.

B. God wants to be everything to the human life. Only when man has God will there be hope for his life.

IV. How to have hope

A. Do not ignore the sense of emptiness. The sense of emptiness tells you that you need God, Who is the hope of life.

B. Recognize that God can be everything to the human life.

C. Repent and turn to God.

D. Receive the Son of God, Jesus Christ. To have the Son of God is the way to have God. Once man has God, his life will be full of hope.

Subject One Hundred Seventy-four

THE EXCELLENCY
OF THE KNOWLEDGE OF CHRIST

Scripture: Phil. 3:7-9

I. The futility of everything

A. Point out that nothing in the universe is really a gain to man.

B. Give concrete examples to show this. For example: education, money, and family, etc., may not be gains to man. Sometimes the more money a man has, the more harm it does. When you mention the futility of everything, bring in the subject of sickness and death. Whether one has education, money, or friendship, this cannot be escaped; whether it be parents, wife, children, or others, none can keep sickness and death away. When death comes, everything is over.

C. Conclude that everything is vain and futile.

II. All things are as dung

A. As far as knowing Christ is concerned, all things are of no avail. So the nature and value of all things are as dung.

B. Dung is a changed form of food. Parents, children, reputation, and position are all forms of food, but eventually they become dung. Everything in the world changes, and when it changes it becomes dung.

C. Dung is the most useless and valueless of all things.

III. The Most Excellent One in the universe

A. Everything in the universe is vain and futile, without weight or value. Only Christ is the Most Excellent One.

B. Christ is the embodiment of God. God is the center of the universe; He is also the reality of the universe. Hence, God is the true value of the whole universe. Because Christ is the embodiment of God, He is the Most Excellent One.

IV. To know Christ

A. Since Christ is the Most Excellent One, to know Him is the most excellent of all things.

B. All forms of knowledge are vain; they only add sorrow to man. Only the knowledge of Christ is real and solid, and only this will give man real happiness. So the knowledge of Christ is the most excellent thing.

V. The result of the knowledge of Christ

A. Not only will the knowledge of Christ give you the Most Excellent One of the universe, but it will also give you the righteousness of God. In Christ your sins will be forgiven and you will be accepted by God.

B. In Christ you will also obtain the life of God.

VI. How to know Christ

A. Recognize that everything is futile, that it is nothing but refuse.

B. Despise and forsake all the vain and futile things.

C. Receive Christ as your life and Savior.

Subject One Hundred Seventy-five

THE PEACE OF THE CROSS

Scripture: Col. 1:20

I. The problem in the universe

A. The biggest problem in the universe is disharmony among all the creatures. Everything in the universe has this problem with God.

B. The reason the creatures are in disharmony with God is that man is in disharmony with God. This is due to man's sin. For example, mosquitoes and insects bite, and animals kill each other. This is all because man is out of harmony with God, which is the result of man's sin. When sin came in, the whole universe became full of chaos.

II. The peace of the universe

A. The universe is out of harmony because of man's sin. Therefore, before the universe can have peace, man's sin must be removed.

B. Man's sin was removed when Christ shed His blood on the cross. Thus, through the shedding of His blood, Christ made peace in the universe.

III. The function of the peace of the cross

A. The peace of the cross firstly reconciles man to God.

B. The peace of the cross also reconciles all things in the universe to God.

IV. How to obtain the peace of the cross

A. Confess your own sin and your disharmony with God.

B. Confess that Jesus died on the cross for your sins.

C. Accept the Lord Jesus to be your Savior and your peace with God.

Subject One Hundred Seventy-six

SEPARATED AND ALIENATED FROM GOD

Scripture: Col. 1:21

I. Separated from God

A. Man was originally created by God; he belonged to God and lived before God.

B. Due to his sin, man was separated from God. Not only is there a barrier between man and God, but there is also a distance between the two.

II. Alienated from God

A. Not only is man separated from God passively, but he is also alienated from Him actively. Separation from God is a forsaking of God, but alienation is a rebellion against God. Separation is a departure from God, but alienation is an assault upon God.

B. The life of man today is not merely one that is separated from God, but it is one that is daily antagonistic toward God. Use examples to prove this.

III. How to be reconciled to God

A. Confess that you are separated and alienated from God.

B. Repent to God.

C. Believe in Jesus Christ, the Son of God, as Savior.

Subject One Hundred Seventy-seven

TURNING FROM IDOLS TO GOD

Scripture: 1 Thes. 1:9

I. Man forsook God

A. Man is created by God and belongs to God.

B. Due to his sin, man forsook God.

C. Man today is living a life of forsaking God.

II. Man worshipped idols

A. Sin causes man to forsake God. It also causes him to worship idols. The result of man's sin is the worship of idols.

B. Man worships idols because he has sinned and has lost God. God is the source of all peace and blessing. To lose God is to lose all peace and blessing. Once man lost the source of peace and blessing, he turned to idols. The more man sins, the more he loses his peace, and the more he loses his peace, the more he wants it. This psychological craving for peace and blessing turns him to idols. No one who worships idols loves them. All the idol worshippers are just trying to utilize the idols.

C. The life of man today is a life of idol worship. Some idols are tangible; others are intangible. Whatever takes the place of God in a man is an idol. Whatever a man relies on, apart from God, is also an idol.

III. The fallacy of idols

A. Idols are false; hence, they are a deception.

B. List facts to show that idols are false.

IV. The reality of God

A. God is real and therefore trustworthy.

B. Use examples to show how secure it is for man to trust in God.

V. Forsake idols and turn to God

A. Since idols are a deception, we should forsake them. Those who would not forsake them are fools. They are either deceiving themselves, or are deceiving others.

B. Since God is trustworthy, we should turn to Him. If we do not turn to Him, we are in a deception, either deceiving ourselves or deceiving others.

VI. How to forsake idols to turn to God

A. Recognize the fallacy of idols and the reality of God.

B. Destroy all of the idols in your home.

C. Repent and turn to God.

D. Receive the Son of God, Jesus Christ, as your Savior.

E. Worship and serve God through the Lord Jesus Christ.

Subject One Hundred Seventy-eight

"CHRIST JESUS CAME INTO THE WORLD TO SAVE SINNERS"

Scripture: 1 Tim. 1:15

I. Who is Christ Jesus?

A. "Christ" signifies that He is God.

B. "Jesus" signifies that He is man.

C. The compound name of "Christ Jesus" means that God came as man to save men and to become the Savior of mankind.

II. Why did Christ Jesus come into the world?

A. Christ Jesus did not come into the world by accident or without a purpose.

B. Christ Jesus came into the world in order to save sinners.

III. Who are the sinners?

A. All men are sinners. As long as you are a man in this world, you are a sinner.

B. Christ Jesus came into this world in order to save sinners, that is, to save you. As far as I am concerned, He came to save me; as far as you are concerned, He came to save you.

IV. How can man receive the salvation of Christ Jesus?

Develop this point.

Subject One Hundred Seventy-nine

THERE IS ONE GOD AND ONE MEDIATOR

Scripture: 1 Tim. 2:5

I. There is only one God

A. As there cannot be two heads in a household or two kings in a nation, so there cannot be two Gods in the universe.

B. This God is the Creator and the Ruler of the universe. He is also the Savior of mankind.

II. There is only one mediator

A. In human history there have been many wise and famous men, yet not one has claimed to be, nor has been recognized as, a mediator between God and man.

B. Only Jesus Christ said that He is the mediator between God and man. The Bible says that He is the one, the only mediator.

III. How Jesus became the mediator

A. He was God coming as man. He had both divinity and humanity, so He was qualified to be the mediator between God and man.

B. He was crucified and His blood was shed for our sins to remove the hindrance between God and man. So He became the mediator between God and man.

C. He resurrected and imparted His life to man so that man could have God's life and be one with God. Through this process He became the mediator between God and man.

IV. How to receive Jesus as your mediator

Develop this point.

Subject One Hundred Eighty
"A RANSOM FOR ALL"

Scripture: 1 Tim. 2:6

I. The condition of "all"

A. This "all" refers to all men on this earth.

B. All men have sinned, and have been condemned by God's righteous laws. So the condition of men is that they are under the condemnation of the law.

C. Since men are under the condemnation of the law, men are sentenced to perdition.

II. "A ransom for all"

A. Jesus Christ is the ransom for all. He gave Himself to become the ransom for all.

B. Jesus is God-become-man coming to be man's Savior.

C. As man's Savior, Jesus has redeemed man from the condemnation of the law and delivered him out of perdition.

D. Jesus redeemed man by giving Himself, that is His soul-life, as a ransom.

E. The blood Jesus shed on the cross is the ransom for all so that man may be freed from the condemnation of the law and from perdition.

III. How to partake of Jesus' ransom

Develop this point.

Subject One Hundred Eighty-one

GOD MANIFESTED IN THE FLESH

Scripture: 1 Tim. 3:16

I. The mystery of God

A. This universe is a mystery, an unsolvable puzzle.

B. The reason the universe is a puzzle is that its creator is mysterious.

C. The creator of the universe is God. God is hidden, so God is mysterious.

D. God's being hidden does not disprove His existence. Actually, God's being hidden serves only to prove His existence. The greater a person is, the more he is hidden. The more common a person is, the more he is seen. You see the average people on the street every day, but you hardly ever see a head of state personally. God is hidden because He is the head of the universe.

II. God's manifestation

A. Anything that is in existence can be hidden, but not forever. With existence comes manifestation.

B. An important person often manifests himself in a different form. Although he is semi-hidden or hidden in a different form, he nevertheless is manifested through it.

C. God was manifested in such a semi-hidden way in a person called Jesus of Nazareth. When men looked upon Jesus, they saw Him as a man and as God. If you say that He is a man, He is not just a man. If you say that He is God, He also appears as a man. He is God incarnated, and He is God's manifestation.

III. The purpose of God's manifestation

A. God wants to be one with man.

B. God created man so that man might become His container to contain God Himself.

C. Man without God as the content is an empty and meaningless vessel.

D. "God manifested in the flesh" means that God put on the flesh so that through that one body He might eventually be able to put Himself into thousands upon thousands of bodies. Through this process God can be one with man.

E. Man has sinned and is separated from God. Before God can become one with man, He must accomplish redemption for man.

F. He accomplished redemption by His death and resurrection. His death abolished man's sins, and His resurrection imparts His life into man.

G. When man receives His life, he is one with Him.

IV. What to do with this God

A. Confess that you and your life are empty, without a center and without reality.

B. Confess that God is the reality and the meaning of your living.

C. Confess that God was incarnated in the flesh, and that He died and resurrected to accomplish redemption for us.

D. Receive Jesus, the One who was God manifested in the flesh, as your Savior.

Subject One Hundred Eighty-two

"THE WASHING OF REGENERATION AND RENEWING OF THE HOLY SPIRIT"

Scripture: Titus 3:5

I. Man's defilement

A. Man was defiled due to the fall of Adam. This was not merely an outward defilement, but also an inward defilement of life and nature.

B. Such a defilement of life and nature was caused by the injection of Satan's life and nature into man.

II. Man became old

A. Because man's life and nature were defiled by Satan, man became old.

B. Because man became old, he experiences corruption, weakness, sickness, and death.

III. The washing of regeneration

A. Since man's life and nature were defiled and corrupted, God's salvation is not to change the life that man has, but to regenerate man. God regenerates man so that man may have God's life in addition to his own life.

B. Once God's life gets into us, it causes us to be separated from our old life and nature. Such a separation is a kind of washing, which washes away our defiled life. So regeneration is a washing.

C. The washing of regeneration is mainly for washing away our defiled life, not our defiled behavior.

IV. The renewing of the Holy Spirit

A. When God saves us, He not only regenerates us so that we may receive His life, but He also puts the Holy Spirit within us so that we may receive His Spirit.

B. The Holy Spirit is within us to renew us from our old, created, and corrupted life. God's life is washing away our defiled life, and the Holy Spirit is renewing that same defiled and corrupted life into a new life.

C. The renewing of the Holy Spirit is not merely to change

a man's living in an outward way. It is to renew his old nature into a new nature.

V. How to receive the washing of regeneration and the renewing of the Holy Spirit

A. Confess that your created life is filthy and that your nature has become old.

B. Abhor your own life and nature.

C. Repent and turn to God.

D. Receive the crucified and resurrected Christ as your Savior.

Subject One Hundred Eighty-three

JESUS TASTED DEATH FOR MAN

Scripture: Heb. 2:9

I. The end man deserves

A. The end man deserves is death.

B. Man's death sentence came from sin.

C. Since man lives in sin, his end shall be death.

II. Jesus tasted death for man

A. Man's death has its source in his sin. When Jesus tasted death for man, He bore man's sin.

B. That Jesus bore man's sin meant that He received the punishment for sin. That punishment was death.

C. Describe how Jesus tasted death for man, how He was forsaken by God, and how His heart melted like wax. He suffered the burning of the fire of God's wrath. These experiences are tastes of death.

III. The results of Jesus tasting death

A. Man's sins were forgiven.

B. Man has been freed from the suffering of death.

C. Those who believe in Him do not perish and will be resurrected if they die.

IV. How to receive the effects of Jesus' substitutional death

Develop this point.

Subject One Hundred Eighty-four

JESUS IS ABLE TO SAVE TO THE UTTERMOST

Scripture: Heb. 7:25

I. Jesus is God coming as man

A. Jesus is God coming as man to become man's Savior.

B. Because His power is the power of God, there is no limit to His power.

II. Jesus' redemption is eternal

A. Because He is God coming as man, and God is eternal, His redemptive work on the cross is eternal.

B. Eternal means limitless and measureless. His redemptive work has an eternal, measureless effect.

III. Jesus is living forever

A. Jesus not only died to accomplish redemption, but He also resurrected.

B. Jesus not only resurrected, but now He is living forever.

IV. Jesus is always interceding

A. Jesus died and resurrected not only to become man's Savior, but also to become his intercessor before God.

B. Just as His redemptive work is eternal, so also is His intercession for man.

V. Jesus is able to save to the uttermost

A. Jesus is God coming as man, whose redemption is eternal; He is living forever and always interceding. Thus, because He is fully qualified, He is able to save men to the uttermost.

B. "To the uttermost" means that He is able to save men not only for all time and eternity, but also to the uttermost in extent.

VI. How to receive the salvation of Jesus

Develop this point.

Subject One Hundred Eighty-five

ETERNAL REDEMPTION

Scripture: Heb. 9:12

I. The need for redemption

A. Man is sinful before God.

B. God is righteous and so is His law. The law has a righteous requirement because of man's sins.

C. When man's sin confronts God's righteousness, there is a need for redemption.

II. The meaning of redemption

A. Redemption resolves man's sins before God according to the requirement of God's righteousness.

B. Because of God's righteousness, sinful men must die. So in order to redeem them, there must be another death. Only another death can satisfy the requirement of God's righteousness, and only such a death can redeem men from their sins.

III. The type of redemption

A. In the time of the Old Testament, before redemption was accomplished, God set up a type of redemption.

B. Redemption was typified by the offering of goats and bulls. Goats and bulls were killed, and blood was shed to accomplish atonement for man's sins.

C. The death and shed blood of goats and bulls was only a shadow, not the reality; while it made atonement for sins, it could not redeem men from their sins.

IV. The accomplishment of redemption

A. Redemption was accomplished on the cross. The Lord Jesus bore man's sins on the cross and suffered the punishment for sins. Thus He fulfilled the requirement of God's righteousness and accomplished redemption for man.

B. The redemption of the Lord Jesus is not a symbol, but a reality. The blood of goats and bulls in the Old Testament time was only a symbol, but the redemption of Christ on the cross is a real accomplished fact.

V. The nature of redemption

A. Redemption is eternal.

B. "Eternal" not only refers to time, but in nature it also denotes a completion, something accomplished once for all.

C. So Christ's redemption, being eternal, is applicable and available to all men at any time.

VI. How to partake of Christ's redemption

Develop this point.

Subject One Hundred Eighty-six

WITHOUT THE SHEDDING OF BLOOD, THERE IS NO FORGIVENESS

Scripture: Heb. 9:22

I. The requirement of God's righteousness: death

II. The significance of shedding of blood: death

III. The meaning of shedding of blood: God's righteous requirement is satisfied

IV. The result of shedding of blood: men's sins are forgiven

V. The shedding of Jesus' blood

A. In the Old Testament all the sacrifices were killed and their blood was shed. This was a symbol of the blood-shedding of Jesus.

B. The shedding of Jesus' blood signifies His death for us. The meaning of His shed blood is that God's righteous requirement is satisfied. Thus, the effect of His blood being shed is that our sins are forgiven.

C. Without the shed blood of Jesus, God's righteous requirement could never have been satisfied, and man's sins could never have been forgiven. But the shed blood of Jesus has satisfied God's righteous requirement so that man's sins can be forgiven.

VI. How to partake of Jesus' blood

Develop this point.

Subject One Hundred Eighty-seven

THE PURIFYING OF THE CONSCIENCE BY THE BLOOD

Scripture: Heb. 9:14

I. The function of the conscience

A. God is the ruler of the universe, so He is also the ruler of man.

B. God rules man by means of man's conscience. So in function, the conscience represents God to rule man.

C. Whatever is condemned by the conscience is also condemned by God.

II. The function of the blood

A. God's righteousness causes God to condemn man; however, Christ bore man's sins and died for man, thus satisfying God's righteous requirement.

B. In the sight of God, the blood of Jesus cleansed man from sin, thereby abolishing God's condemnation of man.

III. The purifying of the conscience by the blood

A. As Jesus' blood has cleansed man from sin in God's sight and has abolished God's condemnation of man, so it has also taken away the condemnation of man's conscience.

B. By Jesus' blood taking away the condemnation of man's conscience, man's conscience is purified so that there is no longer the feeling of shortcoming in the conscience.

C. The purifying of the conscience with its feeling causes man's conscience to be at peace before God.

IV. The result

As the blood of the Lord Jesus cleanses man's conscience, it not only gives peace to man's conscience, but also enables man to serve God.

V. How to partake of this cleansing

Develop this point.

Subject One Hundred Eighty-eight

AFTER DEATH THE JUDGMENT

Scripture: Heb. 9:27

I. It is reserved for men once to die

A. Men deserve death.

B. Death came from sin.

C. No one can escape death. Give some examples to describe how man cannot escape death.

II. After death comes judgment

A. Death is not the end but a beginning. Man's life is short, and this short life is ended by death. But after death there is eternity. This eternity is ushered in by death.

B. Whatever man does in this age will be judged in eternity. Many commit crimes and escape the punishment of the law and the shame of public opinion. Many think they will be safe from punishment once they die. But what man does cannot be resolved by his death. Actually death is not the end of all things. Everything will be judged in the coming eternity.

III. The results of judgment

A. There is not one who has never committed a sin in this age, so in eternity no one can escape God's righteous judgment and condemnation.

B. The result of condemnation is perdition.

C. Perdition means to go to hell.

IV. The way to escape

Give a strong conclusion on how to escape death and judgment.

Subject One Hundred Eighty-nine

A NEW AND LIVING WAY

Scripture: Heb. 10:20

I. The path of man's living

A. The path of man's living is a path that is far away from God.

B. This path is a path of committing sins.

C. This path is also a path of going into death.

II. God's saving way

A. The Lord Jesus bore man's sins and died for man.

B. The Lord resurrected and imparted His life into man.

III. A new and living way

A. God's saving way is a way God has prepared for man. This way is through the Lord's crucifixion, the shedding of His blood, and through His resurrection. This way enables man to come near to God.

B. This way was never open before, so it is a new way; and this way is in Christ's resurrection life, so it is also a living way.

C. This way does not have the hindrance of sin; rather, it has the power of life, drawing us close to God.

D. This way not only brings man near to God, but also allows man to be one with God. Not only can man enjoy all the blessings that God bestows upon him, but he can also enjoy God Himself.

IV. How to partake of this way

Develop this point.

Subject One Hundred Ninety

THE NECESSITY OF BELIEVING THAT GOD IS

Scripture: Heb. 11:6

I. God is

A. The creation of the universe proves that God is.

B. The order of the universe proves that God is.

C. Man's physical body and mentality prove that God is.

II. God is hidden

A. Although God exists, He is hidden.

B. Because God is Spirit, He is hidden to materialistic man. As a result, the materialistic man cannot see or touch the Spirit.

C. God's honor, greatness, and holiness cause Him to hide Himself from man who is low and filthy.

III. You must believe that God is

A. You must believe because God is hidden.

B. You must believe because God is Spirit and cannot be seen by man's naked eye.

C. You must believe because God is honorable holy, and we are low and filthy. Thus for man to touch God, there is no way other than the way of believing.

IV. The results of believing in God

A. By believing in God you receive His life.

B. Believing in God causes you to have the sensation of being enlightened within.

C. Through your believing you become well-pleasing to God.

V. How to believe

A. Confess that you are a sinner before God.

B. Repent and come forward to God, believing that He is.

Subject One Hundred Ninety-one

JESUS IS UNCHANGING

Scripture: Heb. 13:8

I. Jesus is God

A. Prove that Jesus is God.

B. As God is eternal and unchanging, so Jesus is unchanging.

II. Jesus is eternal

A. Jesus died and rose again.

B. Jesus lives today and will be living forever.

C. What Jesus did in the past He is doing today, and in the future He will still be doing the same.

D. Likewise, what Jesus was able to do in the past He is able to do now, and will still be able to do in eternity.

III. Jesus is real

A. As Jesus was so real to people when He was on the earth, so He is also real to men today.

B. Jesus is real because He is living. Because Jesus is living forever, He will be real forever.

C. Since Jesus is real, the deliverance and healing He gives to us is real.

IV. How to partake of this unchanging Jesus

Develop this point.

Subject One Hundred Ninety-two
THE PRECIOUS BLOOD OF CHRIST

Scripture: 1 Pet. 1:18-20

I. Man's indebtedness before God

A. Man is sinful.

B. God is righteous.

C. For man and God to be reconciled, the price of redemption must be paid.

II. The blood of Christ

A. As the indebtedness encumbered upon man must meet the requirement of God's righteousness, it is the highest possible indebtedness.

B. Because the highest price is demanded, nothing of man can pay it, not even man's good works, man's own righteousness, man's morality, or good behavior.

C. Only the blood of Christ can fulfill God's requirement, so Christ's blood becomes the only acceptable payment. This is why Christ's blood is the precious blood. The word "precious" indicates the unique value of the blood of Christ.

D. Christ's blood is the precious blood not only because of its high value, but also because of His supreme nature. His blood is not like the blood of goats or bullocks; that is, the blood of the created lives. His blood is the blood which the Creator shed for His creatures.

E. Since His blood possesses such a supreme nature and unique value, its effectiveness is unlimited.

III. The function of the precious blood

A. It enables man to have his sins forgiven.

B. It enables man to be justified.

C. It cleanses man's conscience.

D. It reconciles man to God.

E. It enables man to obtain God's life.

IV. How to partake of the precious blood of Christ

Develop this point.

Subject One Hundred Ninety-three

JESUS BORE OUR SINS

Scripture: Gal. 3:13b; 1 Pet. 2:24

I. Jesus was hanged upon the tree

A. Jesus was hanged upon the tree; that is, Jesus was crucified on the cross.

B. Crucifixion was a death penalty during the days of the Roman Empire.

C. When Jesus was crucified on the cross, He was suffering the death penalty.

II. Jesus Himself bore our sins

A. Jesus suffered the death penalty not because He was sinful, but because He bore our sins.

B. As Jesus was dying on the cross, God put all our sins upon Him. Jesus' crucifixion was the way ordained by God to deal with our sins.

C. During Jesus' crucifixion on the cross, the heavens and the earth were darkened. This signifies that Jesus was forsaken by God when He bore our sins upon the cross.

III. The results of Jesus' bearing our sins

A. Now we can have our sins forgiven

B. Now we can be justified by God.

C. Now we can obtain the life of God.

IV. How to partake of the sin-bearing Jesus

Develop this point.

Subject One Hundred Ninety-four

DEAD UNTO SINS AND
LIVING UNTO RIGHTEOUSNESS

Scripture: 1 Pet. 2:24

I. Living unto sins and dead unto righteousness

A. The real condition of man is that man is living unto sins and dead unto righteousness. When you mention a crime, everyone is living. But when you talk about righteousness, everyone is dead.

B. Give examples to prove that man has the instinct to commit sins. For instance, a child does not need to be taught to lie.

C. Also give examples to prove that in doing good works man is as weak and impotent as a dead person.

II. God's saving way

A. We are incurable. The nature of our life is prone to sin and cannot work righteousness.

B. Yet, in God's regeneration, we receive His life in addition to our original life.

C. When God's life gets into us, we are born again and our old life is replaced by a new life.

III. Dead unto sins and living unto righteousness

A. As soon as God's life enters into man, man is dead unto sins and living unto righteousness.

B. Give examples to prove that a man is dead unto sins as soon as he is saved. Point out that formerly he was proud in committing sins, but now he is not.

C. Then give examples to illustrate a man living unto
righteousness. Point out that now he is lively and full
of strength in doing good and working righteousness.

IV. How to have such a change

A. Confess that you are weak and incapable of doing
good, and that all you can do is commit sins.

B. Repent, turn to God, and receive God's life into you.

Subject One Hundred Ninety-five

THE RIGHTEOUS ONE SUBSTITUTED
FOR THE UNRIGHTEOUS ONES

Scripture: 1 Pet. 3:18

I. Jesus is the righteous One

A. Jesus is God coming as man.

B. Jesus was born in holiness without the nature of sin.

C. Jesus has never committed sin. Once He asked publicly, "Who among you can prove that I have sinned?"
When He was examined before His crucifixion, no one
could find sin in Him.

D. Jesus is the sinless and the righteous One.

II. We are the unrighteous ones

A. We are sinners.

B. We were born in sin.

C. We have committed sins and grew up in sin.

D. We are altogether, one hundred percent sinners.

III. The righteous One substituted for the unrighteous
ones

A. The righteous One substituted Himself for the unrighteous ones; that is, the Lord Jesus substituted Himself
for us.

B. On the cross the Lord Jesus became our substitute by
bearing our sins, shedding His blood, and dying for us.

C. Because He bore our sins and died for us on the cross,
our sins are forgiven before God. Because He died for

us, we can be delivered from death and can obtain eternal life.

IV. How to partake of Jesus' substitution

Develop this point.

Subject One Hundred Ninety-six

THE LORD'S BLOOD CLEANSES US FROM SIN

Scripture: 1 John 1:7

I. The Lord Jesus bore our sins on the cross and shed His blood for us

II. The function of the Lord's blood

A. Because Jesus bore our sins and shed His blood, His blood can cleanse us from our sins.

B. The cleansing of the Lord's blood is always effective.

III. The meaning of being cleansed from sins

A. The Lord's blood cleanses us from our sins; that is, it erases our record of sins before God.

B. When we are cleansed by the Lord's blood, all record of our sins is erased before God.

IV. How to obtain the cleansing of the Lord's blood

Develop this point.

Subject One Hundred Ninety-seven

GOD'S FORGIVENESS AND CLEANSING

Scripture: 1 John 1:9

I. God's forgiveness

A. God's forgiveness is based upon the redemption of the Lord Jesus.

B. God's forgiveness removes our record of sins.

II. God's cleansing

A. God's cleansing is by the blood of the Lord Jesus.

B. God's cleansing washes us from every sin. Forgiveness erases the record of sin. Cleansing removes the stain of sin.

III. The basis of God's forgiveness and cleansing

A. God's forgiveness and cleansing are based upon God's faithfulness. God's faithfulness is according to God's Word. God's Word in the Bible promises us that He will forgive us and cleanse us. When we believe in Jesus, He is bound by the faithfulness of His Word to forgive and cleanse us.

B. God's forgiveness and cleansing are based upon God's righteousness. God's righteousness is according to God's work. The redeeming death of the Lord Jesus, which dealt with our sins, is God's work. Today when we believe in the Lord Jesus, God is bound by His righteousness to forgive us and to cleanse us.

IV. The extent of God's forgiveness and cleansing

A. He cleanses us from *all* our unrighteousness.

B. He forgives and cleanses the sins of *all* believers.

V. How to obtain God's forgiveness and cleansing

A. Repent and confess your sins to God.

B. Receive the Lord Jesus and His redemption.

Subject One Hundred Ninety-eight

JESUS IS THE PROPITIATION FOR OUR SINS

Scripture: 1 John 2:2; 4:10

I. Sin separates man from God

A. Man's sins violate God's righteousness.

B. God's heart draws Him toward man in love, but God's righteousness has forced Him to forsake man. Therefore, His love cannot reach sinful man.

II. The Lord Jesus propitiates for us

A. The Lord Jesus bore man's sins according to the requirements of God's righteousness.

B. The Lord Jesus propitiated the very matter which formerly prevented God's love from reaching man.

III. God provides in love

A. The Lord Jesus as our propitiation is the provision of God's love.

B. Because God, in His love, wants to be gracious to man while at the same time God's righteousness puts requirements upon man, God provided man with the Lord Jesus as the propitiation.

Note: The point is not that God was angry and would not forgive man, and that the Lord came to propitiate God's wrath. We have to be clear. The One who conciliates the situation is God Himself. God's heart causes Him to deal with man in love, but God's righteousness puts requirements upon man. Therefore God Himself provided man with the Lord Jesus as the propitiation to propitiate the contradictory situation between God's love and God's righteousness.

IV. How to obtain the propitiation of the Lord Jesus

Develop this point.

Subject One Hundred Ninety-nine
GOD IS LIGHT AND GOD IS LOVE

Scripture: 1 John 1:5; 4:8

I. God is light

A. Light is a matter of nature.

B. Light has the function of shining.

C. God as light denotes the function of that nature of God which is shining.

D. Once man touches God, he receives light. He is no more in darkness.

II. God is love

A. Love is a matter of sentiment.

B. Love has the function of imparting warmth.

C. God as love denotes the function of the sentiment of God which imparts warmth.

D. Once man touches God, he receives warmth and departs from coldness.

III. How God is expressed as light and love

A. He shows forth His light in His Son Jesus.

B. He shows forth His love through the cross.

C. God caused His Son to accomplish redemption through the cross to become man's Savior, that man may obtain Him as light and love.

IV. How to obtain God as light and love

A. Confess that you are in darkness and in coldness.

B. Receive the Son of God, Jesus Christ, as your Savior.

C. Have fellowship with God through Christ.

Subject Two Hundred

HE THAT HAS THE SON HAS LIFE

Scripture: 1 John 5:11-13

I. The Son of God is God in another form

A. The Son of God is Jesus Christ. Jesus Christ is God come as a man in order to save man.

B. The Son of God is God made manifest to man.

II. God's life is in the Son of God

A. God is in His Son, so God's life is also in the Son.

B. The life that is in the Son of God is the eternal life.

III. He that has the Son of God has life

A. Life is within the Son of God. If man wants to obtain life, he must receive the Son of God.

B. Once man receives the Son of God, he has God and also the life of God.

IV. The proof of having life

A. 1 John 5:12 says, "He that hath the Son hath the life."

B. The proof that someone has obtained life is that his living has changed. Describe how once a man receives the Lord, his life is changed.

V. How to obtain the Son of God

A. Confess that you do not have God's life.

B. Believe in the Son of God.

C. To believe means to receive the Son of God as Savior with our heart and our spirit.

Subject Two Hundred One

KNOWING THAT YOU HAVE ETERNAL LIFE

Scripture: 1 John 5:12, 13

I. The meaning of eternal life

A. Eternal life is life that is eternal.

B. Eternal life is God's life.

II. Eternal life is in the Son of God

A. God put His eternal life into His Son.

B. He that has the Son of God has eternal life.

III. The proof of having eternal life

A. You can know whether you have eternal life. *Emphasize that it is wrong if one does not know whether he has eternal life.*

B. The words of the Bible prove that we have eternal life. Here it says, "These things have I written unto you, that ye may know that ye have eternal life..."

C. Based upon the words of the Bible, one should know that he has eternal life.

D. If one does not believe in God's word, he makes God a liar.

E. We should reject our own feeling rather than disbelieve the words of the Bible; we should distrust ourselves rather than make God a liar.

Subject Two Hundred Two

THE WHOLE WORLD LIETH IN THE EVIL ONE

Scripture: 1 John 5:19

I. Men are captives of the evil one

A. Once men followed the evil one to commit sin, they became captives of the evil one.

B. As soon as a man is born, he is in the position of a captive.

II. Men are in the power of the Devil

A. To say that man became the Devil's captive means that man fell into the power of the Devil.

B. To be in the power of the Devil is to be dominated by him.

III. Men are lying in the hands of the evil one

A. Men are not only dominated by the Devil, but they are also manipulated by him.

B. To be dominated means that one is refused his freedom; even worse, to be manipulated means one is led to act unwittingly, with no consciousness of being manipulated.

C. To dominate is to deny one the freedom to do anything; to manipulate is to make one do something without the realization of what he is doing. A man lying in the hands of the Devil is like a patient on the operating table who, having been anesthetized, allows the doctor to operate freely.

D. Give examples to show how man is in the Devil's hand, committing sin without consciousness and without self-control.

IV. How to escape from the hands of the Devil

A. Confess that you are in the hands of the Devil.

B. Believe in Jesus as your Savior because He has destroyed the Devil and nullified the works of the Devil.

Subject Two Hundred Three

THE LAMB THAT WAS SLAIN

Scripture: Rev. 5:6, 9; 1:5; 7:14, 17; 13:8

I. The Lamb is Christ

A. Christ came to redeem men.

B. Christ's redemption was accomplished through His coming as the Lamb of God. As the Lamb He was slain and His blood was shed for men.

II. To be slain is to be crucified

A. Christ was crucified on the cross because He bore man's sins.

B. Christ was crucified to satisfy God's righteous requirement.

III. The effectiveness of the Lamb's being slain

A. It enables us to depart from sins.

B. It washes us clean and white.

C. It qualifies us to receive the life of God.

IV. How to obtain the Lamb that was slain

A. Confess that He was slain for you.

B. Receive Him as your Savior.

Subject Two Hundred Four

THE WRATH OF THE LAMB

Scripture: Rev. 6:12-17

I. The Lamb is Christ

A. The Lamb symbolizes Christ as man's Savior Who accomplished redemption.

B. Whenever the Bible refers to Christ as the Lamb, it alludes to His being the Savior for the redemption of man.

II. The tender love of the Lamb

A. Whenever the Bible mentions the Lamb, there is the thought of tender love conveyed.

B. The way Christ appears as the Lamb is also tender-loving.

C. When Christ was being offered up for the redemption of man, He was like a lamb being led to the slaughter; He was without murmuring or hatred.

D. When Christ bore man's sins on the cross, He was the Lamb full of tender love.

III. The wrath of the Lamb

A. While the Lamb was tender-loving for the redemption of man, Revelation 6 refers to the wrath of the Lamb.

B. The wrath of the Lamb is not caused by man's sins,
but by man's unbelief and rejection. Even though man
is sinful, God is able to redeem him; but man's unbelief and rejection kindle God's wrath.

IV. The time of the wrath of the Lamb

A. The time of His wrath will be at the end of this age.

B. There is the possibility that the age could end at any
moment.

V. The consequence of the wrath of the Lamb

A. When the Lamb is wroth, the heavens and the earth
will be turned upside down and men will be struck
with sudden terror and fear.

B. All those who heard the gospel and did not believe,
but rather rejected Him, will be in that calamity.

VI. How to escape the wrath of the Lamb

A. Do not put off confronting God until tomorrow. Tomorrow may be the day of His wrath. Repent and believe
in Him today.

B. Today you can receive Him as the loving Lamb. Confess
that He is your Savior and open your heart to Him.

Subject Two Hundred Five
THE ETERNAL JUDGMENT

Scripture: Rev. 20:11-15

I. The conclusion of the last days

A. The last days of the universe will be concluded by
judgment.

B. Of all God's judgments the greatest will be His judgment upon men of all generations at the end of the
present heavens and earth.

II. God's judgment

A. God's judgment at the end of the present heavens
and earth will be executed at the great white throne.
Whiteness signifies righteousness and purity. All of
man's unrighteousness and filthiness will be reflected
in front of that throne of judgment.

B. God's judgment will be based upon the books before Him. These are the records of all of men's words and deeds. God's judgment will be made according to these records.

C. God's judgment in that day will be made according to what we do today.

III. The result of God's judgment

A. All those whose names are not written in the book of life will be cast into the lake of fire.

B. All those whose names are written in the book of life are the ones who have believed in the Lord Jesus and have obtained His life.

C. The result of the judgment is that all those who did not believe in the Lord Jesus will be cast into the lake of fire.

D. To be cast into the lake of fire is to perish forever.

IV. How to avoid the eternal judgment

A. Repent and turn to God.

B. Receive the Lord Jesus as our Savior. This is also to obtain God's life so that our names may be written in the book of life. Only those whose names are written in the book of life can escape the eternal judgment.

Subject Two Hundred Six

THE WATER OF THE FOUNTAIN OF LIFE

Scripture: Rev. 7:17; 21:6; 22:1, 17

I. The fountain of life

A. God is the fountain of life.

B. This fountain issues from the Son of God. God is in His Son Jesus Christ as the fountain of life.

II. The water of the fountain of life

A. The water of the fountain of life is the life of God.

B. This water of life is flowing out of God's Son to be received by man.

III. The function of the water of life

A. As water is for quenching thirst, so also is the water of life. It quenches the thirst of human living.

B. Water is not only for quenching thirst, but also for enjoyment. So also is the water of life to man. It not only quenches man's thirst, but also gives man eternal enjoyment.

C. The water of life also delivers man from death.

IV. How to obtain the water of life

A. To obtain water you must drink.

B. You do not need to pay any price because it is freely given by God. Everyone can drink freely.

C. To drink freely is not to depend on your works, but simply to believe and receive.

Subject Two Hundred Seven

THE TORMENT OF HELL

Scripture: Rev. 14:9-11; 21:8; Mark 9:43, 48

I. Hell is the portion of God's wrath

(In Rev. 14:10 cup means portion.)

A. Because of God's love toward man, He accomplished redemption for him.

B. If a man refuses to repent, he remains under God's wrath.

C. The totality of God's wrath is hell.

II. There is fire and brimstone in hell

A. Fire burns man.

B. Brimstone chokes man.

C. The lake of fire which burns with brimstone is unquenchable.

III. There are worms that do not die in hell

To be bitten by mosquitoes, bugs, or fleas is already

unbearable, but imagine the torment from the worms in hell which do not die with the unquenchable fire!

IV. How to escape hell

Develop this point.

Subject Two Hundred Eight

WHO SHALL BE IN THE LAKE OF FIRE

Scripture: Rev. 21:8

I. Those who will be in the lake of fire

A. The fearful. These want to believe in Jesus but are afraid of others' mocking.

B. The unbelieving. These would not receive the Lord Jesus as their Savior.

C. The abominable. These do not believe in the true God, but rather worship idols. This is like an evil woman who loves another man besides her own husband and commits abominations.

D. The murderers. Once a man worships idols, it is easy for him to commit sins and to hate and kill others.

E. The fornicators. Today's newspapers, magazines, and movies are full of fornication.

F. The sorcerers. These include fortune-tellers, sooth-sayers, astrologists, etc.

G. The idolaters. Abomination and idolatry are nearly the same. The difference is that abomination refers to the nature of idol worship, whereas idolatry refers to the act of idol worship.

H. The liars.

I. All men are at least one of these eight kinds of people. Whoever is none of these, please raise your hand.

II. How to escape the lake of fire

A. Repent.

B. Believe in Jesus.

Subject Two Hundred Nine

THE PLEASURES OF THE NEW JERUSALEM

Scripture: Rev. 21:10; 22:5; 7:15-17

I. The New Jerusalem is a shining city (Rev. 21:21, 18; 4:3)

A. The street is pure gold signifying God's divine nature.

B. The gates are pearls signifying our entrance into the city through Christ's redemption.

C. The wall is jasper signifying the riches of the divine life in the believers.

II. The New Jerusalem is God's dwelling place

A. There is the throne of God and of the Lamb (Rev. 22:1).

B. There is the glory of God shining through the Lord Jesus as the lamp (Rev. 21:23).

III. The New Jerusalem is full of the enjoyment of the blessing of life

A. There is the tree of life (Rev. 22:2).

B. There is the water of life (Rev. 22:1).

IV. The New Jerusalem is where God's eternal care is manifested

A. God's light will shine over it.

B. Christ will be shepherding there.

V. In the New Jerusalem there is no more hunger, thirst, tears, darkness, or suffering

A. There will be no hunger or thirst (Rev. 7:16).

B. There will be no darkness (Rev. 22:5).

C. There will be no tears (Rev. 21:4).

D. There will be no suffering (Rev. 21:4).

VI. How to enter into the New Jerusalem

A. Repent and believe in the Lord Jesus.

B. Through believing, your name will be written in the Lamb's book of life. Only those whose names are written in the book of life can enter into the New Jerusalem (Rev. 21:27).

Subject Two Hundred Ten

WHO WILL BE IN THE NEW JERUSALEM

Scripture: Rev. 21:27

I. Who will be in the New Jerusalem?

A. Those who repent and believe in Jesus.

B. Those who receive the Lord Jesus as their Savior.

C. Those whose sins are forgiven.

D. Those who have obtained God's life.

E. Those whose names are written in the book of life.

F. Those who follow the Lamb.

II. How to enter into the New Jerusalem

Develop this point.

Part III
Special Topics

In the following outlines there are eight groups, each consisting of several topics which are suitable for special gospel preaching meetings.

GROUP 1
MATTERS RELATED TO MAN

Subject Two Hundred Eleven

THE ORIGIN OF MAN

Scripture: Acts 17:24-29

The main purpose of this subject is to prove that God exists.

I. Man's origin is God, because man is created by God

II. The amazing structure of man's body proves that man is created by God

In passing, argue against and show the absurdity of the theory of evolution.

III. The chemical composition of the human body proves that man is created by God

   A. The Bible says that man is made of dust, and the chemical composition of the human body is the same as dust.

   B. When you are speaking, mention in detail the function of different members of the human body, how they are utterly marvelous and could never have come about through mere evolution.

IV. Therefore, we must conclude that if there is man, there is God

If you and I exist, there is God. Man's existence proves that God exists.

Subject Two Hundred Twelve

THE NATURE OF MAN

Scripture: Jer. 17:9; Mark 7:21-23; Rom. 7:14, 18; Gen. 8:21

I. The characteristics of man express the nature of man

Every object has its own characteristics. Because man is

living, his characteristics express his nature. What an
object is depends on its characteristics; what man is
depends on his nature. In other words, with an inani-
mate object it is a matter of characteristics, while with a
living person it is a matter of nature. If we want to study
the subject of man, we cannot avoid studying the nature
of man.

II. Man's nature, is it good or bad, virtuous or evil?

A. First, discuss what the sages of both the East and the
West have had to say. Some have said that the nature
of man is good while others have said it is evil.

B. Then, using the Bible, prove that human nature is
evil. When speaking of the evil nature of man, you
should mention that the nature of man at the time of
creation was good (Eccl. 7:29); but later, because sin
came in causing man to fall, man's nature became
evil. The evil nature came from Satan. Satan defiled
and overcame man's good nature. So, we may say that
today man's nature is evil. Use the words of the Bible
to show this clearly.

III. Conclusion

A. Man's nature is evil beyond repair.

B. Man needs another life with another nature.

Subject Two Hundred Thirteen

THE DEEDS OF MAN

Scripture: Rom. 3:10-18

I. Man's deeds express his nature

A. What man does is a result of what he is; what he is is
based upon his human nature. Since man's nature is
evil, so his deeds also are evil.

B. Being in such a condition, man needs to realize that
he is a sinner.

In speaking of man's evil deeds, focus upon the sins
mentioned in Romans, plus some others. By this,
you should touch people's feeling and cause them to

realize that they are sinners. Pick out a few sins such as lying, stealing, and adultery, discussing them thoroughly and severely. First talk about the principle, then illustrate by examples. Do not touch the deeds of man superficially, but rather dig out the sins that are within him. Depict man's condition when he commits sins; do this in such a way that the audience may have the feeling of sin and be convicted.

II. How to be saved from sins

Develop this point.

Subject Two Hundred Fourteen

THE NEED OF MAN

Scripture: John 3:3; Jer. 13:23; Heb. 9:22

I. Man's need is based upon his condition

Because man's nature is evil and his behavior is corrupted, there is the need to deal with his evil nature and evil deeds.

II. Man's self-improvement and good behavior

A. Sages and human philosophers throughout the generations have discovered the corrupt situation of man and have often tried their best to help it. The result is that man either tries to correct himself or to do good.

B. To try to improve oneself is an attempt to make up for the lack in one's nature. To do good is to try to make up for the failure in one's deeds.

III. Man's self-improvement and good behavior are both useless

A. Self-improvement cannot change the evil nature of man, just as the leopard cannot change his spots and the Ethiopian cannot change his skin.

B. The principle of man's living by good behavior is basically wrong. Because to do good is a fundamental duty or responsibility of a human being, it cannot be regarded as an accomplishment even if a man were to succeed in doing good. Moreover, neither could good behavior hide the sins which may have been committed previously. For example, it is futile if by doing good a man attempts to erase his sin of having murdered somebody.

IV. Man needs a saving way which includes two aspects

A. Man's evil deeds need to be erased. Man needs a salvation whereby his sins may be taken away and the record of them may be erased.

B. Man's evil nature must be replaced. Because his evil nature cannot be corrected or improved, it must be replaced.

V. God's way of salvation

A. The Lord Jesus shed His blood for us and ransomed us from sin. Thus, God's salvation takes care of man's evil deeds.

B. Through this salvation we are regenerated and receive a new life, God's life, which replaces the original evil nature. Such a salvation also takes care of man's evil nature.

Subject Two Hundred Fifteen

THE SAVIOR OF MAN

Scripture: Acts 4:12; 1 Tim. 1:15; Luke 2:10-11; 19:10

I. Man needs a Savior

Since man needs the way of salvation (refer to Subject 214), man needs a savior. There must be a savior in order that the way of salvation might be accomplished.

II. The Lord Jesus is not a teacher but a Savior

A. Throughout all the generations not one sage, philosopher, or religious person could call himself the Savior. At most, such people have been merely religious leaders or teachers.

B. Only the Lord Jesus Christ called Himself the Savior. The Bible declares that He is the Savior, and also myriads of Christians throughout the generations testify that He is the Savior. *Emphasize this point.*

III. He is able to save

A. The Lord Jesus is God becoming man to be our Savior.

B. Since He is God, nothing is impossible with Him. He can both redeem man and deliver him from sin.

Subject Two Hundred Sixteen

THE SALVATION OF MAN

Scripture: Matt. 20:28; 1 Pet. 2:24; John 12:24; 1 Pet. 1:3

The subject of this message is the cross.

I. Since a savior is one who saves man, he must accomplish redemption for man

II. Throughout the generations no sage, human philosopher, or religious leader has ever claimed to have accomplished redemption for man

III. The Savior is Jesus

A. Jesus Himself said that He would accomplish redemption for man, give up His life for man, and be a ransom for man.

B. *Stress the cross in this section.* He hung upon the cross in order to bear our sins. The cross is the way of salvation which God prepared for man. When Jesus was on the cross, God put upon Him the sins of all men.

C. The Savior not only said that He would give up His life to be a ransom for man, but also that His death would release His life. Because of His resurrection, man is able to obtain His life and be born again.

IV. Christ's crucifixion, the shedding of His blood, and His death and resurrection are our salvation

A. Christ's blood takes care of our sinful deeds.

B. Christ's life takes care of our sinful nature.

Subject Two Hundred Seventeen

THE WAY OF SALVATION FOR MAN

Scripture: Acts 2:37, 38; 16:30, 31; 10:43; John 3:36; 1:12; 6:51; 4:14; Rom. 10:8-10, 13

I. **Both the Savior and His salvation are available**

II. **The need is for man to receive**

A. If a man is to receive the Savior and be saved, he must confess that his nature is corrupt and his deeds are evil. He must repent. To repent is to turn one's thoughts and intents to God; this includes hating, confessing, forsaking, and departing from one's sins.

B. Once a man repents, the following step is to believe in the Lord Jesus.

1. Believing cannot be inherited. Do not think that you are saved because your father or grandfather are pastors or elders.

2. Believing is not joining a religion or going through a baptismal ceremony.

3. Believing is not believing some doctrine.

4. Believing is more than agreeing.

5. Believing is not merely to acknowledge. To acknowledge that Jesus is the Savior crucified for us is still not enough.

6. Believing is receiving. To receive is to eat and to drink. The Bible invites man to receive Christ by eating and drinking Him as the bread of life and the water of life. The Bible likens God's salvation to a feast. At a feast you must use your own mouth to eat and drink in order to receive the food. Others cannot believe for you. If three generations of your forefathers believed in the Lord, or even if you yourself have been baptized and believe some doctrines, you are still not saved. You must let the Lord Jesus come into you. Merely agreeing and acknowledging are both useless. Eating and drinking the Lord Jesus as your bread and water will bring salvation to you.

III. How to receive

A. Call upon the Lord Jesus.

B. Pray to Him according to the inner feeling. Do not compose a prayer. If you feel sinful within, just confess your sin-fulness; if you are conscious of a certain sin, then confess that sin.

Subject Two Hundred Eighteen

THE PROOF OF MAN'S SALVATION

Scripture: 1 John 5:12-13; John 6:47; 3:18; Acts 10:43; 1 John 3:14

I. You can know that you are saved

Every man is aware of it when he receives something important. The Savior and His salvation are exceedingly great. When a man is saved, he must not be unaware of it. It is not right for him to receive the Savior and His salvation without realizing it.

II. How can you know that you are saved? In other words, what proof is there that you are saved? There are two sides to the proof

A. One side is God's Word. God's Word proves that you are saved.

1. John 6:47 says that whosoever believes in the Son has eternal life. Once you have believed in the Lord Jesus, you have eternal life. If you still say that you do not have eternal life, either you are lying or God is lying.

2. Furthermore, God's Word says that once you have believed, you are forgiven. Then are your sins forgiven? You must answer this question according to God's Word.

3. His Word also says, "He that hath the Son hath the life." Do you have the Son of God? If you have the Son of God, you must have the life of God.

B. The other side of the proof is the change in your life

and living. Once you receive the Lord and obtain the Lord's life, your living must have some changes. Formerly you loved gambling and the sinful things; now they have lost their attraction.

III. Feelings are unreliable

Do not depend upon your feelings as they are unreliable. If you realize what God's Word says and that some changes have taken place in your life, that is sufficient proof that you are saved. Do not emphasize feeling but rely upon the fact that you are saved. It is like having money in your pocket. Whether or not you feel it, it is a fact that the money is there.

Subject Two Hundred Nineteen

AFTER A MAN IS SAVED

Scripture: Matt. 3:8; 2 Cor. 5:14; Rom. 12:1; Eph. 6:18; 2 Tim. 3:16-17; Heb. 10:25; Acts 2:42

I. He needs to be baptized
II. He needs to deal with sins
III. He needs to consecrate himself
IV. He needs to pray and read the Word
V. He needs to attend meetings regularly and have fellowship with other Christians

GROUP 2
MATTERS RELATED TO SIN

Subject Two Hundred Twenty

THE ORIGIN OF SIN—SATAN

Scripture: Isa. 14:12-14; John 8:44; Ezek. 28:13-17

I. How sin came in

A. Satan was originally an archangel created by God.

B. Because he was proud and exalted himself, wanting to

be equal with God, sin came in. It was through Satan's rebellion that he became God's enemy.

II. What is behind all sin

A. The principle of sin is pride, self-exaltation, self-will, not caring for God's desires, and disobedience to God.

B. Because Satan was the first one to exalt himself and rebel against God, he became the one from whom all sin originates.

Subject Two Hundred Twenty-one

THE ONE COMMITTING SIN—ADAM

Scripture: Rom. 5:18-19; 3:10-18

I. Sin transmitted to man

A. Although sin originated with Satan and was initiated by him, it was passed on to man and committed by man. Explain how Satan tempted Adam to commit sin in the garden of Eden.

II. Man being a sinner

A. Because Adam followed Satan and was tempted by Satan, sin entered into man. Since that time all men have been sinners. Man's committing of sin did not begin at his birth, but it began nearly 6,000 years ago. From the time of Adam until now man has been committing sin.

B. Today you also commit sin. Use examples of man's living and conduct to show that he commits sins.

Subject Two Hundred Twenty-two

THE ONE WHO CONDEMNS SIN—GOD

Scripture: Gen. 18:25; John 8:7-11; Exo. 34:7

I. God should condemn sin

A. God created us.

B. He also rules over us.

C. It follows that if we sin, He ought to condemn our sins.

II. God can condemn sin

A. Only God is without sin.

B. Hence, He alone can condemn our sins.

III. God will condemn sin

A. God is righteous.

B. His righteousness demands His judgment on our sins.

Subject Two Hundred Twenty-three

THE ONE WHO REDEEMS US FROM SIN— CHRIST

Scripture: Isa. 53:6; 1 Pet. 2:24; Heb. 9:12

I. Man needs redemption

A. Man is sinful.

B. Man, being sinful, has neither the right nor the power to redeem himself from sin.

II. Christ is man's Redeemer

A. Christ is God, coming to redeem us. Only He could and would redeem man from sin.

B. Christ redeemed man from sin through His death on the cross. The penalty He paid on the cross accomplished redemption on man's behalf.

C. Christ died on the cross, bearing our sins in His own body.

D. The redemptive work of Christ on the cross is complete and eternal.

Subject Two Hundred Twenty-four

THE ONE WHO FORGIVES SIN—GOD

Scripture: 1 John 1:9

I. The One who forgives sin

A. The One who condemns sin is the One who forgives

sin. Only He who is qualified to condemn is qualified to forgive.

B. Thus, only God can forgive our sins.

II. The basis of God's forgiveness

A. The forgiveness of God is based upon Christ's redemption and is executed through His righteousness.

B. The forgiveness of God is also based upon His faithfulness and is according to His word. Not only has God sent Christ to accomplish the work of redemption for us, He also gives us His word to proclaim the fact of redemption. If we believe in His proclamation, He has to forgive us because of His faithfulness and because of His word.

III. The completeness of God's forgiveness

Because Christ's redemption is complete and eternal, God's forgiveness is also complete and eternal.

Subject Two Hundred Twenty-five

THE ONE WHO IS FREED FROM SIN—
THE BELIEVER

Scripture: Acts 10:43; 26:18; Rom. 6:7; 8:1-2

I. How can man be freed from sin?

A. Christ has accomplished redemption and God has promised forgiveness.

B. So now, if a man believes, he can be freed from sin.

II. To be freed from sin has two meanings

A. To be freed from sin means to be freed from sinful acts. This also means that the history of sins is erased and the judgment on sins is removed.

B. To be freed from sin means to be freed from the nature of sin. This is because the power of sin is broken and the pains of sin are over.

III. Once a man believes and is freed from sin, he is immediately justified

Subject Two Hundred Twenty-six

THE ONE WHO BEARS SIN—SATAN

Scripture: Matt. 25:41; Lev. 16:7-10; Rev. 20:10

I. Who should bear sin?

A. Since sin originated with Satan, it should ultimately be borne by him. Although Satan transmitted sin to man, God sought to remove it from him and to give it back to Satan. To do this the Lord Jesus bore sin for a short while on the cross, but that was only the bearing of man's sentence for sin; sin itself is ultimately and eternally to be borne by Satan alone.

II. How sin will be borne

A. Although man was deceived into receiving the burden of sin from Satan's hand, thus becoming a sinner, God has no intention for man to bear sin. As soon as a man believes in the redemptive work accomplished by Christ, he is freed from sin.

B. If he does not believe, he will have to help Satan to bear sin for eternity. Thus Matthew 25:41 says that the unbelieving ones shall enter into the eternal fire prepared for the Devil. The lake of fire is not for man, but for Satan. If you follow Satan, you will have to share his judgment.

GROUP 3
MAIN POINTS OF THE GOSPEL

Subject Two Hundred Twenty-seven

GOD

Scripture: Rom. 1:19-20; Acts 14:15-18; 17:24-29

I. The creation of the universe proves the existence of God

II. The order of the universe proves the existence of God

III. The biological structure of man proves the existence of God

IV. The psychological structure of man proves the existence of God

Subject Two Hundred Twenty-eight

THE DEVIL

Scripture: John 8:44; 1 John 5:19; 3:8

I. **Everything in the universe has its opposite**

A. Positive and negative, up and down, good and evil, true and false, are opposites.

B. White and black, light and darkness, heaven and earth, are also opposites.

C. Hence, as there is a God, there must also be a Devil.

II. **All the contradictions in the universe come from this opposition between God and the Devil**

A. Since there exists both God and the Devil, a conflict occurs.

B. All the opposite pairs such as good and evil, light and darkness, white and black, true and false, are contradictions existing in the universe.

III. **All the tragedies and miseries in the universe originate from the Devil**

A. Since there is not only God but also the Devil, there appear not only bright, good, and happy things, but also dark, evil, and miserable things.

B. All the dark, evil, and miserable things come from the Devil.

IV. **All the sins of man come from the Devil**

A. No one sins voluntarily and willingly, but everyone sins because he cannot help it.

B. This is because the whole world lies in the hand of the Devil.

V. **The Devil, which is Satan, is the enemy of God**

A. The existence of falsehood proves the existence of

truth in the same way that the existence of forged
bank notes proves that there are genuine ones.

B. The existence of a Devil proves the existence of God.

Subject Two Hundred Twenty-nine

MAN

Scripture: Gen. 1:26-27; 1 John 3:8a; Rom. 3:10-12; Heb.
9:27; Rev. 20:11-15

I. Man is made by God and for God

Man was innocent in his original state.

II. Man followed after Satan

By this he became corrupted and forsook God.

III. Man sinned

IV. The end of man's sin is death

After death there is judgment, and after judgment, there
is the lake of fire.

Subject Two Hundred Thirty

SIN

Scripture: Rom. 1:28-32; Mark 7:21-23

The book of Romans mentions twenty-one kinds of sins,
and the Gospel of Mark mentions thirteen. There are
altogether thirty-four kinds of sins. A few towards which
the feelings of the sinners are sensitive can be chosen
and expounded in detail.

Subject Two Hundred Thirty-one

THE SAVIOR

Scripture: Matt. 1:21; Luke 2:11; John 4:42; Acts 4:12

I. Man needs a savior because he is sinful

II. Throughout the entire history of mankind no one ever claimed to be the Savior

III. **Only the Lord Jesus said that He is the Savior**

IV. **The Lord Jesus is God coming not only as man but as the Savior**

(Refer to Subject 215.)

Subject Two Hundred Thirty-two

REDEMPTION

Scripture: Matt. 20:28; Heb. 9:12; Rom. 3:24

I. **The Lord desires to save**

He came as the Savior to accomplish the work of redemption. This work was accomplished through His death on the cross where the Savior bore man's sins and died in man's place.

II. **Salvation is through His death and resurrection**

Not only did the Savior die to redeem us and to free us from sin, but He rose from the dead that man may receive His life and thus be regenerated.

III. **Man's need is salvation**

Man's need is not that he be reformed or improved, but that he be redeemed and regenerated. (Refer to Subject 216.)

Subject Two Hundred Thirty-three

BELIEVING

Scripture: Mark 1:15; Acts 16:31; Rom. 10:10-13

I. **The Savior's redemption having been accomplished, there is the need for man's receiving**

II. **Before he receives, man must first repent**

III. **After repenting man needs to believe, and this believing is his receiving**

IV. **In this receiving he should call upon the name of the Lord**

(Refer to Subject 217.)

Subject Two Hundred Thirty-four

SALVATION

Scripture: Acts 16:31; 10:45; John 3:36; 1 John 5:13; Luke 19:8-9

I. As soon as man believes, he is saved

II. Salvation is of two aspects

On the one hand, man receives forgiveness of sins; on the other hand, he receives the life of God.

III. Assurance of salvation is based upon the word of the Bible

The Bible guarantees our salvation.

IV. One proof of man's salvation is that there is a change in his life

GROUP 4
QUESTIONS ENCOUNTERED
CONCERNING THE GOSPEL

Subject Two Hundred Thirty-five

GOD, THE DEVIL, THE SPIRIT OF MAN, AND THE SOUL

Scripture: Rom. 1:20; John 8:44; 1 John 3:8; Matt. 16:26; Luke 12:20; 16:19-31

I. There is a God

II. There is a Devil

Give examples of people being possessed by demons, speaking for demons, and performing demonic works. All of these have the devil as their source and sin as their consequence.

III. There is the spirit of man

A. Prove the existence of the human spirit by the human conscience. Although the conscience cannot be seen, everyone feels the effect of its working, and has to recognize its existence. The conscience is the main part of the spirit.

B. Prove the existence of the human spirit by life. The difference between a dead person and a living one is life, and life is simply the spirit (Luke 8:55).

IV. There is man's soul

A. Show that there is a soul by using the illustration of love. Although it cannot be seen, love no doubt exists and is one of the functions of the soul.

B. The death of a man also proves the existence of the soul. A man's death is simply the departure of his soul from his body. Although the body is still present, the man is said to have departed, meaning that the soul has left the body.

C. Use the story of the rich man and Lazarus in Luke 16 to further substantiate that there is man's soul. While in Hades the rich man was able to recall things that had happened during his earthly life. Although his body was buried, it was his soul that was remembering his life on earth.

Subject Two Hundred Thirty-six

JESUS IS GOD

Scripture: John 1:1; 10:30; 14:9

I. Jesus said that He is God

If you want to know who a man is, you have to ask him. Throughout history no philosopher, religious leader, or sage has dared to claim to be God. Only Jesus said that He is God.

II. His deeds prove that He is God

He performed miracles and spoke words of wisdom and life.

III. His disciples professed that He is God

IV. The Bible says that He is God

V. The experience of the believers throughout the centuries confirms that He is God

VI. **The power of His salvation proves that He is God**

VII. **The prayer of the believers bears witness that He is God**

Subject Two Hundred Thirty-seven
JESUS BECOMING MAN

Scripture: John 1:14; 1 Tim. 3:16; 2:5

I. **The necessity of Jesus becoming a man**

A. Being God Himself, He could not come near to man and contact man unless He were to become a man.

B. Without becoming a man, He could not sympathize with man since He had not passed through man's experience.

C. Without becoming a man, He could not bear the sins of man.

II. **The plausibility of Jesus becoming a man**

A. If He could create man out of nothing, much more He could be conceived through a virgin.

B. Since He established the law of human reproduction, He can establish another law of reproduction.

C. Even science itself confirms this possibility.

III. **The fact of Jesus becoming a man**

Using the Bible for this section, show that He was conceived of a virgin, that He was born in a manger, and that the glad tidings of His birth were announced by the angels. *Develop this with other related facts.*

Subject Two Hundred Thirty-eight
JESUS BEARING SIN

Scripture: 1 Pet. 2:24; Isa. 53:5-6, 12

I. **The purpose of His becoming a man was to bear the sins of man**

A. His death on the cross was for the redemption of man from sins.

B. His blood was shed for many, for the remission of sins.

II. How can He bear the sins of those who are not yet born?

A. Although man is limited by time, God is not under the same limitation. For example, some people make preparations for their descendants even before the latter are born. Consider how the railway was laid long before you were born. When you want to travel by train, you do not have to ask that the tracks be laid again.

B. God is not limited by time because He is eternal. Look at the circle in the figure. Where is the beginning and where is the end? As in a circle there is neither beginning nor ending, so also in God's provision the cross is timeless, taking care of your sins before they were even committed in time.

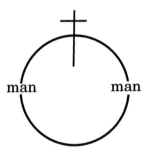

III. How can the blood of Jesus cleanse our sins?

A. It is not the physical applying of some blood on your body that cleanses you.

B. His blood is a symbol. It is a symbol of God's righteous demand being fulfilled.

Subject Two Hundred Thirty-nine

THE RESURRECTION OF JESUS

Scripture: 1 Cor. 15:36-38; John 12:24; Acts 2:32; 3:15; 5:30; 1 Cor. 15:14,17

I. Jesus resurrected from the dead

A. Not only spiritually, but also physically and psychologically.

B. His tomb was empty.

C. After His resurrection, He asked His disciples to touch His side, proving that He was risen physically.

II. In His resurrection He is the divine life-seed

If a seed with life concealed within it can sprout after being buried in the ground, how much more can Jesus, being God, with the divine life inside Him, sprout forth again to bear fruit.

III. The Lord's saving power proves His resurrection

A. Give examples and tell stories of the present and real saving power of the Lord Jesus.

B. The gospel of the Lord is a gospel of power.

C. Power proves that He is living.

D. All the founders of the different religions lay dead in their tombs—only Jesus resurrected.

IV. The power of answered prayer proves the Lord's resurrection

A. Today whenever a man calls on the name of the Lord, his prayer is answered.

B. This experience of prayer being answered is a proof of the resurrection of Jesus.

Subject Two Hundred Forty

THE ASCENSION OF JESUS

Scripture: Acts 1:9-11; 2:33; 5:31

I. Being resurrected, Jesus lives in this universe, in the heavens.

II. The witnesses of His ascension

A. His disciples saw His ascension.

B. The angels also saw it and bore witness to it.

C. His ascension happened in time and space.

D. It was not a figment of man's imagination or an abstraction, but an accomplished historical fact.

III. The authority of His name proves Jesus' ascension

A. The Bible says that when He ascended He received a name which is above every name.

B. Whenever man calls on that name, the authority in it is manifested, and prayers are answered.

IV. Today the whole world recognizes Jesus

This is also a proof of His ascension. The whole world uses His birth as the basis of its calendar. When a person's birthdate is recognized as the basis of a people's calendar, to the same person does that people belong. Thus the whole world unconsciously recognizes Him as the Lord of all.

Subject Two Hundred Forty-one

THE COMING AGAIN OF JESUS

Scripture: Matt. 16:27; Acts 1:11; 1 Thes. 4:16-17; 2 Thes. 1:7-10; Phil. 3:20-21

I. Jesus Himself said that He will come again.

II. In His ascension the angels mentioned that He will come again.

III. All His disciples said that He will come again.

IV. His coming is with signs

A. The Bible tells us that the greatest of the signs are the restoration of the nation of Israel and the increase of tribulations.

B. Even the astronomers and the geologists tell us that the tribulations on the earth are increasing.

C. Since the signs preceding His coming are being fulfilled, His coming will definitely come to pass.

V. His coming is for two things

A. He will rapture those that believe in Him.

B. He will judge the unbelieving ones.

VI. How will He regard you at His coming?

Develop this point.

GROUP 5
THE CHAIN OF HUMAN LIFE

Subject Two Hundred Forty-two

THE FIRST LINK—SIN

Scripture: Rom. 5:12

I. Man is born, raised, grown, and immersed in sin

II. Give examples to prove the sinfulness of man's behavior

Subject Two Hundred Forty-three

THE SECOND LINK—DEATH

Scripture: Rom. 5:12; 6:23; Ezek. 18:4

I. Death comes from sin, and hence is joined to sin

The more sin a man commits the faster he dies.

II. There are four steps in death

A. The spirit is dead, lacking any sense of morality, and without knowledge of God.

B. The body will die.

C. The soul will be cast into Hades.

D. At the end of the world, the body, soul, and spirit will be reunited to be thrown into the lake of fire.

III. Man lives in death today

He is not living daily, but is dying daily.

Subject Two Hundred Forty-four

THE THIRD LINK—JUDGMENT

Scripture: Heb. 9:27; Rev. 20:11-13

I. There is a coming judgment

All the iniquity and unrighteousness that a man commits in his lifetime cannot be erased merely by death. There will be a judgment.

II. In His word God said that man will suffer His judgment

III. The future judgment is after a man's death

The death of a man is not his end, but the beginning of a second stage.

IV. The future judgment will be according to man's deeds today

V. The future judgment is altogether just and righteous

It will be the judgment before the great white throne.

VI. Unless a man believes in the Lord Jesus today, in that judgment he will stand condemned

Subject Two Hundred Forty-five

THE FOURTH LINK—HELL

Scripture: Rev. 20:15; 21:8

I. Hell as God's jail

A. When someone commits a crime he is judged and then put into jail.

B. The universe is governed by God.

C. When man transgresses the law of God, he must be put into God's jail.

D. This universal jail is called hell.

II. Hell being the lake of fire

A. In the future, after God has judged man, He will send all the sinners to the lake of fire.

B. The lake of fire is what we commonly know as hell.

C. *Describe the pains and the torment in hell.*

GROUP 6
THE GOSPEL OF LIFE

Subject Two Hundred Forty-six

THE CONDITION OF MAN

Scripture: Rom. 3:23; John 3:18; Psa. 51:5; Jer. 17:9; Rom. 7:18; Eph. 2:1

I. Man commits sinful acts

II. **Man has a sinful nature**

III. **Man is under the judgment of God—the punishment for sin**

IV. **Man is under the rule of sin and therefore under the power of sin**

V. **In reality man is altogether a sinner**

VI. **Man is not only a sinner, he is a dead person**

He is dead in his sins, having no feeling for sins whatsoever.

Subject Two Hundred Forty-seven
THE WAY OF GOD'S SALVATION

Scripture: Isa. 53:6; Rom. 3:24; 1 Cor. 1:4; 2 Cor. 5:21

Before speaking about the way of God's salvation, first emphasize that the way of man is to establish his own righteousness and to improve himself.

I. **Through redemption God's salvation solves the problem of man's sinful acts**

God sent His son Jesus Christ to redeem man from sin.

II. **Through resurrection God's salvation solves the problem of man's sinful nature**

God raised His son from among the dead that man may have God's sinless life.

Subject Two Hundred Forty-eight
THE SAVIOR OF LIFE

Scripture: John 1:14, 4; 10:10

I. **The Savior is God coming to be a man**

II. **Within this Savior is the powerful life of God**

III. **The purpose of God coming to us as the Savior is to impart this powerful life into us**

IV. **There is only one Savior of life**

All the philosophers, religious founders, and sages throughout the ages are unable to impart life to man. They are all dead teachers. Only Jesus is the living Savior.

Subject Two Hundred Forty-nine

WHAT IS LIFE?

Scripture: 1 John 1:1-2; Heb. 7:16; *Hymns,* #602

I. **The life that the Savior gives to man is the life of God, an eternal life**

II. **Since this life is eternal, it is not only everlasting, but also fully unlimited**

III. **This life is bright and shining, holy and righteous, kind and gentle**

IV. **This life is powerful**

V. **This life contains the nature of God and all the riches in that nature**

VI. **The Savior wants to impart this life to man**

Subject Two Hundred Fifty

THE WAY FOR MAN TO RECEIVE LIFE

Scripture: Acts 11:18; John 3:16

I. **Confess**

Man needs to confess that his own nature and behavior are corrupt and that he is dead in sin.

II. **Repent**

III. **Believe**

IV. **Call**

Man needs to call upon the name of the Lord.

Subject Two Hundred Fifty-one

THE ASSURANCE OF HAVING RECEIVED THIS LIFE

Scripture: 2 John 5:10-13

I. **Assurance through God's Word**

A. The Word of God is the assurance that a saved one possesses this life.

B. If one does not believe what the Word of God says, he is making God a liar.

II. Our feelings are undependable

Do not depend on your feelings; depend on the Word of God.

Subject Two Hundred Fifty-two

THE PROOF OF HAVING RECEIVED THIS LIFE

Scripture: Ezek. 36:26; Titus 3:5; 1 John 3:14

I. A person is changed psychologically
II. Changed in the feeling of his conscience
III. Changed in temperament
IV. Changed in mind
V. Changed in inclination
VI. Changed in life
VII. Changed in behavior
VIII. Changed in his whole being

GROUP 7
THE MEANING OF LIFE

Subject Two Hundred Fifty-three

THE SUPERIORITY OF MAN

Scripture: Gen. 1:26-27

I. Man as the "soul" of all creation

The Chinese say that man is the "soul" of the whole creation. Man is superior to all the rest of creation.

II. The body of man

The body of man is superior to that of any other creature. The human body is the most beautiful, the most dexterous, and the most useful. It is stronger than that of any other creature.

III. The spirit of man

The spirit of man is unique. No other creature has a spirit. Because of this spirit, man can worship and receive wisdom. This wisdom makes him superior and noble.

IV. Man's life the highest

Therefore man's life is the highest of all created life.

Subject Two Hundred Fifty-four

THE MEANING OF MAN

Scripture: Gen. 1:26; Rom. 9:21-23

I. Since man is so superior, there must be a meaning for man's existence

II. What is the meaning of man?

Is it to study? to work? to eat? to clothe himself? to marry? to raise a family? to serve others? Is man merely for these things? No one can give an answer to this question.

III. Man as God's vessel

The Bible tells us that not only is man created by God, but that he is also created for God. Man has been created to be a vessel to express the image of God. Hence, the real meaning of man is God. The meaning of man is to be for God. If man does not have God, he will be meaningless.

IV. Today everyone who feels that life is meaningless feels so because he is not giving himself for God's purpose with man

Subject Two Hundred Fifty-five

THE NEED OF MAN

Scripture: John 4:13; 7:37

I. Man's body

Man's body needs four basic things: food, clothing, shelter, and transportation.

II. Man's soul

Man's soul has psychological needs. These are related to his mind, emotion, and will. He seeks to meet these needs through such pleasures as education, music, sports, and cultural or social activities.

III. Man's spirit

The spirit of man also has its need. The need of the spirit is the deepest and the most real need of man. This need is the need for God Himself. The reason God made a spirit in man is so that man may have need of Him and be able to receive Him. In the same way that God made man's stomach for digesting food, He made the spirit of man for receiving Himself.

Subject Two Hundred Fifty-six

THE SATISFACTION OF MAN

Scripture: John 4:14; 6:35; 7:38

I. Man's satisfaction is not found in material things

Even after a man has accumulated great wealth, he is not satisfied.

II. Man's satisfaction is not found in psychological things

Even after man has received honor and fame, he is still not satisfied.

III. Man's real satisfaction is found in his spirit

This satisfaction comes when God enters into man's spirit. Only God can satisfy the human spirit.

Subject Two Hundred Fifty-seven

THE REAL LIFE

Scripture: Eph. 3:19

I. God is man's true life

Since God is the meaning of life and the satisfaction of man, He is the true life of a man. If a man is without God, not only is his an empty life, but also a false life.

II. The real life is one that is filled with God inwardly

III. The real life is one that is absolutely living for God

IV. The real life is also the living out of God Himself

Subject Two Hundred Fifty-eight

HOW TO RECEIVE GOD
AND MANIFEST HIS LIFE

Scripture: Acts 26:20; John 1:12-13; Rom. 12:1-2

I. Confess that you need God

II. Repent and turn to God

III. Receive the Son of God as your Savior

IV. Consecrate yourself to God

V. Practice being one spirit with the Lord

GROUP 8
WHAT IS THE CHRISTIAN FAITH?

These messages are an introduction to the Christian faith from an objective standpoint. They are investigative and deductive in nature.

Subject Two Hundred Fifty-nine

GOD IS

Scripture: Heb. 11:6; Rom. 1:19-20

I. Where does the creation come from?

A. Does evolution explain the creation? Give evidence, such as the laws of nature, to show that the theory of evolution is unreliable.

B. There has to be a Creator in the universe. Perhaps you

regard Him as the Supreme Being, God, the Divine Force, or the Mighty One; nevertheless, He is the Creator. Use the Bible to prove this point. The Bible says that the universe is created by God.

II. The basis of the Christian faith is that God is

A. From the existence of the universe deduce the origin of the universe.

B. From the origin of the universe deduce the existence of God.

Subject Two Hundred Sixty

GOD HAS WRITTEN TO MAN

Scripture: Heb. 1:1-2; 2 Tim. 3:16

I. God desires to have fellowship with man

Since there is a God in the universe, this God must have a relationship with His creatures. Since He is a Being with much intellect, emotion, and affection, naturally He would like to fellowship with His creatures. Among the creation, the best object of fellowship is man. Hence, God would have fellowship with man.

II. How does God fellowship with man?

Men fellowship among themselves mainly through speaking and writing. The fellowship between God and man is also in these two ways. When it is possible, He communicates with man face to face. When this is not possible, He conveys His thoughts to man through writing.

III. God fellowships with man through the Bible

A. Among all the writings of the human race there is only one book given by God to man. In the entire history of mankind, no book except the Bible was written by God. *Strongly emphasize that the Bible is inspired by God.*

B. Is the Bible inspired by God? If the Bible is written by God, it must contain the following few points:

1. It must claim that it is a book written by God Himself to man.

2. It must reveal the origin and the consummation of the universe.

3. It must speak of the relationship between God and man.

4. It must present the highest standard of morality.

5. It must be powerful.

6. Its prophecy has to be fulfilled.

No other classic satisfies the above six requirements. Only the Bible is qualified. Hence, the Bible is the unique book written by God to man. (See *The Normal Christian Faith*, by Watchman Nee, pp. 33-49.)

Subject Two Hundred Sixty-one

GOD COMING AMONG MAN

Scripture: John 1:14; 2 Tim. 3:16

I. Two reasons why God came to man

A. He came that man may approach Him.

B. He came that man may understand Him. In order to do these two things, God had to become a man. (Relate the story in *The Normal Christian Faith*, pp. 51-53.)

II. God coming among man

Throughout these six thousand years, only one person has ever been God among us. From Adam to Moses, there is only one person—Jesus of Nazareth, who claimed to be God. If He is God, He must have the following qualifications:

1. He must have told us that he was God.

2. He must be superior in words and deeds.

3. He must have supernatural power.

4. He must have the words of his prophecies fulfilled.

Only the Lord Jesus satisfies the above four requirements. Hence, the Lord Jesus is God coming to man as a man.

Subject Two Hundred Sixty-two

MAN IS SINFUL

Scripture: Rom. 3:23; 7:18

God, coming among man to have contact with him, would naturally encounter much difficulty on man's side. This is because the nature of man is corrupted and the behavior of man is sinful. He, being a holy God, has to solve these two problems before He can fellowship with man.

Subject Two Hundred Sixty-three

THE WAY OF GOD'S SALVATION

Scripture: Rom. 3:24; 1 Pet. 1:4

Since the righteous God wants to fellowship with man, and since man is sinful and corrupted, He needed to find a way to solve the problem of both man's sinful acts and man's sinful nature. In order to solve this problem, He shed His blood for man that man might be redeemed from sin. He also gave His very life to man that man might be free from his sinful nature. So, His way of salvation needed to be one that, on the negative side, redeemed man from sin, and on the positive side, imparted life to man. The salvation mentioned in the Bible is indeed of this nature.

Subject Two Hundred Sixty-four

GOD WANTS MAN TO RECEIVE HIS WAY OF SALVATION

Scripture: Mark 1:15; Acts 2:38; 16:31; Rom. 10:9-10

God has completed the work of salvation. Surely He wants man to receive this, since all that He has done is for man. The way to receive this salvation is by repentance and believing.

Subject Two Hundred Sixty-five
SAVED BY BELIEVING

Scripture: Mark 16:16; Acts 16:31; Rom. 10:10

God's salvation is, on the one hand, real, and on the other hand, it is already accomplished. When man receives it, he will be immediately saved.

Subject Two Hundred Sixty-six
SALVATION RESULTS IN CHANGE

Scripture: Luke 19:8-9

Use examples to prove this both from the Bible and from what you have seen and experienced. One good example is the case of Zaccheus.

Index

The 266 gospel subjects have been classified into 31 categories as an aid to those who preach the gospel. Some of the gospel subjects cover two or three aspects, so they are listed under two or three categories. Some subjects refer primarily to a category, others treat it in a secondary manner. A subject that refers primarily to a category is not in parentheses, a subject that treats it secondarily is.

Category	Subject Numbers
15. The Savior (Christ)	7, 35, 43, 46, 47, 55, 61, 64, 80, (84), 85, 96, (98), 124, (130), (133), 160, 161, (174), 178, 179, 181, 191, (200), 203, 215, 223, 231, 237, 248, 261
16. What the Lord is	79, (113), 115, 116, 118, 236
17. Redemption	(6), (19), (25), (28), 29, (30), 38, (46), 47, (60), 68, 78, 98, 120, (121), (142), 147, 159, 162, 164, 165, (167), (175), 180, 183, 184, 185, 189, 193, 195, (203), 216, (223), 232, 238, 247, 263
18. The precious blood	25, 31, 42, 60, 67, (120), 143, 169, 186, 187, 192, 196, 197
19. Eternal life	9, (57), (97), 99, 100, (102), (103), (104), (107), 110, 111, (115), (120), (137), 155, 182, 194, 200, 201, 206, 214, 249, 250, 251, 252
20. Resurrection (ascension, second coming)	121, 147, 171, 239, 240, 241
21. The Holy Spirit	57, 90, 119, 182
22. Repentance	87, 122, 123, 125, (135), (217)
23. Believing	(34), 71, 73, 76, (94), 97, (108), 109, 110, 122, 129, (133), 135, (143), (144), 157, (217), 233, 264, 265
24. Salvation	51, 117, (128), 133, 158, (172), 217, 218, 219, 234, 265, 266
25. Stories of salvation	31, 32, 34, (73), (76), 82, (95), 107, 126, 127, 132
26. Deliverance	(81), 114, (136), 168, 225
27. Peace and blessing	36, 63, 136
28. Gospel and religion	17, 66, 81, (124), (126), (127), 128, (136), 137, (214)
9. The law and grace	(22), 27, 84, 94, (142), (143), 145, 152, 154, (167), (169), (171), 172
'rgiveness of sins ' justification	39, (69), 83, 93, 125, 129, 130, 142, 144, 146, 151, 197, 224
ing, decision	33, 51, 54, (62), (88)